Transforming Teaching for Mission

First Fruits Press

The Academic Open Press of Asbury Theological Seminary
204 N. Lexington Ave., Wilmore, KY 40390
859-858-2236
first.fruits@asburyseminary.edu
asbury.to/firstfruits

APM

Transforming Teaching For Mission

Educational Theory and Practice

The 2014 proceedings of
The Association of Professors of Missions

Edited by
Robert A. Danielson
Benjamin L. Hartley

2014 APM Annual Meeting
St. Paul, MN
June 19-20, 2014

Transforming Teaching for Mission: Educational Theory and Practice
The 2014 Proceedings of the Association of Professors of Missions.

Published by First Fruits Press, © 2014
Digital version at http://place.asburyseminary.edu/academicbooks/10/

ISBN: 9781621711582 (print),
9781621711742 (digital), 9781621711759 (kindle)

Transforming teaching for mission : educational theory and practice : the 2014 proceedings of the Association of Professors of Missions.
    v, 326 pages ; 23 cm.
    Wilmore, Ky. : First Fruits Press, ©2014.
    ISBN: 9781621711582 (pbk.)
    1. Missions – Study and teaching – Congresses. 2. Missions – Theory – Congresses. 3. Education – Philosophy – Congresses. 4. Teaching – Methodology – Congresses. I. Title. II. Danielson, Robert A. (Robert Alden), 1969- III. Hartley, Benjamin L. (Benjamin Loren) IV. Association of Professors of Mission annual meeting (2014 : St. Paul, Minn.) V. Association of Professors of Mission. VI. The 2014 proceedings of the Association of Professors of Missions.
    BV2020 .A876 2014

Cover design by Jon Ramsey

About the Association of Professors of Mission

ROBERT DANIELSON, ADVISORY COMMITTEE MEMBER

The Association of Professors of Mission (APM) was formed in 1952 at Louisville, Kentucky and was developed as an organization to focus on the needs of people involved in the classroom teaching of mission studies. However, the organization also challenged members to be professionally involved in scholarly research and share this research through regular meetings. In the 1960's Roman Catholic scholars and scholars from conservative Evangelical schools joined the conciliar Protestants who initially founded the organization.

With the discussion to broaden membership to include other scholars from areas like anthropology, sociology, and linguistics who were actively engaged in mission beyond the teaching profession, the decision was made to found the American Society of Missiology (ASM) in 1972. Since the importance of working with mission educators was still vital, the APM continued as a separate organization, but always met in conjunction with the ASM at their annual meetings.

The APM continues as a professional society of those interested in the teaching of mission from as wide an ecumenical spectrum as possible. As an organization it works to help and support those who teach mission, especially those who often lack a professional network to help mentor and guide them in this task. Through its influence, the APM has also helped establish the prominence and scholarly importance of the academic discipline of missiology throughout theological education.

Table of Contents

Conference Proceedings

Foreword

Benjamin L. Hartley, President

It was my privilege to serve as President of the Association of Professors of Mission (APM) for 2014 even if it was not exactly according to plan. Sister Madge Karecki, Director of the Office of Mission Education and Animation of the Archdiocese of Chicago, had intended to serve in this capacity this year. Early in the year, however, she accepted an invitation to serve as President of St. Augustine College in Johannesburg, South Africa and needed to resign as President of the APM. I mention this because the original germ of an idea for our theme, "Transforming Teaching for Mission" was hers; I sought to be faithful to her idea as I developed it in the months prior to our June 2014 gathering.

The field of missiology – and the Association of Professors of Mission along with it – is in the midst of mult-faceted re-assessment as more than a few publications in recent years make plain.[1] The welcomed

---

1 See, for example, Dwight Baker, "Missiology as an Interested Discipline – and Where Is It Happening?" *International Bulletin of Missionary Research* 38 no. 1 (January 2014): 17-21; Paul Kollman, "At the Origins of Mission and Missiology: A Study in the Dynamics of Religious Language," *Journal of the American Academy of Religion* 79 no. 2 (June 2011): 425-458; John Roxborogh, "Missiology after "mission"?" *International Bulletin of Missionary Research* 38 no. 3 (July 2014): 120-124; Michael A. Rynkiewich, "Do We Need a Postmodern Anthropology for Mission in a Postcolonial World?" *Mission Studies* 28 (2011): 151-169. Re-evaluations of the definition of mission are

growth of our sister society, the American Society of Missiology (ASM), since their strategic planning meetings in June of 2010 (in which APM also participated) is contributing to this re-assessment as well. Even the 2012 decision made by the American Society of Missiology and the APM to meet in a new location after a decades-long practice of gathering at the Society of the Divine Word's Techny Towers Conference and Retreat Center in Illinois is prompting a fair bit of stock-taking as old habits of interaction in a familiar place are disrupted by new meeting locations.

As a professional society comprised of professors devoted to excellence in teaching about mission we always need to be about the task of posing fresh questions about the teaching of mission in the training institutes, seminaries, colleges, and universities to which we belong. After the APM's establishment in 1952, the first theme addressed at the 1954 gathering of the Association of Professors of Mission sought to do this very thing. That meeting was described simply as "syllabus sharing" and involved an informal discussion of teaching issues as missiologists. In the sixty years since that first gathering there have been a number of annual meetings which have had a similarly broadly-encompassing topic for consideration.

The 2014 Annual Meeting of the APM explored mission pedagogy (or, more precisely, andragogy) with a particular focus on how the teaching of missiology engages with educational theorists and teaching methods which include but also extend beyond missiology's cognate fields of history, biblical studies, anthropology, and theology. The teaching of missiology has benefited from a number of different movements and individuals from related fields which have constructed and critiqued educational theory. The "scholarship of teaching and learning" has grown considerably in the past two decades and now includes its own professional society (The International Society for the Scholarship of Teaching and Learning) and a number of academic journals. The Society for Intercultural Training, Education, and Research (SIETAR) shares similar goals to the APM, and some missiologists contribute to this professional society. The method of "shared inquiry" in the discussion of classic texts made popular by the

---

also evidence of this re-assessment in this field. See, for example, two rather strikingly different proposals by way of definition: Titus Presler, "Mission is Ministry in the Dimension of Difference: A Definition for the Twenty-first Century," *International Bulletin of Missionary Research* 34 no. 4 (October 2010): 195-202, 204; Paul Avis, *A Ministry Shaped by Mission* (London: T&T Clark, 2005).

Great Books Foundation also merits further investigation as missiologists discern together which texts are most generative for the teaching of key themes in mission.

Among individual contributors to educational theory, Ivan Illich (1926-2002) stands out as perhaps the most controversial critic of missionary practice, but his writings on the philosophy of education most famously articulated in *Deschooling Society* (1971) continue to be influential. Other leaders in adult education such as Paulo Freire, Parker Palmer, Susan Daloz Parks, and Ted Ward have likewise made important contributions in educational theory and practice and have, in different ways, transformed the teaching of mission. I benefited myself from the influence of Professor Ted Ward at Michigan State University even after he left that institution in the courses and programs related to the field of international development which still bore his imprint.

Our conference on June 19-20 at The University of Northwestern in St. Paul, Minnesota explored the connections among the above areas of inquiry by inviting three plenary speakers who were not self-described missiologists but were nonetheless sympathetic to the goals of our professional society.

We had three plenary speakers at the 2014 Conference. (Short bios of these three individuals are provided elsewhere in this volume.) Dr. Mary Hess gave a lively and challenging presentation entitled "Adult Learning in a World Leaning into God's Mission." Her presentation contained a number of short video clips about social media, contemporary shifts in epistemology, and thoughtful questions as to how best teach mission in light of these dramatic changes in western culture today. Dr. Daniel Born's presentation was an analysis of missionary fiction and discusses the Great Books Foundation's method of "shared inquiry." Time restraints on his presentation prevented him from sharing at length about this method of teaching at our June gathering, but he does this in the paper included in this volume. Finally, Dr. Grace Cajiuat's interactive presentation encouraged participants at the APM to reflect on important interpersonal and intercultural questions about our teaching – especially in how we encourage learning in classrooms of increasing diversity. Because of the nature of Dr. Hess's and Dr. Cajiuat's presentations we are not able to reproduce their contributions as they were presented. Youtube videos obviously cannot be portrayed in any book, and copyright restrictions on other images prohibit us from reproducing them. A brief summary of their presentations is provided here with a listing of internet URL's for some of the video clips.

Our 2014 APM gathering continued the practice of the last several years of inviting persons to present papers in parallel paper session "tracks." This year we had fifteen papers organized into five tracks:

1. Classroom Case Studies and Strategies for Mission Education

2. Theological Considerations for Mission Education

3. Rethinking the Mission Curriculum

4. Anthropological/Sociological Considerations in Mission Education

5. Mission Education Outside the Classroom.

Twelve of the fifteen papers presented at our June 2014 gathering are included in this volume. Three of our participants chose to publish their work in other venues, and so their work is not included here.

This year's conference also introduced a few new practices which our professional society has either not done before or has not done for some time. First, the APM leadership organized formal breakfast meetings between seasoned professors of mission and younger APM members in order to encourage the sharing of pedagogical insights. Such conversations often happened informally in previous years, but in order to be more hospitable toward younger members of our society we decided that creating intentional opportunities for such interactions would be beneficial. We also re-introduced a practice – common in earlier years of our society's history – of having a dedicated time at the APM for members to discuss together how they teach certain kinds of courses in the mission curriculum. Finally, in recognition of the long-standing and fruitful interaction between the APM and the Overseas Ministries Study Center (OMSC) in New Haven, Connecticut the APM this year also invited OMSC resident missionary Rev. Ernest Chung to preach for us during our opening worship. This is a practice we hope to be able to continue in future years as well.

I trust you will enjoy reading the collected papers in this volume. If this volume serves as an introduction to the Association of Professors of Mission because you have not been able to join us at our annual meetings, then I hope it will encourage you to join us in the future. You are welcome!

APM

Conference Papers

APM

Opening Plenary Address

Great Books and Missionary Fictions

DANIEL BORN

DOI: 10.7252/Paper. 000037

About the Author

Daniel Born earned his PhD in English from the Graduate Center of the City University of New York, where he studied with Irving Howe and Alfred Kazin. He is the author of *The Birth of Liberal Guilt in the English Novel: Charles Dickens to H. G. Wells*, and has edited several books, including *The Great Books Foundation Science Fiction Omnibus* and *The Seven Deadly Sins Sampler*. He grew up in Brazil as the son of Mennonite missionaries, and currently lives in Chicago. A former chief of staff and vice president at the Great Books Foundation, he is lecturer in the M.A. literature program at Northwestern University's School of Continuing Studies.

Good morning, colleagues and friends.

Many thanks to my good friend Ben Hartley, who invited me to your meeting in St. Paul. Let me begin with a few disclaimers: first, I am not a professor of mission, and my scholarship in your field is light if not downright flimsy. Second, I come to today's topic by way of my experience as a missionary kid in Brazil during the 1960s and 70s, which makes much of what I have to say merely anecdotal. That experience tempers or you might say, warps my scholarship and my teaching of literature-- and since the World Cup is underway as we speak, may subject me to temporary bouts of insanity. Finally, I want to reflect with you about certain literary texts that we might teach as professors of mission, and to ask together with you what kinds of literary narratives, and narratives about mission, might be considered great books. I believe that is a question we can fruitfully pursue.

What is a great book, and what criteria do we bring when we make that designation? Do any missionary stories qualify as great books, and if so, why should we care? In his article, "Missionaries as Heroes and Villains," published six years ago in IBMR (*International Bulletin of Missionary Research*,) Jonathan Bonk suggested that "Public perceptions of missionaries have typically oscillated between eulogy and vilification. Both extremes contain elements of truth, but neither can tell the whole truth," (Bonk 2008:113). Let me acknowledge my debt here to Bonk while suggesting that most fictional narratives about missionaries that have lasting literary value usually complicate the categories of hero and villain. In other words, the Manichean terrain of superhero good and evil must be abandoned in favor of the realm of the human. I will argue today that the most insightful narratives about missionaries—those narratives worth teaching—work in the gray area of experience between absolutes, the area where most humans live. By the same token, the best narratives about missionaries do not treat faith and doubt as mutually exclusive, either-or categories, but in fact demonstrate that faith and doubt are locked in a far more complicated relationship.

I would argue that missionary fictions that either celebrate or debunk the missionary project fall short of "great books" status because they have already arrived at their foregone conclusions before they get started. Because we know where such books are taking us, they do not hold lasting interest. The problem with hagiography and skeptical debunking is that both genres preclude the need for interpretive work by their readers. In the final part of my talk, I want to explore at least one example of a literary narrative that attains "great book" status in part because it invites multiple interpretive questions rather than transparent understanding. Great books cannot be reduced to PowerPoint bullet points; rather, they are the kinds of works that promise to deliver lively interpretive argument long after their authors are dead. We will consider an excerpt from Japanese writer Shusaku Endo and discuss it in terms of "shared inquiry," a text-based, Socratic method of discussion promoted by the Great Books Foundation today. This method developed out of the pioneering practice of Mortimer Adler and Robert Hutchins beginning first at Columbia after World War I, and then at the University of Chicago in the decades roughly between 1930 and 1950. I want to return to the Great Books pedagogical tradition later in this presentation. For those of us involved in adult education, such a practice has useful classroom benefits, not the least of which is selecting texts that will stimulate rather than stifle classroom discussion.

Young Adult Missionary Fiction

Since I come from a tradition that is pietist and confessional, let me begin by way of some personal remarks. In 1963, at the susceptible age of seven, I read my first missionary story, one of the Jungle Doctor books written by Paul White. My father was a seminary student at the Mennonite Brethren seminary in Fresno, getting a master's in missiology. I started making a regular habit of checking out books at the Butler Avenue MB Church library after the Sunday morning service was over. The Jungle Doctor books, like most action-adventure written for boys, what we might today call young adult or YA fiction, establish a triumphalist narrative of Christianity overcoming the forces of darkness. (I use the word "darkness" intentionally here.) Invariably, Jungle Doctor demonstrates the superiority of Christianity over native animistic religion, as well as the liberating benefits of western medicine over the superstitions of the local witch doctor, a villainous figure usually intent on keeping the local population enslaved. Still, I think I liked the Jungle Doctor books for other reasons. First, he had that very cool hat. [Exhibit A: Pith helmet demonstration]

Second, the Jungle Doctor showed himself daring and open-minded in his dealings with local culture. The most vivid memory I have of Jungle Doctor is how he sat down with Masai warriors and shared their favorite drink, a tasty beverage that mixed cow's blood and milk. Edward

Said and other postcolonial theorists would call this the most blatant kind of exoticizing or "othering" of foreign cultures, but I would contend it is also perhaps the beginning of cross-cultural understanding: to meet with another culture means the sharing is not always in one direction. Sometimes one needs to drink a cup of blood. And by the same token, several anthropologists and some Brazilians I knew considered our sport of football to be among the most dehumanizing of sports; our Super Bowl may be the most lasting and elaborate shrine to barbarism invented. There is more than one message to take from Jungle Doctor, isn't there, and I am not sure it is an altogether harmful YA series.

A notion of missionary work as heroic, risky, swashbuckling adventure dominates the children's literature of mid-century, not only the Jungle Doctor books, but also the Danny Orlis and the Sugar Creek Gang books. The latter introduced me to important subject matter including alcohol addiction, bear-killing, and urban life in Chicago. These are the literary descendants of adult Christian fiction penned in the late nineteenth and early twentieth centuries, books few of us have read, but which are nicely summarized by Jamie S. Scott in an essay titled "Missions in Fiction." With titles like *The Sky Pilot: A Tale of the Foothills* (1899) and *The Preacher of Cedar Mountain: A Tale of the Open Country* (1917), these books, according to Scott,

> all portray the missionary as a man mighty in flesh and spirit in the standard colonial and imperial romance model of fearless crusader, lone adventurer, and chaste lover. These novels proceed from action scene to action scene, exciting the sensibilities of a cloistered urban audience with descriptions of natural calamities and wild animal attacks, robberies and frontier bar brawls, tragic heroines and Roman Catholic perfidy (Scott 2008:122).

While Scott mentions these books as embodiments of muscular Christianity, he doesn't mention the original book that launched that tradition: the British boy's classic, *Tom Brown's School Days* (1857), written by Thomas Hughes and inspired by headmaster Thomas Arnold at Rugby School. The boilerplate for Tom Brown, who must face all manner of bullies and worldly temptations, is slightly updated roughly one hundred years later for Bernard Palmer's Danny Orlis books, the staple literature of midcentury American Christian boy heroes. Orlis combines physical derring-do and mental agility. Imagine Billy Graham's soul, Derek Jeter's athleticism, and the technical know-how of 1980s TV escape artist MacGyver all welded together, and you might come close to the miracle that is Danny Orlis. This Boy Scout travels close to the Lord. The advertising copy from Moody Press in 1970 conveys it:

> Adventure, mystery, suspense—these make up every Danny Orlis story. From the northern Canadian wilderness to the steaming jungles of Guatemala, Danny meets danger and mystery as well as everyday problems in the homeland. He is a capable outdoorsman, a skilled athlete—and above all a consistent Christian. Quick action, quiet courage, and level-headed thinking often save the day as Danny uses his resources to the fullest. His ability to apply biblical solutions to every situation makes him a unique personality whose experiences often provide realistic guidelines for Christian youth facing similar difficulties (Sword of the Lord Bookstore, 2014).[1]

An ironic smile crossed my lips as I transcribed these words from the website to the text of this paper. Then I realized that, minus the irony, this more-or-less describes my father. Not all books have to be great. Even formula fiction has its uses.

Adult Missionary Fiction

While my subject here today is missionary fiction, it must be granted that the apogee of missionary swashbuckling adventure was no novel, but in fact a real event during the late 1950s in the proverbial steaming jungles of Ecuador. That story is well-known to this audience: the killing of young North American evangelicals who had tried to make contact with a tribe who called themselves the Waodani and were known to their neighbors simply as the Aucas, or "enemy." According to their tribal neighbors, the Aucas were notoriously violent killers with a high murder rate among their own kind. It was only a short time between the five missionary men's radio silence from aboard their Piper Family Cruiser aircraft to the discovery of their speared and hacked bodies downstream from "Palm Beach," the makeshift river landing strip where they first made face to face contact with the Aucas. The American news media went wild. *Life* magazine headlined the story in its January 30, 1956 issue, "'Go Ye and Preach the Gospel': Five Do and Die," (1956:10) with a full-spread photo layout including shots of the widows commiserating in a kitchen, the natives standing and sitting in all their naked glory back in Ecuador, and the pillaged remains of the Piper aircraft on a strip of sand. Elisabeth Elliot, wife of murdered missionary Jim Elliot, would write a memoir, *Through Gates of Splendor* (1957), and a documentary film by the same title was produced in 1967. Elliot became a celebrity on the evangelical talk circuit.

Elliot's bestseller probably inspired thousands of missionaries, including my parents, to hear and heed the divine call. This was one of the first "grownup" books I read as child, encouraged by my parents, especially my mother. This story, combined with the furlough visit of my father's old seminary buddy Arlo Heinrichs, a Wycliffe Bible translator working in the Brazilian Amazon, suggested to me that the truth was far more amazing and exotic than any fiction could simulate.[2] Heinrichs brought back from Brazil a cured and shellacked anaconda skin, rolled up neatly in a package the diameter of a small barrel. Extended on our front lawn in Fresno it was twenty, maybe twenty-four feet long, and a couple of feet wide, a veritable runway in miniature, adorned with spectacular geometric scales. We and the neighbors were blown away. The kids all wanted to touch it, and we did. This was in 1964, and when I think about it now I have to say it was more exciting than the Beatles. A year later, my father, mother, my two brothers and I boarded a Boeing 707 at LAX, dressed in our Sunday best. We were on our way to southern Brazil where my parents would begin a year of language study before heading further south to join the faculty of the Mennonite Brethren seminary in Curitiba.

1965 was also the year that writer Peter Matthiessen published his novel *At Play in the Fields of the Lord*, a finalist for the National Book Award and one of the most effective and unrelenting debunkings of missionary work ever written (Matthiessen 1965). Matthiessen labors hard—maybe a little too hard—to show that the missionary enterprise is not so blameless as some had thought; indeed, he sketches what is by now a familiar (almost hegemonic) critique that missionary work accompanies neo-liberal capitalist and imperialist oppression, whatever gospel truths evangelical missionaries might hold dear. At certain key points it also riffs off of Elliot's nonfiction account of the Auca tragedy. Matthiessen's two aggressively secular characters, the soldiers-of-fortune Wolfie and the Cheyenne American Lewis Moon, advertise themselves as experts in "Small Wars & Demolition"; they understand clearly that they are instruments of mayhem and if all goes well, profit, as they do their part to clear the jungle of its Indians so that the forces of economic development can go forward unimpeded.[3] As far as the two fundamentalist missionary couples depicted in the novel, Matthiessen does a good job of differentiating them as individuals; they don't merely come across as interchangeable sock puppets for Moody Bible Institute, where they received their theological training. In Matthiessen's story, both marriages will crumble under the pressure of evangelizing the Niaruna tribe from the base of Madre de Dios, a squalid frontier jungle town that seems to be have been lifted straight from the pages of a Conrad novel.

As the novel progresses, Matthiessen's missionaries reveal themselves in distinctly individual ways as all too human. Leslie Huben, the former basketball star and missionary overachiever, shows himself incapable of loving his beautiful wife. It's as if Matthiessen wants to say Leslie might be a pretty boy and successful evangelist, but he's not a real man. Leslie also holds patently contemptuous views of the natives he is trying to convert; at one point in the action, we are told that he "prayed almost daily for barbed wire to fence the mission hut so that the Indians, with their lice and smoky smell and dirty fingers, would give them a little privacy (Matthiessen 1965:136)."

Martin and Hazel Quarrier, patterned after the grotesques of a Flannery O'Connor short story, lose their ten-year-old son Billy to fever (mind you, in a stroke of sick poetic justice, the Niarunas are going to be infected and decimated by the flu conveyed from Andy to Lewis Moon.) When Billy dies, Hazel goes insane. She has to be put on a plane and flown back to North Dakota. Martin Quarrier is Matthiessen's most sympathetic missionary because he is capable of doubt. This includes misgivings about certain missionary tactics, including the use of bartered goods to entice the Indian population. As Elliot told us about the five martyrs to the Aucas, their attempts to reach the tribespeople began with drops of gifts including cooking pots, colored buttons, and ribbons. Similarly in *At Play*, the missionaries leave gifts out on a makeshift rack for the Indians to take, and Quarrier develops a bad conscience about these mercenary tactics, especially when the Niaruna try to exchange a young Indian woman for the missionary goods. We should note that Matthiessen didn't have to invent this sordid occurrence; in the Auca adventure as chronicled in *Life* magazine, a young woman of fourteen or fifteen years of age was offered by the Indians as part of their barter, and the five missionary men nicknamed her "Jezebel" (*Life* magazine 1956:14).

Martin commands more reader sympathy than the pious hypocrite Leslie because he also recognizes his own flaws, including a wandering eye for other women—both Indian and white. He is deeply attracted to Andy. (Hector Babenco's casting of Darryl Hannah as Andy in the 1991 film was a stroke of genius. Tom Berenger as Moon and John Lithgow as Martin weren't too bad, either.) In the end, though, Matthiessen's real interest in the novel is Lewis Moon, the Cheyenne American who in his youth converted to Christianity in the States, became a poster-boy for tribal missions, and then backslid into his current soldier-of-fortune nihilism. By the end of the novel, it is clear that Moon represents reawakened native pride; there is a certain irony in the original North American native "going native" in South America and joining the Niaruna as a kind of honorary member; in this sense Matthiessen's novel anticipates his nonfiction work *In the Spirit of Crazy Horse* (1983), about the American Indian Movement uprising in North Dakota, as well as his commitment to ecological preservation as conveyed in *The Snow Leopard* (1978).

Multitudes of fictional debunkings of the missionary effort have percolated through the literary culture since the 1960s, too many for us to detail here. Some of these include notable works of science fiction, a genre perpetually caught up in first encounters between Homo sapiens and other sentient species.[4] As far as literary fiction goes, I would mention just one other work. Barbara Kingsolver's *The Poisonwood Bible* (1998), shows the spirit of Matthiessen but little comparable skill; Kingsolver's villain, Baptist missionary Nathan Price, never excites much reader antipathy because he displays all the personality of a cardboard cutout, and his daughters' and wife's voices do not differentiate much from Kingsolver's own flat-footed polemic on the evils that missionaries do.[5] She has not written a novel so much as a tract. Still, surprisingly, in spite of its imaginative failure, her novel attracted many sympathetic critics.

One of the few literary novels in recent years to portray missionaries with sympathy and complexity is Robert Stone's *A Flag for Sunrise* (1981). This is Stone's best novel in a long and distinguished writing career. Like Matthiessen, Stone also bears the Conradian imprimatur. Set in Central America during a revolution pitting Marxist-inspired guerrillas against right-wing army thugs, *A Flag for Sunrise* has as its most compelling character a young American nun, aptly named Justin, who will be tortured to death by a Central American comandante who naturally believes she is part of a leftist plot to overthrow his country. Before her death, she will have a sexual encounter with the American operative Holliwell, a CIA spook who, like the soldier-of-fortune Wolfie in *At Play* is a lonely skeptic and survivor who sees through every illusion but in the end cannot articulate what is worth living for. Stone, like Matthiessen, seems more sympathetic to Catholic missionaries than to Protestants; the Catholics convey more anthropological sensitivity and political awareness. It also makes sense to read *A Flag for Sunrise* against the backdrop of the revolution in El Salvador. The four Catholic women missionaries raped and murdered by paramilitary forces in El Salvador in December 1980[6] did not get quite as much attention that the five martyred evangelical men received in *Life* magazine in 1956. Still, Stone's narrative makes little sense without some understanding of the bloody crossroads of theology and politics tearing Central America apart in the 1970s and 1980s. Stone's Catholics, like Matthiessen's, at least have the wherewithal to recognize that an apolitical theology is probably an illusion.

Missionary Fiction Which Qualifies as Great Books

There are missionary fictions, which I believe qualify as great books. Not many, but a few. And here I want to offer a definition of what a great book is. In order to do that, let me take a step back and briefly recap how the Great Books movement began in the twentieth century and what it has become.

Most of us make a connection to the Great Books by way of a dusty set of books ("Great Books of the Western World") in grandma's attic. This publishing project, one of Mortimer Adler's many ventures, had its heyday in the 1950s. Less well known but carrying greater consequence is the pedagogical revolution that the Great Books movement helped to launch. John Erskine, a professor at Columbia University, originated this with his "War Studies" course for American soldiers in Europe during World War I. The course was so popular that Erskine taught it back on the home campus after the war, renaming it "General Honors." Distinguished by Socratic discussion based on close reading of seminal texts, the Erskine approach traded in boring scholarly lectures for seminar-wide discussion; participation by all class members was encouraged. We might consider the method a forerunner to "active learning." To this day a couple of courses based in the Great Books method are required of all Columbia undergraduates: "Literature Humanities" and "Contemporary Civilization."[7]

Mortimer Adler was a young teaching assistant at Columbia who caught the Great Books fever from Erskine. When Hutchins hired Adler to come to the University of Chicago, Adler quickly put his imprimatur on the undergraduate curriculum; he engineered an entire undergraduate liberal arts program in the Great Books. Versions of this curriculum are still taught at St. John's College and Shimer College in Chicago, although Adler and Hutchins' ambitious program at the University of Chicago was largely dismantled after Hutchins' retirement there as chancellor in 1951. Meanwhile, Adler and Hutchins launched the Great Books Foundation in 1947, an adult education network of book groups devoted to discussing the great works of Western literature. In the 1960s, the Foundation expanded its efforts to K-12 education in the form of Junior Great Books.

The novelty of the Great Books approach was to make discussion participants truly participate. Typically, the discussion leader does not lecture, but asks questions meant to stir dialogue. With that in mind, let's turn our attention to the reading that has been distributed to you prior to this morning's session. It is a selection from Shusaku Endo's novel *Silence* (1966; transl. 1969), and it has received considerable attention from scholars and writers including Philip Yancey, William Cavanaugh, and David J. Bosch (Yancey 1996; Cavanaugh 1998; Bosch 1994). But rather than summarize the critics, which is what our scholarly impulse would lead us to do at this moment, let us proceed in Great Books discussion fashion. What I would ask you to do at your table is put the excerpt in front of you and then write down these two questions:

> (1) Is Ferreira telling the truth when he says "there is something more important than the Church, more important than missionary work" (258)?
>
> (2) Does Christ speak to Rodriguez? (259)

Reread the excerpt. Write your answers to these two questions, referring specifically to supporting passages in this text. When you are finished, briefly discuss your answers with those at your table, and after about ten minutes, we will convene our entire gathering here for general discussion. Finally, in closing, I will say a few words about interpretive questions in shared inquiry, and not only how these questions can open up a text to conversation, but indeed help us figure out what a great book is. [Exhibit B Discussion: What is Shared Inquiry, and how can I use interpretive questions as a classroom strategy?]

Notes

1. This promotional blurb copy can be found everywhere from Sword of the Lord Bookstore (swordbooks.com/dannyorlisseries.aspx) to Goodreads online, with interesting variations. The Sword of the Lord online bookstore replaces "steaming jungles of Guatemala" with "the rugged mission field of Mexico." The link between heroic action-adventure and Christian formation is fully laid out at the conclusion of *Tom Brown's School Days* roughly a century earlier: "Such stages have to be gone through, I believe, by all young and brave souls, who must win their way through hero-worship, to the worship of Him who is the King and Lord of heroes. For it is only through our mysterious human relationships, through the love and tenderness and purity of mothers, and sisters, and wives, through the strength and courage and wisdom of fathers, and brothers, and teachers, that we can come to the knowledge of Him . . ." (Hughes, 357).

2. Heinrichs's thoughts about translation work with the Piraha Indians are discussed by John Colapinto in his article about former missionary and now linguistic theorist Dan Everett, "The Interpreter," *The New Yorker*, 16 Apr. 2007.

3. It is worth noting here that Hector Babenco's screen adaptation of Matthiessen's novel was also an influence on James Cameron's cinematic hit, *Avatar*. A summary of Cameron's comments to this effect are summarized at the online site *Morning Spoilers* (http://io9.com/5338570/james-cameron-admits-avatar-is-dances-with-wolves-in-space).

4. I discuss some of these narratives about interplanetary and interstellar missionaries in "Character as Perception: Science Fiction and the Christian Man of Faith," *Extrapolation* 24.3 (Fall 1983), 251-271. Narratives on the debunking end of the spectrum would have to include Arthur C. Clarke's "The Star" (1955) and Michael Moorcock's *Behold the Man* (1966). Other narratives conveying a more ambiguous message include James Blish's *A Case of Conscience* (1958) and Harry Harrison's "The Streets of

Ashkelon" (1962). Walter M. Miller, Jr.'s *A Canticle for Leibowitz* (1959) celebrates the church as the necessary cradle of civilization in a nuclear post-apocalyptic landscape anticipating that of Mel Gibson's Mad Max movies.

5. I am partial to my brother Brad Born's review of Kingsolver in *Mennonite Life*, 56.1 (March 2001), "Kingsolver's Gospel for Africa: (Western White Female) Heart of Goodness." He writes, "The ideological clumsiness that threatens the novel's artistry appears in the opening pages. Immediately one encounters Kingsolver's heavy hand at work, hammering out the fearful symmetry of the abusive white male, the fundamentalist Christian zealot, and the ugly American, all incarnated in Nathan Price, the arch missionary villain" (1). Brad argues that the novel can be criticized on the same grounds that Chinua Achebe attacked Conrad's *Heart of Darkness*, except that in Kingsolver's case, "only... American female heroines are granted the dignity of complexity, of inner struggle. If you pay attention to Kingsolver's writing, she's interested in characters like herself, women who domesticate and assimilate distant tragedies into a personal, feminine American self" (5).   At http://archive.bethelks.edu/ml/issue/vol-56-no-1/article/kingsolvers-gospel-for-africa-western-white-female/

6. See Milt Freudenheim and Barbara Slavin, "Guerrillas Regroup as Carter Switches On Salvador Arms," *New York Times*, 25 January 1981. According to the Carter administration, the El Salvadoran junta had taken "positive steps" in its investigation of the rape and murder of the four Catholic missionaries.

7. See David Denby, *Great Books: My Adventures with Homer, Rousseau, Woolf, and Other Indestructible Writers of the Western World* (New York: Touchstone, 1996), especially his introduction, pp. 11-19. I have written previously about the Great Books movement, especially focused on the contributions of Mortimer Adler and Robert Hutchins, in "Utopian Civic-Mindedness: Robert Maynard Hutchins, Mortimer Adler, and the Great Books Enterprise," in *Reading Communities from Salons to Cyberspace*, ed. DeNel Rehberg Sedo (Houndmills, Basingstoke: Palgrave Macmillan, 2011), 81-100.

Works Cited

Blish, James
    1958   *A Case of Conscience.* New York: Ballantine Books.

Bonk, Jonathan J.
    2008   "Missionaries as Heroes and Villains," *International Bulletin of Missionary Research,* 32 no.3 (July).

Born, Brad
    2001   "Kingsolver's Gospel for Africa: (Western White Female) Heart of Goodness," *Mennonite Life,* 56 no.1 (March).

Born, Daniel
    1983   "Character as Perception: Science Fiction and the Christian Man of Faith," *Extrapolation* 24 no. 3 (Fall): 251-271.

    2011   "Utopian Civic-Mindedness: Robert Maynard Hutchins, Mortimer Adler, and the Great Books Enterprise," in *Reading Communities from Salons to Cyberspace* edited by DeNel Rehberg Sedo. Houndmills, Basingstoke: Palgrave Macmillan, 81-100.

Bosch, David J.
    1994   "The Vulnerability of Mission," in James A. Scherer and Stephen B. Bevans, eds., *New Directions in Mission & Evangelization 2: Theological Foundations,* Maryknoll, NY, 73-86.

Cavanaugh, William T.
    1998   "The God of Silence: Shusaku Endo's Readings of the Passion," *Commonweal* (13 March): 10-12.

Clarke, Arthur C.
    1955   "The Star," *Infinity Science Fiction* (November).

Connor, Ralph
    1899   *The Sky Pilot: A Tale of the Foothills.*

Denby, David
    1996   *Great Books: My Adventures with Homer, Rousseau, Woolf, and Other Indestructible Writers of the Western World.* New York: Touchstone.

Elliot, Elizabeth
    1957   *Through Gates of Splendor.* Spire Books.

Endo, Shusaku
    1980   *Silence.* New York: Taplinger.

Everett, Dan
    2007   "The Interpreter," *The New Yorker*, 16 April.

Freudenheim, Milt and Barbara Slavin
    1981   "Guerrillas Regroup as Carter Switches On Salvador Arms," *New York Times*, 25 January.

Harrison, Harry
    1962   "The Streets of Ashkelon," *New Worlds.*

Hughes, Thomas
    1857   *Tom Brown's School Days.* New York: Grosset & Dunlap.

Kingsolver, Barbara
    1998   *The Poisonwood Bible.* New York: HarperCollins.

Life magazine
    1956   "Go Ye and Preach the Gospel: Five Do and Die," *Life* 40.5 (January 30): 10-19.

Matthiessen, Peter
    1965   *At Play in the Fields of the Lord.* New York: Random House.

    1978   *The Snow Leopard.* New York: Viking Press.

    1983   *In the Spirit of Crazy Horse.* New York: Viking Press.

Miller, Walter M. Jr.
    1960   *A Canticle for Leibowitz*. New York: Lippincott.

Moorcock, Michael
    1966   "Behold the Man," *New Worlds*.

Scott, Jamie S.
    2008   "Missions in Fiction," *International Bulletin of Missionary Research*, 32 no.3 (July).

Seton, Ernest Thompson
    1917   *The Preacher of Cedar Mountain: A Tale of the Open Country*.

Stone, Robert
    1981   *A Flag for Sunrise*. New York: Knopf.

Sword of the Lord Bookstore
    http://www.swordbooks.com/dannyorlisseries.aspx. Accessed on 15 September 2014.

Yancey, Philip
    1996   "Japan's Faithful Judas"(Parts 1 and 2), http://www.2think.org/endo.shtml and http://www.2think.org/endo2.shtml. Accessed 15 September 2014.

APM

Classroom Case Studies and Strategies for Mission Education

Transformative Learning versus Informative Learning in Facilitating Mission Studies

GLORY E. DHARMARAJ

DOI: 10.7252/Paper.000033

About the Author

Glory Dharmaraj served for a number of years as a staff member of the United Methodist Women's Division in New York City. Most recently, Glory Dharmaraj is the co-author with Jacob Dharmaraj of *Mutuality in Mission: A Theological Principle for the 21st Century (2014).*

In the first annual conference meeting on June 25, 1744 held in Old King's Foundry, London, John Wesley emphasized three key elements in his extensive conversation with the Methodist clergy and lay preachers: "What to teach, how to teach, and what to do" (Mason 1862, B). Adapted to this article's focus on facilitating mission studies, the Wesleyan key elements still remain the same, though this paper is not focused on doctrine, discipline and practices. Instead it seeks to examine what to teach, how to teach, and what to do in light of transformative learning. Drawing a distinction between transformative learning and informative learning, this article explores the process of how an environment for transformation can be created with the constructive role of "transformative spirituality" (Keum 2013: 12-14).

The roots of the United Methodist Women's mission studies go way back to the ecumenical Central Committee on United Study in 1900. Beginning in 1901, the committee published a mission study annually for the use of mission study groups of women in local churches (Robert 1997: 260-261). Ecumenical Schools of Christian Mission, with preparation for teaching, began in 1904 with the efforts of the Federal Council of Churches, and then the National Council of Churches in the U.S. In 1999, the mission studies for the United Methodists began to be published by the General Board of Global Ministries of the United Methodist Church, and now solely by the United Methodist Women.

Every year, the United Methodist Women National Office trains leaders in three mission studies covering three different areas. One focuses on spiritual growth, another on a geographical area in the world, and the third one on a specific issue. This year's mission studies are *How Is It With Your Soul?* by Priscilla Pope-Levison and Jack Levison, *The Roma of Europe* by Larry Beman, *The Church and People with Disabilities: Awareness, Accessibility, and Advocacy* by Peggy Johnson. The spiritual growth study is produced in English, Spanish, and Korean annually. In addition, there are youth and children's studies, also. All these studies are developed by the United Methodist Women National Office.

In facilitating the mission studies to the study leaders regionally across the U.S., intentional efforts are taken to create an environment for transformative learning with access to both transformative and popular educational methods. The learning community for the study selected for this article is comprised of adult learners, pastors, and laity who facilitate these studies in the various United Methodist conferences. Transformative and popular educational methods emphasize learner-centered education over teacher-centered; awareness-raising education over depositing of information; empowerment for action over maintaining the status quo; and critical pedagogy over mere lecture method.

A key text which revolutionized adult education aimed at emancipatory knowledge in the late mid-twentieth century is *Pedagogy of the Oppressed* by Paulo Freire where he emphasizes education as a process which centers around critical reflection on one's personal and collective reality that leads to engagement in actions. Critical reflection is a component integral to transformative learning methods used in facilitating mission education.

Adult Learning as A Process and a Journey

A key Scripture I have used at the beginning of facilitating mission studies for adults is Matthew 13: 1-23. From a popular educational point of view, as interpreted by Helene Castel, this parable can offer insight into a "process of the seed being mixed with the soil" and this process is "not a gentle journey" but "a journey that is actively engaged with all the elements in the system of the soil and not controlled by the sower (the teacher). It is a deep earthy interaction…" (Castel 1999:7). Castel invites her class to imagine the possibility of plowing being done after sowing in ancient Palestine.

Whether this practice in ancient Palestine was predominant or not, for transformative learning process today, it is helpful to look at the parable closely as something about an interaction between the soil and the seeds, the condition of the soil and the effect of the soil on the seeds. A key insight the story offers is how the elements of the soil interact deeply with the seeds in order to bring forth results. The interaction of the soil and the seeds is a process, a mutual process. Transformative learning is also a process.

It has been said that we learn only 10% by reading; 20% by hearing; 30% by seeing; 50% by both seeing and hearing; 70% by sharing and discussing with each other; 80% by experiencing, and 95% by facilitating the study for someone else or a group. Transformative learning takes this seriously into account.

What is Transformative Learning?

In the language of the parable of the sower, transformative learning enables the learners:

- To move from being a mere seeing community to a perceiving community.

- To move from being a mere hearing community to an actively listening community.

- To listen to stories and share knowledge from both the heart and head levels.

- To name the resistant soils, systems that are hard and that choke lives at the margins of society.

- To understand with our hearts, align with the forces of transformation, God's reign in the world.

- Be moved to be difference-makers, bearers of fruit, a thirty-fold, a sixty-fold, and a hundred-fold.

Transformative learning is a "deep structural shift in one's consciousness, mindset, feelings, and actions" (O'Sullivan, Morrell and O'Conner 2006: xvii).

In the language of theological education for engagement in mission, as summarized by the conveners of the session on "Theological Education and Formation" at the World Missionary Conference of Edinburgh 2010, education is geared towards wholeness:

- The ear to hear God's word and the cry of God's people;

- The heart to heed and respond to the suffering;

- The tongue to speak to both weary and arrogant;

- The hands to work with the lowly;

- The mind to reflect on the good news of the gospel;

- The will to respond to God's call;

- The spirit to wait on God in prayer, to struggle, and to be silent, to intercede for the church and the world (Kim and Anderson 2011:158).

Though mission study methods to be outlined in the article are not the same as theological education methods, there are key outcomes which relate to both.

Key Steps in Transformative Learning

Using the spiritual growth study for 2012, *Immigration and the Bible* by Joan M. Maruskin, as an example, let me examine the ways in which I facilitated this spiritual growth study. Transformative learning starts with sharing stories from our different backgrounds and identities, relating to the issue under study. As stories from the mission study texts unfold, and concepts evolve, stories are shared from the different contexts of the learners.

The pedagogical strategy further includes reading the Bible through the eyes of the migrant, immigrant, and refugee. In fact, Maruskin's central thesis is that the "Bible is the ultimate immigration handbook. It was written by, for, and about migrants, immigrants, refugees, and asylum seekers" (Maruskin 2012: 3). Enabling reading through the perspectives of people at the margins offers a range of insights into the pain and cry of the least of these. Reading the stories from the Bible, as a community of people from different cultural backgrounds inside a class setting, and reflecting on what God is saying in specific contexts is both an individual and collective learning process.

Braiding the stories of immigrants, along with the insights from reading the biblical stories, the adult learners are led to further reflection. As reflections unfold, the participants identify patterns, similarities, and differences in the stories they hear from each other. The facilitator makes sure that while reflection takes place, voices of those not present at the table are included, since in analyzing the relations of power in the interconnected structures of class, race, gender etc., it is vital to include a diversity of voices. This part of the learning process is often known as critical reflection or critical thinking.

In this, self-examining one's presuppositions and social locations, as a study leader, is important. Elaine Enns and Chad Myers suggest that persons engaged in transformative work map their social power in light of race, class, gender, educational achievement etc., (Enns and Myers 1970:36). They name such an exercise "testing the soil of power and privilege" (1970:28). In a "Social Power Inventory and Worksheet for Individuals and Groups in the United States" that Enns and Myers have developed, on a scale of four in their mapping of social identities, four stands for the most powerful, three somewhat powerful, two not powerful, and one least powerful. This social mapping is based on perceptual realities. In the social mapping, as posited by Enns and Myers, the score of people with a graduate degree will be four and people with no high school education will be one; skin color white will be four; black one (1970: 36). The mapping includes attractiveness, professional status, gender, citizenship, language etc., and can be extended to include age, disability etc.,

Being aware of the social locations of the participants as well as the complexity of social realities can be helpful to the facilitator, since participants respond from their own social locations, assumptions, and perspectives. In order to lead the class in the critical reflection process collectively, such a tacit understanding is valuable, since the class members struggle with key issues in the mission study, as they name the issues, contradictions, as well as the systemic barriers.

Diagrammatically, the process of critical reflection can be represented by a spiral, starting with sharing one's experiences relating to the issue, reading the Bible through the eyes of the migrant and immigrant, locating patterns of similarity and dissimilarity, naming the barriers and resistance to change, discerning God's voice in the readings and at work in the world, looking for clues of transformation, and coming up with actions. The process is repeated again with the cycle of experience, reflection, and action. The spiral image captures the flow of the transformative method as it involves experience, reflection on experience, social analysis, strategies for transformation, and action.

Intersectionality

In the critical reflection, a key component is social identity and location of the person doing the analysis. Often social identities are connected to each other, and they are not isolated entities. The reality of interconnectedness or intersectionality of class, gender, race, national origin, language, disability, and so on cannot be dismissed in the critical reflection.

The term "intersectionality" is both a revealer of the layered and complex nature of the issue at hand, and also a tool available to address the issue. The term intersectionality was first coined by Kimberlé Crenshaw in 1989. A lawyer by profession who worked among battered women, Crenshaw named an experience which several of the women whom she encountered embodied. These women underwent multiple layers of oppression due to their race, class, sexuality, language, locality, etc. In their daily lived existence, these multiple oppressions intersected. Crenshaw has identified the site of multiple oppressions and named the place of such an experience. A woman of color, with no education, and who speaks a language other than the dominant language, and who has difficulty living above the poverty line embodies the impact of many strikes against her. (Crenshaw 1989: 1241–1299). It is important to address the convergence of these knotted oppressions as a whole using a holistic approach to solve the problem. Therefore it is of value to put on the lens of intersectionality. It is a tool for understanding and application for persons engaged in mission.

In facilitating the mission study, the reality of intersectionality is discussed, and its impact analyzed, as the clues and actions for transformation are geared towards the mission work of shalom, fullness of life for everyone. Since intersectional oppressions and shalom are mutually exclusive, in order to engage in the work of shalom, fullness of life for everyone, it is helpful to shape our tools for greater engagement in God'smission by naming the intersectional and fluid nature of identities, and not compartmentalize the various categories.

Transformative Spirituality

Equally important is the spiritual identity of the adult learner as a child of God. Recalling one's baptism, naming one's baptismal identity as a child of God, and claiming it as a call for all the baptized believers to "resist evil, injustice, and oppression in whatever forms they present themselves…" (*The United Methodist Hymnal* 1989: 34).

Transformative spirituality includes addressing personal sins as well as corporate sins and systemic evil. Raymond Fung from Hong Kong bemoans the fact that often the churches today have "no notion of sinned-againstness," and goes on to say, "The gospel should not only call on the people to repent of their sins but also must call on them to resist the forces that sin against them" (Fung 1980: 332-333). The hall mark of transformative spirituality is addressing sin as well as *sinned againstness,* the systems that perpetuate poverty, war, conflict, and that constantly push people to the margins of society and living.

Edinburgh 2010 Common Call includes a call for critical reflection saying, "Disturbed by the asymmetries and imbalances of power that divide and trouble the church and world, we are called to repentance, to critical reflection on systems of power, and to accountable use of power structures." This is reinforced in the official statement of mission and evangelism, approved by the central committee of the World Council of Churches in 2012, in its specific discussion on transformative spirituality (Keum 2013:12-14). Transformative spirituality undergirds transformative learning in addressing the cry of the needy, the sinned against people here and elsewhere.

The Bible has been and can be interpreted in a narrow way to support the oppressive systems. Transformative spirituality disturbs those of us comfortable with the injustices and imbalances of power that divide people, and offers us the courage to stand in solidarity with the least of these. Transformative spirituality or mission spirituality enables us to read the Bible from the perspectives of the least of God's children—be it the migrant, the poor, and the least of these with the God of Shalom, as they name the systems and barriers. As faith community, the class struggle to be in alignment with the values of the reign of God, the kingdom of God, the Shalom which is everyone's right, and which Jesus came to embody and make open to everyone.

As the class works on action plans, stories of struggle in the Bible, reading the Bible through the eyes of the least of these, reclaiming our baptismal identity and the sustenance of Holy Communion, walking in solidarity with the least of these, respecting their being change agents, are part of the transformative spirituality part of being the church in the world.

Feeding the roots of transformation today includes seeding justice, love, and peace, and identifying allies who are engaged in addressing the same social justice issue. This is the pedagogical core then; the basics of this kind of learning. Facilitating mission studies is learner-centered. Learners themselves are agents of change and interveners in places of injustice to transform them. Study leaders are not unquestioned authorities. They examine their own presuppositions and social locations. They are enablers and creators of safe environments for trust and sharing. The learning process may be messy sometimes but it is like the soil and seed which exist in a womb of mutuality. Mission education venue is like a seedbed where seeds are sown and saplings nurtured that will sprout into transformation.

Use of Social Tree as an Informal Method of Analysis

The lecture method is only minimally effective in facilitating the mission study. Intentionally the leader is called a facilitator, not a conveyor of mere content, as a teacher. Discussions, role play, panels, simulation exercises, and skits are some of the methods used in facilitating the study. I will share two examples, one the use of social tree and another, a dialogue on informative and transformative learning. The use of a social tree is a method often used and adapted by popular educationists (Barndt, 1989: 31).

In this exercise, the participants are seated in small groups, and asked to imagine a socially-well tree and a socially-ill tree, and draw these two trees both side by side on newsprint. The facilitator invites each group to imagine if an ideal community were a tree, what could be the roots, trunk, branches, leaves, and fruits? In other words, the facilitator invites the participants to communicate what an ideal community looks like pictorially or in words using different colored pencils. The naming is done through picture as well as words, as the case may be. The adult learners use post-its to move their concepts on the tree from one part of the tree to the other, as in small groups, they come up with an alternative vision.

In the same fashion, the participants are invited to imagine a socially-ill community. If it were a tree, what could be the roots, trunk, branches, leaves, and fruits. The participants communicate a broken-down community in the picture and in words. What the pictures are supposed to convey are the interrelated nature of the parts. The ideal tree is an alternative vision. These two contrasting pictures are used to demonstrate how issues need to be addressed at the root level, while offering charity measures as a temporary solution to problems.

The facilitator enables the participants to do critical reflection using the named parts of the socially-ill tree and leading them to envision action steps taken towards an alternative vision imagined by the groups. The various components of the critical-thinking process come into play in a pictorial way. For the basic data about the economic and social conditions in a particular community in the U.S. the participants are encouraged to visit *The American Community Survey* at www.census.gov/acs.

Cross-Cultural Contextualization

Cross-cultural contextualization in the United Methodist Women Mission educational settings is a challenge and opportunity to the study leaders. Rightly done, the mission study becomes a gift to the margins.

Often non-Hispanic and non-Korean study leaders are called at the regional level to equip themselves for facilitating the conference-level Hispanic and Korean study leaders etc., The spiritual growth texts are translated into Spanish and Korean annually, and they are aimed to provide methodology that is culture-specific.

Contextualization is the freedom to learn the text from one's own respective cultural context. It is also the freedom from seeing the world in a contextually-homogenized setting. Context of the learner is a key element in transformative learning. The context is fluid, dynamic, and it is constructed constantly. It is not static. Images, symbols, language, objects, worldviews and identities are some of the elements that shape one's context. Culture defines contextualization as it "attempts to see a culture not as a static system, but rather a system that is always in the process of change because of stimuli from within and from without" (Neely 1995:8). A key question for contextualization then is the ability to see through the lens of the respective cultural readership: seeing it from the underside versus seeing it from the location of privilege.

Regional Mission Study Leader as Connector

Facilitators of the study at the regional levels do have Hispanic and Korean leaders in their classes who teach the study in their respective languages. Often the facilitators have a conversation with them in an informal setting, discussing methods of teaching that might make meaningful connections between the key themes of the text and the living experience of the participants in the respective cultural groups.

- What is the Korean/Hispanic experience that provides the framework within which the text can be understood and experienced fully?

- Among the particular target group, how do the daily experiences of the women vary from those of men? Help the participants claim their daily experience of struggle in the Hispanic context, and the daily experience of the Korean context.

- What are some of the cultural components of the target group?

  » Immigration in Korean/Hispanic contexts

  » Hybridity (belonging to two or more identities)

  » Diaspora (living in more than one world, the locality of one's country of origin and the country of their residence)

  » Ritual and other symbols

  » Use of stories

- What are some of the contextually-oriented methods that can be added as options when facilitating this mission study?

- Designing a learning environment to suit diversity within the target group.

Serving Contexts Within the Context

Max Stackhouse once asked the question, "How do we know a context when we see one?" He himself responded to his question by asking other questions such as "How big is a context? How long does it last? Who is in it? Who is out of it? And how do we know?" (Neely 1995: 8). Geography, language, ethnicity, political systems, economic systems, social systems, class, gender, age, language, values, identit,y etc., form the larger context.

As for the Hispanic and Korean participants, they often function in their respective cultural contexts within the larger context of the dominant culture. A context within the context speaks of a layered existence. The language study leaders serve the contexts within the context. The regional mission study leader is encouraged to be aware of this context of the language groups within the larger context, and facilitate spaces for such contexts within the context to flourish. That is, the regional mission study leader equips language study leaders to enable their participants to see their different stories and multiple belongings, from their different social sites against the backdrop of larger systems and structures. The language study leaders enable the participants to tell their stories in their own respective contexts, against the backdrop of the narratives of the dominant stories and systems. Mission study class rooms facilitate the space for interconnectedness for the language group leaders to serve a context within the context.

Mission education class prepares the way for the church to be in the world in new ways with a contextual communication and constant conversation between the center and the margins. The center creates and facilitates spaces for multiple voices and the margins shape and influence the center. In summary, facilitating mission study is more than the act of studying; it is study that leads to action in order to make a difference. A story in the Babylonian Talmud captures this timeless truth. Rabbi Akiva and Rabbi Tarfon debate the question, "Which is greater, study or action?" Rabbi Tarfon answered saying that action is greater. Rabbi Akiva answered saying that study is greater. The listening elders agreed with Rabbi Akiva that study is greater than action because it leads to action (*Babylonian Talmud, Kiddushin* 40b). At the end of facilitating the mission study, I have made use of the following dialogue which I wrote to drive home the summary of the distinction between informative and transformative educational methods.

Dialogue Between Information Education and Transformative Education

Two Study Leaders and One Mission Study

I am a study leader.	I am a study leader.
I teach in the conference Mission u this year.	I teach in the Mission u this year.
My name is INFORMATIVE education.	My name is TRANSFORMATIVE education.
Mine is a banking model of education.	Mine is a transforming model of education.
I deposit knowledge.	Learners and the leaders together produce knowledge.
Mine is a top-down model.	Mine is learner-centered.
I am the "sage on the stage."	I am a "guide on the side."
I transmit *authoritative* knowledge.	I facilitate *emancipatory* knowledge.
I thrive on an auditorium-style class room.	I prefer a class room suited for small-group discussions.

I am a study leader.	I am a study leader.
I control knowledge production.	I work with critical pedagogy.
I provide information and expertise.	I create space for collaborative learning.
I add to the already existing-structures of knowledge.	I lead the leaders *out* from an established habit of mind.
Learners are consumers of facts.	Learners are agents of change.
I want my learners to imitate me.	I empower my learners to reflect on their experiences.
Are not learners "received knowers?" Deepening an individual's reserach base?	Aren't they "connected owers?" Connecting themselves and their stories to structures of domination and marginalization?
Invest in information. That is a starting point.	Broadening collective knowledge by listening to the voices from the margins. Learners bring their experiences, diverse gifts, and identities. Reflection of experiences and understanding other worldviews. That is a starting point.
Research + reading = Accumulated knowledge.	Critical reflection & collective analysis = *Conscientization*.
Is not our goal to cover the content of the study?	Is not our goal to change people from being consumers of content to transformers of lives?
You use big words like the United Methodists who talk about *transformation of the world*.	Transformation is the key word.

I am a study leader.	I am a study leader.
Isn't reality being-in-itself?	Isn't reality being- in-community?
Living out of oneself.	Living out of relationship.
Between God and me.	Between God-to-human, human-to-human, human-to-creation.
Isn't reality being-in-itself?	Isn't reality being- in-community?
Living out of oneself.	Living out of relationship.
Between God and me.	Between God-to-human, human-to-human, human-to-creation.
The core relation of human beings is to God.	The core relation of human beings is to God and neighbor.
Who is my neighbor?	Transformative learning is all about "Neighborology."
Plain truth.	*For a plain people.*
Called Methodists.	Called United Methodists.
Who strive for personal holiness.	Who strive for both personal holiness as well as social holiness.
My name is INFORMATIVE education.	My name is TRANSFORMATIVE education.

Works Cited

Anonymous
  1744   *Minutes of the Methodist Conferences, from the First, held in
          London, by the Late Rev. John Wesley, in the year 1744*, vol.
          1. London: John Mason, 1862.

Barndt, Deborah
  1989   *Naming the Moment: Political Analysis for Action.* Toronto,
          Canada: The Jesuit Centre for Social Faith and Justice.

  1989   *Babylonian Talmud, Kiddushin* 40 B. http://on1foot. org/
          text/babyloniantalmud-kiddushin-40b.

Castel, Helene
  1999   "Reflections on How Adults Learn and Change in Justice
          Education: "Taking Learners as Seriously as the Issues."
          Unpublished paper presented to the National Seminar
          of the Women's Division, General Board of Global
          Ministries, The United Methodist Church. August 1983.
          Updated June.

Enns, Elaine and Chad Myers
  2009   *Ambassadors of Reconciliation: Diverse Christian Practices
          of Restorative Justice and Peacemaking.* Vol. 2. Maryknoll,
          NY: Orbis Press.

Fung, Raymond
  1980   "Human Sinned-Againstness." *International Review of
          Mission*, 69(275): 332-333.

Kim, Kirsteen and Andrew Anderson, eds.
  2011   *Edinburgh 2010: Mission Today and Tomorrow.* Oxford,
          UK: Regnum Books International.

Kimberlé Crenshaw
>	1989	"Mapping the Margins: Intersectionality, Identity Politics, and Violence against Women of Color," *Stanford Law Review*, 43(6):1241-1299.

Keum, Jooseop, ed.
>	2013	*Together Towards Life: Mission and Evangelism in Changing Landscapes with a Practical Guide.* Geneva: WCC Publications.

Maruskin, Joan
>	2012	*Immigration and the Bible: A Guide for Radical Welcome.* New York: Women's Division, General Board of Global Ministries, The United Methodist Church.

O' Sullivan, Edmund, Amish Morrel, and Mary Ann O'Conner, eds.
>	2002	*Expanding the Boundaries of Transformative Learning: Essays on Theory and Praxis.* New York: Palgrave.

Neely, Alan
>	1995	*Christian Mission: A Case Study Approach.* Maryknoll, NY: Orbis Press.

Robert L. Dana
>	1998	*American Women in Mission: A Social History of Their Thought and Practice.* Macon, Macon, Georgia: Mercer University Press, 1997. Reprint.

United Methodist Church
>	1989	*The United Methodist Hymnal.* Nashville: The United Methodist Publishing House.

The Pedagogy of Hip Hop in Teaching Missiology

Exploring a Project Based Learning Environment using Elements of Hip Hop Culture as the Curriculum

DANIEL WHITE HODGE

DOI: 10.7252/Paper.000031

About the Authors

Daniel White Hodge, PhD, is the director of the Center for Youth Ministry Studies and Assistant Professor of Youth Ministry at North Park University. He is the author of the forthcoming book *The Hostile Gospel: Post Soul Theological Connections in Hip Hop Culture* (Brill Academic 2014), *Heaven Has A Ghetto: The Missiological & Theological Message of Tupac Amaru Shakur* (VDM Academic 2009), and *The Soul of Hip Hop: Rimbs, Timbs, & A Cultural Theology* (IVP 2010).

Abstract

There is no doubt of the influence Hip Hop has had on the pop-culture scene throughout the Western World. Moreover, with the emergence of the field of Hip Hop Studies and educators such as Christopher Emdin who use Hip Hop to teach science, math, and history, it stands to reason that Hip Hop is much more than just a musical genre. This paper explores the uses of Hip Hop pedagogy in the classroom to teach aspects of missiology (e.g. *missio Dei*, being sent forth). Using a project based learning pedagogical format in which lectures are limited, projects and class interaction is elevated, and the use of the four foundational elements to Hip Hop are utilized (Djing, dance, graffiti art, and MCing), I will demonstrate the power of Hip Hop culture in a learning environment to teach missiological concepts. Finally, I will argue that Hip Hop pedagogy is an effective learning tool to engage the emerging young adult population as it utilizes a multi-discipline approach and contains many aspects in it that are theological and missiological.

The Case for Hip Hop and Missions

With its 'in your face' mantra and passionate pleas for calls to justice, social consciousness, and spiritual reformation (Hodge 2010a, 2010b, One 2003, Outlawz 1999). Hip Hop has begun to show its multi- dimensional traits and many uses (Dhokai 2012, Norton 2014, Petchauer 2011b). There is no reservation that Hip Hop has provided a wealth of material in which to discuss, debate, and engage with. Hip Hop[1], being a culture, lifestyle, and way of life, is also widely misunderstood and often seen, in the Christian church, as secular, humanist, devoid of God, and profane (Hacker 1995, Hodge 2009, 2010b, Hopkins 2001, Reed 2003, Smith and Jackson 2005). As the scholarship of Hip Hop has grown exponentially over the last decade, very little research has been done on the missiological significance of Hip Hop and its wealth of theological messages. Further, the absence of Hip Hop's uses in the classroom for Christian higher educational pedagogy is even more glaring. To give an example, the non-

Christian scholarly world has seen the effectiveness of Hip Hop's uses in the classroom and has begun to adopt various pedagogical strategies in order to embrace the fullness of Hip Hop.

Christopher Emdin, launched a nationwide sensation when he suggested that Hip Hop could be used to teach math and science (Emdin 2007a, 2007b 2008). Emdin suggested that Hip Hop was a multi-disciplinary tool and one that aided students in learning the components of math; he has been very successful and continues to develop this pedagogy (Emdin 2015b). Jason Irizarry has suggested that Hip Hop's music is one which can provide potential for teachers to be informed on how to actually teach. Irizarry suggests that teaching practices can actually be improved from learning the pedagogical frameworks within Hip Hop (2009: 496-498). Emery Petchauer has suggested to us that when students are 'deeply involved' with Hip Hop culture their learning environment and structure is improved and that students are able to apply their experiences with the critical discourses of Hip Hop (Petchauer 2011b). In the music field, Hip Hop, in the obvious sense, has been utilized to teach everything from theory, notation, chord progression, voice structure, and digital notation (Petchauer 2011a, 2011b, 2009, Hill 2009, Emdin 2008, Dhokai 2012). These are just a few of the uses of Hip Hop in the non-Christian setting.

Howard Peskett and Vinoth Ramachandra have suggested that part of missions is about "caring for human suffering" (2003: 39-40) and that working for peace is part of a biblical mandate (167-171). Edward Pentecost has reminded us that missionary theology includes philosophy, theology, anthropology, sociology, communications, world religions, church history, and psychology (1982: 14-18)—all of which are aspects of what Hip Hop culture does (Hodge 2013b, 2013a). Glenn Rogers has also argued that part of missiology's specialization is community response and development along with teaching while developing a theology of mission (2003: 77-98). These are all aspects and mantras of Hip Hop culture (Hodge - 2015 Forthcoming). Should they also not be included in the missiological field as examples of appropriate contextualization? Wilbert Shenk has argued for a contextual and more contemporary form of missions and missiological engagement with popular culture (1999). I would agree and add that Hip Hop culture – global in many ways – is a mission field and also one that is largely under-studied in the field of missiology.

Thus, where is the work in the Christian educational context? Where is the work which makes the case to better learn the Gospel using Hip Hop pedagogy? I argue that Hip Hop is, in fact, a strong pedagogical tool for teaching the concepts of missiology—the *missio Dei* and being sent forth. This essay will demonstrate the uses of a Hip Hop curriculum used in a classroom setting at North Park University in Chicago Illinois by using the foundational four elements of Hip Hop—Djing, MCing, Dance, and Graffiti Art. Using classwork as a form of measurement, I will demonstrate the increases in knowledge toward the *missio Dei* by using Hip Hop as a pedagogical tool. Lastly, I will suggest that Hip Hop pedagogy is an effective learning tool to engage the emerging young adult population as it utilizes a multi-discipline approach and contains many aspects in it that are theological and missiological.

Hip Hop Education Literature

While I realize many reading this essay are not familiar with the concepts, arguments, and field of Hip Hop Studies, the limits of this essay keep me from expanding on the historical dimensions of Hip Hop and to make the case for Hip Hop theology.[2] However, there is a growing body of scholarship that argues for this (George 1998, 2004, Guevara 1996, Miller 2013, Morgan 1999, Neal 2002, One 2003, One 2009, Pinn 2003, Reed 2003, Rose 1994, 2008, Southern 1983, Utley 2012, Watkins 2011, Watkins 2005, West 1993, Zanfagna 2006) and I will mainly focus here, on the literature surrounding Hip Hop pedagogy and education in the classroom.

As Emery Petchauer has reminded us, it is important for researchers to explore the content of Hip Hop's lyrics, but it is inaccurate to assume that listeners interpret, apply, and assign meaning the same way researchers do (2011b: 770). Therefore, it is imperative that Hip Hop be engaged by listeners, communities, and educators; that is, we must approach Hip Hop as both a learner and educator simultaneous as Niyati Dhokai has suggested (2012: 113-114). This maintains, then, that the educator must be willing to change and adapt to the various contexts that emerging adult college students bring to the classroom. Iwamoto, Creswell, and Caldwell (2007) explored what rap lyrics and their meanings meant to eight college students of different ethnicities. In their study, they found that students responses varied and that Hip Hop and rap music were utilized for a varied use in the lives of students (Iwamoto, Creswell, and Caldwell 2007: 343-344). From this, the suggestion is that Hip Hop cannot be viewed as merely a one dimensional construct and that "everybody" interprets the same thing in the music; the educator must be aware of this (Hill 2009, Dimitriadis 2001).

The basic elements of Hip Hop (DJing, dance, MCing, and graffiti art) can also be used in therapeutic sessions. Susan Hadley and George Yancy's (2012) edited volume, *Therapeutic Uses of Rap and Hip-Hop*, argues for just that. Rap is utilized to incorporate aspects of psychotherapy in a contextualized manner by asking clients what their preference is in rap music; then, through careful therapeutic process, songs are dissected and discussed at length as it pertains to the person's areas of concern (Elligan 2012:35-37). Further, Edgar Tyson discovered that rap music and elements of Hip Hop dance can be used in grief therapy with Black males (2013). This type of work in the areas of post-traumatic stress disorder (PTSD) can prove to be useful when dealing with a generation of urban Black males who have experienced intensely traumatic events. Tyson found that the youth, in the process of dealing with their trauma, actually discovered hidden talents they had through the rap music; this aided them in their recovery from PTSD (2013:298-300). Tyson argues that "...neglecting to utilize and examine these Hip-Hop based technologies in youth work also might represent a missed opportunity to successfully intervene in the lives of one of society's most vulnerable populations" (303). That should be impetus for any missiologist to explore Hip Hop further.

Scott MacDonald and Michael Viega (2013) discovered a form of therapy through song writing in the medium of rap (e.g. MCing). By utilizing rap songs and artists who are discussing pain and lamenting, the authors—who are also therapists— found that the music making experience was important and life changing for the youth they were working with (168-170). This study demonstrates the power of music and the continuing positive effect of art in the lives of young people.

Christopher Emdin, whose Ted Talk on Hip Hop pedagogy has been viewed by thousands, has discovered a process of using Hip Hop to teach, inform, and construct mathematic equations. Emdin's work is now being adopted in not only college classrooms, but also K-12 settings in which young people are taught basic concepts in math, science, and even history (2007, 2008). In this pedagogy, the active project based classroom is utilized to allow for students to discuss, engage, question, and learn from the culture of Hip Hop while employing mathematical skills in the classroom from the basic elements of math to calculus. Emdin's approach uses both a contextualized manner of teaching, while also allowing room for the curriculum to change as needed; this is crucial as Hip Hop culture continues to evolve. Key constructs to his teaching philosophy (e.g. project-based and student-centered learning) remain concrete, while the actual pedagogy is movable and allows room for the educator to create new models of learning as the student climate changes to allow for effective teaching and strategy.[3] Emdin's model is worthy for any educator to take note of and creates space for Hip Hop to be used beyond the teaching of just music (Iwamoto, Creswell, and Caldwell 2007, Petchauer 2011a, 2011b, Irby and Hall 2011, Dhokai 2012, Petchauer 2009). The spiritual and theological uses of Hip Hop are missing in this literatire. One must ask, how students also might derive missiological principles from Hip Hop influenced education?

Conceptual Framework

This essay employs the conceptual framework and worldview of Paulo Freire's *conscientização* to explore how Hip Hop could be used in a critical fashion, while still maintaining a missiological position. This primary framework was chosen to accommodate the broader conceptualization of Hip Hop as a voice for the oppressed, liberating minds and souls, and in creating critical thinking skills toward a missiological theory. Freire describes *conscientização* as:

> ...learning to perceive social, political, and economic contradictions and to take action against the oppressive elements of reality... *conscientização* does not lead men to 'destructive fanaticism.' On the contrary, by making it possible for men to enter the historical process as responsible subjects, *conscientização* enrolls them in the search for self-affirmation and thus avoids fanaticism (2000: 19-20)

This definition elucidates metacognition in the framework of liberation theologies and philosophies. That is, with Hip Hop, one is able to imagine a liberated position through the music, art, and social aesthetic of Hip Hop culture (Giroux 1996). Using Freire's modus, Hip Hop, then, is used to help the student 1) think about how to think, 2) think towards liberation, and 3) in a missiological sense, think towards the liberating power of Jesus Christ within dominant structures of oppression and injustice. To this conclusion, Freire raises a Christological point,

> ...the great humanistic and historical task of the oppressed: to liberate themselves and their oppressors as well. The oppressors, who oppress, exploit, and rape by virtue of their power, cannot find in this power the strength to liberate either the oppressed or themselves. Only power that springs from weakness of the oppressed will be sufficiently strong to free both (2000: 28).

A Christian's mission, then, is to help 'free minds' and souls toward a Christ-like worldview.[4] Freire, then, has created a conceptual context for the use of Hip Hop to teach missiological concepts.[5]

In addition to Freire's *conscientização* concept, I also draw from Wilbert Shenk's (1999) work on the contextualizing missions model. Shenk argues for a three-part thesis toward the inclusion and engagement with contextualization (1999: 56):

> Contextualization is a process whereby the gospel message encounters a particular culture, calling forth faith and leading to the formation of a faith community, which is culturally authentic and authentically Christian.
>
> Control of the process resides within the context rather than with an external agent or agency.
>
> Culture is understood to be a dynamic and evolving system of values, patterns of behavior, and a matrix shaping the life of the members of that society.

In this sense, Hip Hop is the contextualizing agent, used in a classroom, with emerging adult students, and allowing that cultural agent (Hip Hop) to create, change, and edify the classroom all the while allowing for the control of the process to reside within the context—in this case being young people and emerging adulthood populations. This, arguably, is a process that connects with Shenk's dynamic and evolving ideology of culture by using a contemporary model of engagement in a classroom setting.

My utilization of critical pedagogy here is not to frame Hip Hop as a complete and true form of critical pedagogy, although there have been Eurocentric attempts to do just that (Stovall 2006) and Afrocentric ones as well (Wells-Wilbon, Jackson, and Schiele 2010). My attempt here, however, is to cohesively outline the general ways that educators and students may engage and construct a Hip Hop pedagogical environment as well as identify the similarities between Hip Hop and missiology vis-à-vis its use in the classroom.

Missiological Uses of Hip Hop in the Classroom

In the fall of 2012, I taught a topics course entitled "The Socio-Theological Discourses of Hip Hop Culture" at North Park University. The course was a hybrid of the flipped classroom,[6] and used Linda Nilson's framework for student-centered learning and outcomes-centered course design (2003: 17-32). The course, which turned into a required general education course, was designed with the student learning process in mind and to give students 1) the opportunity to discover and explore Hip Hop Culture—in this case being the theological context, 2) allow for students to explore, missiologically, the meaning of Christian theology as seen from a Hip Hop perspective, and 3) to utilize new methods of pedagogy derived and rooted in the four foundational elements of Hip Hop. The course description was as follows:

> This course explores the dynamics, cultural variances, theological discourses, and applied methods of Hip Hop spirituality in relationship to adolescent culture. This class introduces students to the issues, culture, and dimensions surrounding Hip Hop spirituality. Close attention will be paid to a theology of Hip Hop and its culture. Through discussion, historical contexts, sociocultural analysis, urban theory, literature, film, and Black Liberation Theology,

a cultural overview of Hip Hop will be drawn to better understand how adolescents and early adults engage in this forty year culture and musical genre; we will also be engaging in the ten foundational elements of Hip Hop culture: DJing/ Turntablism, Breaking, Graffiti art, Break Beats, MCing, Street Knowledge, Street Language, Street Fashion, Entrepreneurialism, and Knowledge of God and Self.

This course introduces students to the challenges and issues involved in Hip Hop studies as it relates to youth ministry, youth culture, and popular culture discourse. Close attention will be paid to various methods of intercultural engagement, the media's response and understanding of Hip Hop, our own understanding of race/ethnicity in relation to Hip Hop studies (which will include but not be limited to African American, Asian, Latino/a, Middle Eastern, and Euro American), youth ministry in the Hip Hop context, and ministry strategies in order to disciple or serve youth who live a Hip Hop ethos. The student will be challenged to become culturally aware and sensitive in their engagement with the past, present and future of Hip Hop. The student will also be able to interpret and analyze the reality of what Hip Hop was, is, and will be. And, the students will be equipped to be cultural ambassadors in their respective communities.

The course was initially open to both undergraduate and graduate students (seminarians). The first class had eleven graduate students and eight undergraduate students. The crucial element in this class was that the seminarian students came from ministry backgrounds—that is, ninety percent of them were actively engaged in a ministry setting. While the full ten elements of Hip Hop were discussed, we focused on the initial four— as previously mentioned. The learning outcomes, using a standard Bloom's Taxonomy approach with active verbs, were:

Analyze individual and culturally diverse approaches to Hip Hop culture. *(You will accomplish this by attending class, viewing films, and participating in class activities.)*

Articulate the ways Hip Hop espouses various theological mantras in connection to the *missio Dei. (You will accomplish this by doing the reading response papers, and final paper/ project.)*

Articulate the relationship between Christ and culture set against a grid of Hip Hop, urban popular culture, and current youth culture patterns. *(You will do this in group discussions, reading response papers, and in the final paper/ project.)*

Identify obstacles to current Hip Hop culture and popular youth and young adult culture. *(You will do this by viewing the films and the group project.)*

Articulate a theologically informed model for understanding, relating to and serving youth involved in Hip Hop culture. *(You will accomplish this in the group project, and in the final project.)*

You will note that assignments were assigned to each of the five learning outcomes of the course. This, following Nilson's (2003) student-centered learning approach, gave students a framework for how each assignment connected to their learning experience. This greatly affected the learning dynamics in class too.[7] In addition, the class had an online component, Moodle, and electronic materials (e.g. articles, websites, and videos) were uploaded along with mini-lectures which aided in class preparation. Having Moodle greatly enhanced the class as lecture notes, syllabi, and all handouts were placed there; a real-time gradebook was also used so that students always knew where they stood in the class and were able to access comments to their work.[8]

In crafting the assignments I sought out colleagues such as Ebony Utley, Monica Miller, Andre Johnson, and Ralph Watkins all of whom are active scholars in Hip Hop Studies, and have taught courses on various topics of Hip Hop and rap music. This gave me an overall sense of how to structure the class. In designing assignments, five key aspects were kept in mind:

Readings and the required literature needed to be attended to.

Active learning[9] was essential for student engagement and learning,

Missiological principles must be kept in mind.

At least two of the main assignments must have a gender, racial, and ethnic diversity component to them.

No testing of any kind (e.g. multiple choice exams, or essay exams). Student success is measured by a) class attendance and participation, b) reading response papers, c) graded in class responses to activities or lectures, and d) a final group city excursion and a final paper or creative project.

The readings for the class were as follows:

Forman, Murray, and Mark Anthony Neal. 2011. *That's The Joint! The Hip Hop Studies Reader.* 2 ed. New York, NY: Routledge. ISBN: 978-0-415-87326-0 (2nd Edition is needed)

Hodge, Daniel White. 2010. *The Soul Of Hip Hop: Rimbs Timbs and A Cultural Theology.* Downers Grove, Ill.: Inter Varsity Press. ISBN: 9780830837328

Miller, Monica R. 2013. *Religion and Hip Hop.* New York, NY: Routledge.

Smith, Efrem, and Phil Jackson. 2005. *The Hip Hop Church: Connecting with The Movement Shaping our Culture.* Downers Grove, Ill.: IVP. ISBN-10: 0830833293 ISBN-13: 978-0830833290

Utley, Ebony A. 2012. *Rap And Religion: Understanding The Gangsta's God.* Santa Barbara, CA; Denver CO.: Praeger. ISBN: 978-0-313-37668-9

From there, the foundation was set to begin creating a class that would actively challenge the student. Lectures were kept to fifteen to twenty minutes (occasionally they went longer depending on the conversation) and immediately following each lecture, there was a form of processing involved for each student (e.g. think, pair, share; 3-2-1 processing) which, very often, involved writing.

Technology (cell phones, iPads, laptops), in this initial class[10], was allowed, but used minimally and/or for a particular assignment. This aided greatly, and the maturity of the graduate students also helped to serve as a "role model" effect for the undergraduates in the class. Class was a three hour block (6:30-9:50 PM; with a 30 minute break) which also enhanced the learning atmosphere of the course.

Each class contained some type of class activity which would help students process the subject matter of that specific class. When we dealt with aspects of the cross and Jesus, we explored artists such as DMX, Tupac, and Lauryn Hill as they discuss Christological messages in their music as they intertwined the sacred, profane, and the secular all into one song—this relating to MCing. Then, lyrics were given to students for a particular song, they were then asked to do a word study on the song, video, and artist (using their technology) and come up with similarities or dissimilarities connected to Jesus and Hip Hop; these projects were done in groups and the students were asked at the beginning "What is the mission God, or, what is God up to in this song, if anything?" The process took an hour, and the discussion forty five minutes. Responses to this assignment from students were:

- I never knew God was active in the Hip Hop community; I always assumed "we" [Christians] needed to go the "them."

- I'm still having a hard time seeing the connecting of Jesus in a song that has the F-word in it, but, the lines to Jesus in Hip Hop and the Hip Hop in Jesus are a lot clearer now.

- God is at work with DMX. God is at work in Hip Hop and we need to listen.

- For the first time, I saw a contextual image of Jesus; these rappers are doing the same thing white theologians like Moody did— rappers just make it sound better!

- Now I can see, a little bit better, how Jesus is connected through and in Hip Hop

These responses, directly from students, helped bridge the next assignment which was to examine the social justice connections between rap music and the New Testament. These two assignments were covered over a period of two classes and then a full debrief session was given with the class. I used

3-2-1 processing to begin the discussion, yet, after about twenty minutes; the discussion always took a shape of its own.[11] Here are some of the themes, as I took my own notes, of these conversations:

- This is the first time I feel like I'm able to engage in class; I've been in seminary now for 2 ½ years and I'm always spoken to.

- God is doing something different within the Hip Hop culture.

- Jesus would have been a Hip Hop head.

- Hip Hop should be used as a missional instrument and cultural tool.

- Never knew Hip Hop was so complex.

- I see Jesus better as a result of Hip Hop[12]

Every other week we had a performance of spoken word, rap, or urban poetry.[13] Each artist was given the scope of the class and then, in turn, focused their material around a theological or spiritual concept. Two such artists were Muslim and discussed the power of the "mission of God" in relation to "the people of God" within oppressive conditions. The artists took about an hour and a half of class to perform and then a discussion followed with the class while the artists were present. If the artist had an album or video, pre-class work was assigned so that the class was aware and knowledgeable of the person or persons. These performances, connecting back to MCing, DJing, and dance, made Hip Hop "come alive" for the students and gave a real-time expression of the pain, struggle and life connected to God and the *missio Dei*. I specifically chose Muslim artists because it gave us a much broader look within the Abrahamic faiths and traditions within Hip Hop culture.[14]

In brief lectures, I, as the educator, made full use of the classroom by walking, moving, and using all three white boards in the class. This follows a pedagogical process which actively places students' attention on both the material and how it is being presented, rather than just speaking from written notes, at the front of the class, from a podium (Nilson 2003).

Students were expected to go on a city outing to some Hip Hop event or venue within the city of Chicago. This project took students beyond the classroom, lectures, and literature which oftentimes, confounds students in their learning process. One must foster the active learning skills outside of the classroom (Hill 2013, Petchauer 2012, Nilson 2003). This city project specifically focused on a Hip Hop event or venue and students, with careful guidelines, were asked to research, engage, and participate (if possible) to explore the socio-theological dimensions of what was happening and how God was at work or the mission of God was being fulfilled.

The real power of this course was that students were able to better see God, understand the Bible and, explore Jesus through a Hip Hop lens, and engage the hegemonic structures of oppression all through a Hip Hop perspective. Two of the African American students in the class told me that this was the first time in their three years as seminary students, learning about "theology," that they felt they had come into a class prepared and not behind their white classmates. A Latina undergraduate student told me that she took the class just to fulfill a credit, but, as a result, was considering ministry to the Hip Hop generation. Five of my Euro-American students relayed to me that this class was one of the "best" in terms of helping explain Liberation Theology, Howard Thurman's theology for the disenfranchised, and James Cone's Black Theology of Liberation. Hip Hop has a multi-disciplinary approach, much like missiology. Further, Hip Hop provides a contemporary feel to "learning" and curriculum design and when used to teach on missiological concepts, provides a rich pedagogical process in which to better understand not just the Gospel of Jesus, but the application of it in real-time settings. That is missional and needed for this generation.

Toward A Hip Hop Missiological Pedagogy

Not everyone can teach a class on Hip Hop. Not everyone should. Little to no understanding of the culture, only having "read" about Hip Hop, and simple ignorance of the field of Hip Hop Studies, could lead to disastrous results. This paper has been concerned with showing a case study example for a class on Hip Hop to teach missiological concepts. Yet, almost any subject can be converted to do just that. The main goal here was to move away from traditional methods and pedagogy of teaching (e.g. lecture, passive learning, and testing), engage students with project-based learning modules, allow students to digest and process a wealth of new information, while still keeping the focus on God and what God was up to in a particular culture. Still, Hip Hop remains a relatively untouched people group by missiologists, and what follows is a brief glance towards what a Hip Hop missiological pedagogy may look like.

The reason Hip Hop and rap can evoke such a connection with this generation and provide a missiological connection is simple; They:

Evoke truth and light within contextual forms of theological inquiries.

Are multi-ethnic in approach and cultural worldviews.

Challenge the norms dominant in culture and religion.

Provide ambiguity yet reveal the mystery of who God is within suffering contexts.

Look for new modes of "church" in a sacred/profane context while still pointing to God as the ultimate "answer" for life—an aspect that the mosaic generation is interested in.

Youth, the Mosaics, postindustrial people groups, and those estranged from religious contexts are not the cultural contexts of fifty years ago. More importantly, with the advent of media, technology, and the age of information, we have a youth culture that is both savvy and technologically creative. For the pastor who is missionally minded, this can present challenges to their theological framework. Hip Hop, while flawed and still human, creates space for those seeking God in alternate ways, to find God and to value the power of what the Bible says in a more relevant contextual form. Hip Hop artists, such as Tupac, act as theologians who can interpret the Bible for a people who are hurting, in need, and desperate for God's love. As Dyson reminds us, Hip Hoppers "…aim to enhance awareness of the divine, of spiritual reality, by means of challenging orthodox beliefs and traditional religious practices" (Dyson 2001: 204). We must give attention to this global culture and the effect it has on our youth – even more so if they are in our youth groups. For example, in my research, some powerful responses came forth when I asked the question "What does Hip Hop make you feel spiritually, if anything?" Here are just a few: "I can feel God smiling on me when I rap," "I found the Bible to be deeper and more real when I listen to Pac," "Hip Hop is our good news…you feel me? I mean, it's like a church and place we can go," and "Hip Hop saved my life. Period. If it wasn't for God working in the rap, I'd be dead now." (Hodge 2009, 2010b). Hip Hop helps the church embrace its mission fully by having a message that youth can and do identify with (Smith and Jackson 2005).

Therefore, missions must look different from what we are used to in order to even begin a conversation with the Hip Hop community, and be what Harvey Cox calls the *laostheou* or "the people of God" in creating a Church (Big C) in which a daily relationship with Christ is at the center—even in the midst of chaos and social inequality (1965, 125). Missions must begin to engage Hip Hop culture as if it were a foreign far off island in the Pacific Ocean and realize that God has been doing something within that culture long before we set foot on its shores.

What is *not* needed is the relationally void[15] style of handing out Christian tracks to complete strangers on the street in hopes that they will "convert" to our belief system. What is *not* needed is this constant "we" and "them" mentality that causes great chasm's between religious and non-religious communities. What is *not* needed is more "religion" for people who need something deeper than just a simple sermon, simplistic five step solutions, and patronizing "I'll be praying for you" statements. What *is* needed is an open mind and an open heart to see where we can be led by those in the Hip Hop community and in turn use the Hip Hop community as a tool for missions in the 21st century and seeing the margins as the center in Christian Mission.

As a concluding comment, missionally engaging Hip Hop is no easy task to be undertaken. Hip Hop is complex and presents not only a Nations Gods and Earth, The Nation of Islam, Zulu Nation, and Zionism. Further, as stated previously, there are parts of Hip Hop culture—as there are in any given culture or sub-culture—which do not give homage to God in any way shape or form. However, this should not dismay the mission-minded individual; we have a great calling such as Paul did when he was in Athens.[16]

If the Great Commission is truly valued by missiologists – which is so often touted in the literature – then the Hip Hop community is worth the missional pursuit.[17] Scholars studying young people in this era have noted that they are falling away from religion, see God as a good thing and not a personal God, identify with a pluralistic form of church, and see sin as relative to the context (Dean 2010, Kosmin and Keysar 2009). Hip Hop, while not a utopian "evangelizing tool," creates space for youth to engage Jesus without the religious mantras present. Hip Hop gives a much purer God and argues for a relationship with God in context and creates a sense of personal consciousness to be spread, once attained, to the community. Hip Hop is a space for young people to find God on their terms and move beyond the four walls of "church" and into a much stronger and purer relationship with God as Hip Hop goes beyond simplistic answers (Hodge 2009: 289-293, Watkins 2011: 97-103). Thus, it behooves us as missiologists to grasp the *missio Dei* within Hip Hop in order to better understand 1) Hip Hop culture; 2) current youth culture; 3) the possibilities of mission to a global culture at a time when societally people are open to hearing about God and spirituality – even if it is in pluralistic circles. A genuine unedited Jesus is more satisfying to people than more words regarding "hell" and "sin."[18] The issues of pain, hurt, oppression, and disenfranchisement are crucial literacies for any minister of the Gospel. God is at work in Hip Hop and even if the appearance of it is offsetting, God is still doing a great work within the culture, music, artists, and youth who listen to its messages.

Notes

1. There are many definitions of what "Hip Hop" is, for the purpose
    of this essay, I will define Hip Hop as an urban sub-culture that
    seeks to express a life-style, attitude, and/or urban individuality.
    Hip Hop at its core—not the commercialization and commodity
    it has become in certain respects— rejects dominant forms of
    culture and society and seeks to increase a social consciousness
    along with a racial/ethnic pride. Thus, Hip Hop uses rap music,
    dance, music production, MCing, and allegory as vehicles to send
    and fund its message of social, cultural, and political resistance to
    dominate structures of norms.

2. In my book, *The Soul Of Hip Hop*, I describe how young people
    aged 14-21 understood God and Christian sacred scripture with
    deeper meaning from artists such as Tupac, DMX, Lupe Fiasco,
    and Lauryn Hill because these individuals spoke from their
    perspective and language (Hodge 2010b Interviews). Artists such
    as Tupac also act as natural theologians who interpret scripture
    and comment upon it no differently than, say, a T.D. Jakes or a Joel
    Osteen do for their constituents (Dyson 2001). Hip Hop pushes
    past the traditionalized white, blonde, blue-eyed, evangelical
    social construct of Jesus and asks for a Jesus that can "reach us,"
    be "real" with us, "feel" us, and relate to us – a contextualized deity
    in a relational stance (Hodge 2010b, Watkins 2011). This type
    of Jesus is one who can relate to youth in urban settings beyond
    the standard evangelical model of both mission and church. This
    type of Jesus also questions authority, seeks to increase social
    consciousness, validates and acknowledges the social isolation as
    valid and real to all the 'hood, and every now and then "puts a
    foot in someone's [butt] to tell a [expletive] he real" (Hodge 2009
    Interview). As ethnomusicologist Christina Zanfagna exclaims,
    "Mainstream hip-hop percolates with unlikely and multifaceted
    religious inclinations. Despite its inconsistent relationship to
    organized religion and its infamous mug of weed smoking, drug
    pushing, gun-slinging, and curse-spewing, rap music is not without
    moral or spiritual content. Hip Hop provides a contextualized and
    relevant form of religious discourse, meaning, and identity for

urban youth and others who are its listeners. As missiologists and youth workers alike, we must give attention to what messages and theological concepts are coming from and out of Hip Hop culture.

3.   This is a critical aspect in the design of new curriculum and pedagogical models of instruction. Linda Nilson reports that the accommodation of various learning styles in the classroom, will make for a better learning environment and stronger metacognition for the respective discipline (2003: 229-235).

4.   This is part of what I argue Hip Hop brings both theologically and hermeneutically, with its message when studied and properly exegeted (2010b).

5.   While Freire was not a missiologist and/or attempting to construct a Christian pedagogy, the concept here is similar to aspects of Christ's mission and the Great Commission; to teach those who are oppressed and oppressors of the life-changing power of the Gospel. This connects with Sherwood Lingenfelter's work on synthesis: pluralism, biblical contradiction, and transformation, in that the missionary must become and adapt toward that culture to better understand it, but to also aid in transforming it too (1992: 20-23).

6.   This is a pedagogical model in which the typical lecture and homework elements of a course are reversed. Short video lectures are viewed by students at home before the class session, while in-class time is devoted to exercises, projects, or discussions (Initiative 2012).

7.   This is measured by 1) course work, 2) class projects, 3) class participation, and 4) final course grades. I take an initial inventory of the class to measure their overall knowledge of course material, a mid-course evaluation (embedded into the course work), and then place those against the final outcomes and grades when the class is finished.

8.   As the class has progressed, I have moved to a 95% all digital classroom. The only thing I print is the syllabus, a student information sheet, and the sign in sheet for each class. Everything else is located online and accessible 24/7 to students. I now utilize TurnitIn for my grading rubrics and paper submissions.

9.   This is a process whereby students engage in activities, such as reading, writing, discussion, or problem solving that promote analysis, synthesis, and evaluation of class content (CRLT 2014).

10.   In subsequent classes I have eliminated it from the class, even more as the class has shifted to an undergraduate class only. However, I am still learning to find the best use of technology in the classroom.

11.   I attribute this largely to the fact that the seminarians in the class were initiators and innovators of the conversation. It was rare that an undergraduate student initiated a conversation. This may have been closely related to the dynamics of the class and that the undergrads may have felt some apprehension with the older students in the class, and, after a while, the pattern emerged that the older students would speak first. Still, the dynamic of having older students in the classroom is imperative, I believe, in aiding the learning process. More classes should, and need to have hybrid components.

12.   This type of statement was also a critical theme throughout my own research. Interviewee after interviewee relayed to me the power of Hip Hop's theology and how they "saw God/ Jesus" better as a result.

13.   Poetry that is specifically about, engaging, or interpretive of the city and urban contexts—related to Hip Hop culture.

14.   While Hip Hop is not entirely spiritual or theological, a majority of its faith traditions lie within Christian, Jewish, and Islamic traditions with variances and contextual approaches for each.

15.   Shaw and Van Engen also tell us that relationships are over communicating any "special" style, message, or sermon and about receptors—the people group—will typically always res,pond better to the Gospel when there is a strong relationship intact (2003: 121-122).

16.   However, this also requires us to be culturally and racially literate in order to breach the spiritual borders and enter into new "territories."

17.   An interesting note here, Daniel Shaw and Charles Van Engen note that to communicate the Gospel message appropriately, one must foster the skill of appropriate communication to the receptors in their context (2003: 114-120). They also follow this with three modes of communication as well: coupling—which involves connecting a new message with the receptors preexisting assumptions, commonality—when message meanings are shared by both the author and the audience alike, and bridging—the authors, or communicators, responsibility to help de-code messages and meanings from the text and/or message. Shaw and Van Engen use this in the context of biblical interpretation and communication, yet, the parallels with Hip Hop and Gospel messages also applies (2003: 117-119). Wilbert Shenk asserts that, "...in order to do its work properly, missiology must keep four aspects continually in view: the normative, the historical, the present, and the future" (Shenk 1993: 18). Hence, with this in perspective, the *present* and the *future* should be focused—at least in part—to and with Hip Hop, and being aware of how one communicates the Gospel is fundamental too. Further, Hip Hop, in its contextual form, embraces John Driver's *Messianic Evangelization* in which the forming of disciples of Jesus is fundamental (Driver 1993: 199). This was a critical finding in my work when I performed interviews on those between the ages of 13-19 who considered themselves to be "Hip Hoppers." They realized a need for a connection with Jesus and cared less about knowing the "rules" and dogma but more about an actual relationship with Christ.

18.   In Knut Alfsvåg's work, the continued debate of the "postmodern" continues. Within those debates the issue of sin and morality typically surfaces and sin is often defined as a relative and culturally defined term. This has impact on how we in our churches define this word and what it means to actually "sin"(2011).

References

(CRLT), Center for Research on Learning and Teaching
    2014   *Active Learning* [cited June 2, 2014]. Available from http://www.crlt.umich.edu/tstrategies/tsal.

Alfsvåg, Knut
    2011   "Postmodern Epistemology and the Mission of the Church." *Mission Studies: Journal of the International Association for Mission Studies*, 28 (1):54-70.

Cox, Harvey
    1965   *The Secular City: A Celebration of its Liberties and an Invitation to its Discipline*. New York: The Macmillan Company.

Dean, Kenda Creasy
    2010   *Almost Christian : what the faith of our teenagers is telling the American church*. New York: Oxford University Press.

Dhokai, Niyati
    2012   "Pedagogical ideas on sonic, mediated, and virtual musical landscapes: Teaching hip hop in a university classroom." *International Journal of Music Education*, 30 (2):111-119. doi: 10.1177/0255761412439925.

Dimitriadis, Greg
    2001   *Performing identity/performing culture: hip hop as text, pedagogy, and lived practice, Intersections in communications and culture*. New York: P. Lang.

Driver, John
    1993   "Messianic Evangelization." In *The Transfiguration of Mission: Biblical Theological and Historical Foundations*, edited by Wilbert R. Shenk, 199-219. Scottdale, PA; Waterloo, Ontario: Herald Press.

Dyson, Michael Eric
    2001   *Holler if you Hear Me: Searching for Tupac Shakur.* New York: Basic Civitas.

Elligan, Don
    2012   "Contextualizing Rap Music as a Means of Incorporating into Psychotherapy." In *Therapeutic Uses of Rap and Hip-Hop*, edited by George Yancy and Susan Hadley. New York, NY: Routledge.

Emdin, Christopher
    2007a "Exploring the contexts of urban Science Classrooms: Part 1-Investigating corporate and communal practice." *Cultural Studies of Science Education*, 2 (2):319-341.

    2007b "Exploring the contexts of Urban science Classrooms: Part 2- The role of rituals in communal practice." *Cultural Studies of Science Education*, 2 (2):351-373.

    2008   "The Three C's for Urban Science Education." *Phi Delta Kappan* no. 89 (19):772-775.

    2015   "Affiliation and Alienation: Hip hop, rap and urban science education." *Journal of Curriculum Studies*, In Press.

Freire, Paulo
    2000   *Pedagogy of the oppressed.* Translated by Myra Bergman Ramos. 30th anniversary ed. New York: Continuum.

George, Nelson
    1998   *Hip Hop America.* New York: Viking.

    2004   *Post-soul nation : the explosive, contradictory, triumphant, and tragic 1980s as experienced by African Americans (previously known as Blacks and before that Negroes).* New York, NY: Viking.

Giroux, Henry A.
    1996   "Towards a Postmodern Pedagogy." In *From Modernism to Postmodernism: An Anthology*, edited by Lawrence Cahoone, 687-697. Malden, MA: Blackwell Publishers.

Guevara, Nancy
  1996   "Women Writin' Rappin' Breakin'." In *Dropping Science: Critical Essays on Rap Music and Hip Hop Culture*, edited by William E. Perkins, 49-62. Philadelphia: Temple University Press.

Hacker, A
  1995   The Crackdown on African-Americans. *The Nation*, July 10, 45-49.

Hadley, Susan, and Yancy George
  2012   *Therapeutic uses of rap and hip hop*. New York, NY: Brunner-Routledge.

Hill, Marc Lamont
  2009   "Beats, rhymes, and classroom life : hip-hop pedagogy and the politics of identity." In: *Teachers College Press*. http://catdir.loc.gov/catdir/toc/fy0904/2008054819.html Materials specified: Table of contents only http://catdir.loc.gov/catdir/toc/fy0904/2008054819.html.

  2013   *Schooling Hip-Hop : expanding Hip-Hop based education across the curriculum*. New York: Teachers College, Columbia University.

Hodge, Daniel White
  2009   *Heaven Has A Ghetto: The Missiological Gospel and Theology of Tupac Amaru Shakur*. Saarbrucken, Germany: VDM Verlag Dr. Muller Academic.

  2010a   "Christ Appropriating the Culture of Hip Hop: The Soul of Hip Hop Pt 2." *Fuller Youth Institute*, 6 (7).

  2010b   *The Soul Of Hip Hop: Rimbs, Timbs, and A Cultural Theology*. Downers Grove, Ill.: Inner Varsity Press.

  2013a   "No Church in The Wild: An Ontology of Hip Hop's Socio-Religious Discourse in Tupac's "Black Jesuz"." *Nomos*, 10 (March 23, 2013):1-5.

2013b "No Church in the Wild: Hip Hop Theology and Mission." *Missiology: An International Review*, 40:4 (4):1-13.

2015 (Forthcoming) The Hostile Gospel: Exploring Socio-Religous Traits in the Post-Soul Theology of Hip Hop, edited by Warren Goldstein, *Critical Studies in Religion*. Boston, MA: Brill Academic.

Hopkins, Dwight N.
2001 "Black Theology on God: The Divine in Black Popular Religion." In *The Ties That Bind: African American and Hispanic American/ Latino/a Theologies in Dialogue*, edited by Anthony B Pinn and Benjamin Valentin, 99-112. New York, NY: Continuum.

Initiative, Educate Learning
2012 7 Things you Should Know About Flipped Classrooms. In *Educause*, edited by Creative Commons. http://net. educause.edu/ir/library/pdf/eli7081.pdf.

Irby, Decoteau J., and H. Bernard Hall
2011 "Fresh Faces, New Places: Moving Beyond Teacher-Researcher Perspectives in Hip-Hop-Based Education Research." *Urban Education*, 46 (2):216-240. doi: 10.1177/0042085910377513.

Irizarry, Jason G.
2009 "Representin': Drawing From Hip-Hop and Urban Youth Culture to Inform Teacher Education." *Education and Urban Society*, 41 (4):489-515. doi: 10.1177/0013124508331154.

Iwamoto, Derek K., John Creswell, and Leon Caldwell
2007 "Feeling the Beat: The Meaning of Rap Music for Ethnically Diverse Midwestern College Student—A Phenomenological Study." *Adolescence*, 42 (166):337- 351.

Kosmin, Barry A, and Ariela Keysar
2009 American Religious Identification Survey. In *ARIS*. Hartford, CT: Trinity College.

Lingenfelter, Sherwood G.
    1992   *Transforming culture: a challenge for Christian mission.*
            Grand Rapids, Mich.: Baker Book House.

MacDonald, Scott, and Michael Viega
    2013   "Hear Our Voices: A Music Therapy Songwriting
            Program and the Message of the Little Saints through
            the Medium of Rap." In *Therapeutic Uses of Rap and Hip-
            Hop,* edited by Susan Hadley and George Yancy, 153-172.
            New York, NY: Routledge.

Miller, Monica R.
    2013   *Religion and Hip Hop.* New York, NY: Routledge.

Morgan, Joan
    1999   *When chickenheads come home to roost: my life as a hip-hop
            feminist.* New York: Simon and Schuster.

Neal, Mark Anthony
    2002   *Soul Babies : Black Popular Culture and the Post-Soul
            Aesthetic.* New York: Routledge.

Nilson, Linda Burzotta
    2003   *Teaching at its best : a research-based resource for college
            instructors.* 2nd ed. Bolton, MA: Anker Pub. Co. Norton,
            Nadjwa E. L.

    2014   "Young Children Manifest Spiritualities in Their Hip-
            Hop Writing." *Education and Urban Society,* 46 (3):329-
            351. doi: 10.1177/0013124512446216.

One, K. R. S.
    2009   *The gospel of hip hop : first instrument.* 1st ed. Brooklyn, NY:
            powerHouse Books : I Am Hip Hop.

    2003   *Ruminations.* New York: Welcome Rain Publishers.

Outlawz, Tupac and The
    1999   Black Jesuz. In *Still I Rise.* Los Angeles, CA: Interscope
            Records.

Pentecost, Edward C.
  1982   *Issues in Missiology: An Introduction*. Grand Rapids, MI: Baker Book House.

Peskett, Howard, and Vinoth Ramachandra
  2003   *The Message of Mission*. Edited by Derek Tidball, *The Bible Speaks Today*. Downers Grove, IL: Inter Varsity Press.

Petchauer, Emery
  2009   "Framing and Reviewing Hip-Hop Educational Research." *Review of Educational Research*, 79 (2):946-978. doi: 10.3102/0034654308330967.

  2011a   "I Feel What He Was Doin': Responding to Justice- Oriented Teaching Through Hip-Hop Aesthetics." *Urban Education*, 46 (6):1411-1432. doi: 10.1177/0042085911400335.

  2011b   "Knowing What's Up and Learning What You're Not Supposed to: Hip-Hop Collegians, Higher Education, and the Limits of Critical Consciousness." *Journal of Black Studies*, 42 (5):768-790. doi: 10.1177/0021934710376164.

  2012   *Hip-hop culture in college students' lives : elements, embodiment, and higher edutainment*. London: Routledge.

Pinn, Anthony, ed.
  2003   *Noise and Spirit: The Religious and Spiritual Sensibilites of Rap Music*. New York: New York University Press.

Reed, Teresa L.
  2003   *The Holy Profane: Religion in Black Popular Music*. Lexington, KY: The University Press of Kentucky.

Rogers, Glenn
  2003   *A basic introduction to missions and missiology*. Bedford, TX: Mission and Ministry Resources.

Rose, Tricia
  1994   *Black Noise: Rap Music and Black Culture in Contemporary America*. Middletown CT.: Wesleyan University Press.

2008   *The hip hop wars : what we talk about when we talk about hip hop--and why it matters.* New York, NY: Basic Civitas.

Shaw, Daniel R, and Charles E Van Engen
2003   *Communicating God's Word in a Complex World: God's Truth or Hocus Pocus.* Lanham, MD: Rowan and Littlefield Publishers Inc.

Shenk, Wilbert R.
1993   "The Relevance of a Messianic Missiology for Mission Today." In *The Transfiguration of Mission: Biblical Theological and Historical Foundations*, edited by Wilbert R. Shenk, 17-36. Scottdale, PA; Waterloo, Ontario: Herald Press.

1999   *Changing Frontiers of Mission.* Maryknoll, NY: Orbis Books.

Smith, Efrem, and Phil Jackson
2005   *The Hip Hop Church: Connecting with The Movment Shaping our Culture.* Downers Grove, Ill.: IVP.

Southern, Eileen
1983   *The Music of Black Americans.* 2nd ed. New York: W.W. Norton and Company.

Stovall, David
2006   "We can Relate: Hip-hop Culture, Critical Pedagogy, and the Secondary classroom." *Urban Education*, 41 (6):585-602.

Tyson, Edgar H.
2013   "Hip-Hop Healing: Rap Music in Grief Therapy with and African American Adolescent Male." In *Therapeutic Uses of Rap and Hip-Hop*, edited by Susan Hadley and George Yancy, 293-306. New York, NY: Routledge.

Utley, Ebony A.
2012   *Rap and Religion: Understanding the Gangsta's God.* Santa Barbara, CA: Praeger.

Watkins, Ralph Basui
2011   *Hip-Hop Redemption: Finding God in the Rhythm and the Rhyme, Engaging Culture.* Grand Rapids, MI: Baker Academic.

Watkins, S. Craig
2005   *Hip hop matters : politics, pop culture, and the struggle for the soul of a movement.* Boston, MA: Beacon Press.

Wells-Wilbon, Rhonda, Nigel D. Jackson, and Jerome H. Schiele
2010   "Lessons From the Maafa: Rethinking the Legacy of Slain Hip-Hop Icon Tupac Amaru Shakur." *Journal of Black Studies*, 40 (4):509-526. doi: 10.1177/0021934708315441.

West, Cornel
1993   *Prophetic Thought in Postmodern Times: Beyond Eurocentrism and Multiculturalism.* Vol. 1`. Monroe ME: Common Courage Press.

Zanfagna, Christina
2006   "Under the Blasphemous W(RAP): Locating the "Spirit" in Hip-Hop." *Pacific Review of Ethnomusicology*, 12:1- 12.

Jesus and the Parables

A Compelling Oral Training Tool

KEVIN OLSON

DOI: 10.7252/Paper.000030

About the Author

Pastor Kevin Olson is working on his Doctorate of Ministry in Servant Leadership Development at Bethel Seminary in St. Paul, MN. He has been serving as the director of the Ambassador Institute based out of Plymouth, MN since it began in 2007. In the past seven years, the Ambassador Institute has been establishing oral training centers in Uganda and India. There are currently 250 students in Uganda and 53 in India. This paper is the result of his experience in both of these countries as well as his studies at Bethel Seminary.

Introduction of a Useful Tool

For the Christian community, the life of Jesus is lifted up as a model to follow for ministry methods. His mandate to make disciples is a preeminent theme for missions and his Word is the foundation for everything that is taught. The student that takes time to look closely into the life and ministry of Jesus can also learn from the methods that he used. *Jesus used parables to make disciples, teach the people, bridge cultures, reveal scriptures, and to transform lives.* This unique oral teaching style has the potential to change ministry vision and practice. Jesus was intentional in his use of parables and we, his disciples, must also unlock the potential behind this technique.

The ministry of Jesus provides a unique look at the use of an oral training method. He used parables and questions regularly as he trained his disciples and taught the masses. Jesus was able to train disciples from a wide variety of backgrounds, multiple languages, and multiple cultures. Even though the bulk of his ministry was focused in the region of Galilee, scripture records that "the people still came to him from everywhere," (Mark 1:45, NIV).

The use of oral training has a relatively short modern history, but its use in biblical history goes back to the beginning of the Bible. It has been used to pass down history, preserve theology, train leaders, and jump the boundaries of time and culture. Looking closely at Jesus' approach can validate this method as an essential cross-cultural tool for missions, a powerful technique for biblical students, and a revolutionary method for communicating across language barriers.

For Making Disciples

The goal of making disciples was central to the work that Jesus was doing. It is possible to educate people so that they know God's Word, understand doctrine, can pass tests and train others but yet miss the goal of making disciples. A simple summary. *A disciple is more than one who knows about Jesus, a disciple is one who is becoming like Jesus.* The goal of transformation is at the core of the use of parables.

One aspect of the use of the parables is to pass on the **knowledge** of the Word of God. It must become a part of the person. As a disciple grows in the knowledge of God's Word, they gain a full understanding of who he is, which also affects who they are. If someone gains the knowledge of God, it will also affect their **character**. The parables uniquely allow a person to see themselves in the story and learn from the people that are illustrated throughout the Bible. The biblical narratives are descriptive of real life and oral learners can understand the results of their actions through the living examples in scripture. The change of a person's character will next be reflected in their **life and ministry**. Love for others, a desire to share God's Word, and a servant spirit are evidence of God's work in the heart of a disciple. The parables are unique in their non-threatening approach to evangelism or outreach and it becomes a natural outflow of the change that has taken place within.

Making disciples is about walking through life with people in such a way that they gain the knowledge of God's Word, their character reflects their Lord and the way that they live is patterned after Jesus. Luke 6:40 says, "Everyone who is fully trained will be *like his teacher*," (Luke 6:40, NIV).

If the goal of training is for disciples to make disciples, then an oral training model must be given serious consideration. Jesus himself started with twelve, then sent out seventy-two, and after his death there were more than five hundred. After Peter's address at Pentecost, three thousand were added to their number. The oral style of training is not solely responsible for this multiplication, but it is the primary tool that Jesus used and it is the way the early disciples passed on what Jesus had taught them.

Avery Willis is often considered the father of the modern oral training emphasis. He wrote and spoke often about the value of oral training. In his book, *Truth that Sticks*, Willis (2010:127) states, "[Jesus'] disciple making was not accidental; it was intentional. ... Jesus intends for us to make disciples as He did. It was His work, and now it is our work. If we follow His example we will intentionally make disciples as He did."

In February of 2009, a biblical oral training program was begun in Uganda called the Ambassador Institute. The training was modeled in part after the parable and question style that Jesus used in order to memorize eighty-four stories with a total of 2200 verses of the Bible.

After two years of study, in January 2011, twenty students completed the entire course. From that group, eight of the graduates became teachers and started seven new classes. The original teacher mentored the eight new teachers so that they could teach the lessons well.

The second class completed their studies in January, 2013 with seventy-one graduates. Out of that class, twenty-five signed up to be teachers and twenty-two classes were started. The next student body will be finishing in the spring of 2015 with two hundred and fifty completing their two years of study.

After the first graduation, Musasazi Wilson (2013), chairman of the students, began to teach three classes. One time he walked three hours to reach the class because his bicycle had broken down. When asked, "Why do you give your time and energy to train others?" He said, "When you have tasted something that is sweet like honey, you want to share it with others."

An oral approach such as Jesus used in the parables can make disciples, but it can also make disciples who in turn make other disciples. It is a training that is deep enough to give the profound truths of God yet it is simple and accessible enough for anyone who is willing to *walk with Jesus* through his Word. It will transform the character of the student so that when he or she is fully trained, they will be like their teacher.

For Teaching People

The purpose of the parable can be seen in both the characteristics of the parables and the manner in which Jesus used them. They were brief stories, sometimes as small as an object lesson. They were simple and repetitive, easy to remember and easy to recite again to others. They were made up of objects, examples and experiences from the crowd's normal daily life. They often connected to the Old Testament and the Kingdom of God. They were engaging for listeners at multiple levels, and the people were shocked, surprised, and challenged. They were appealing and relevant, (Terry 2009:Front Cover).

Warren Wiersbe describes the parables as both mirrors and windows. "As mirrors, they help us see ourselves. They reveal our lives as they really are. As windows, they help us see life and God. You may <u>not</u> have an easy time identifying with some truth in Romans 7 or Ephesians 2, but you probably have little difficulty seeing yourself in one of the parables," (Wiersbe 1979:14). That describes the beauty and the power of the parable. It can be easily understood, easily identified with, and yet pointed and revealing.

Ultimately the purpose of the parable is to teach the people. To do so, they must show us an image of ourselves and a vision of what is beyond. They must engage the listener, connect them to what they know and unveil the mysteries of what they do not understand.

The potential of the parable is in the fact that it is the Word of God. Hebrews 4:12 says that it is "living and active sharper than any double-edged sword, it penetrates even to dividing soul and spirit, joints and marrow; it judges the thoughts and attitudes of the heart." Jesus cut right to the core of peoples' heart. He exposed their motives, and he revealed their hidden agendas.

Jesus used the parables to describe the kingdom of God. In Matthew 13, Jesus portrays a picture of the kingdom of God. He portrays the small seed of faith that grows into a large tree and the bread dough that rises in the pan. He entices the curious to dig for the treasure and seek for the jewel. Finally, he cautions those listening regarding the fact that the judgment is just as real as the anticipated kingdom. In a few short word pictures, Jesus drew in the listener and illustrated a spiritual realm that they couldn't even imagine.

The parables have the potential to teach people the Word of God. They can uncover the mysteries of doctrine and cut to the heart of human beings because it is God who is working in and through his Word. This makes it a unique tool for instructing people and a useful tool to bridge cultures.

For Connecting Cultures

Jesus faced some enormous cultural barriers as he taught radical new concepts. The church was to be built on a living relationship with their heavenly father along with the religion and ritual that they had learned from the rabbinic tradition. Along with the new picture of God was a new revelation of how Jesus saw the various levels of society. Instead of viewing some as less important and others as more important because of their prominence or position, Jesus used a child as the example for his disciples, (Matthew 18:1-5).

Jesus continued his cultural transformation by describing a new set of priorities, the kingdom of heaven, the example of love, the treatment of enemies, the cost of being a disciple, the strength of small faith, the investment of our time and talents, and his own return. Jesus also needed to empower his disciples to pass on what they had received. Jesus empowered fishermen, tax collectors and common people with that life-changing message instead of the synagogue rulers, the Pharisees, or the scribes. These common people would be taking on the role of communicating the Word of God.

It is helpful to consider the challenge that Jesus faced in communicating these radical new concepts to people. The kingdom that Jesus needed to reveal to his disciples was profoundly different from anything they had previously conceived of. The challenge that Jesus faced in trying to pass on information to his disciples was far beyond just a language or a cultural barrier and the nature of the topic was a matter of eternal consequences.

The parables show that Jesus was fully acquainted with human life in its multiple ways and means. He was knowledgeable in farming, sowing seed, detecting weeds, and reaping a harvest. He was at home in the vineyard, knew the times of reaping fruit from vine and fig tree, and was aware of the wages paid for a day's work. Not only was he familiar with the workaday world of the farmer, the fisherman, the builder, and the merchant, but he moved with equal ease among the managers of estates, the ministers of finance at a royal court, the judge in a court of law, the Pharisees, and the tax collectors. He understood Lazarus's poverty, yet he was invited to dine with the rich," (Kistemaker 2002:12-13).

Jesus was able to flow between these various strata of society and relate to each as if there was no social barrier between them. The parables made the connection between them possible because they relate to people on a personal level. The human condition shows that inside there is much in common regardless of how society may view the layers. The challenge of reaching people where they are at is the heart of missions and the modern orality movement is making an impact on the methods that are being used to cross cultures.

Culture is what gives us identity and makes us unique, but culture also separates us from one another. "Culture is what defines a group of people that have similar education levels, beliefs, customs, language and communication methods. Culture connects us, gives us a sense of belonging, familiarity and peace" (Snead 2013:42-43). Yet culture makes it difficult for people to understand one another. Finding a bridge to communicate across these barriers is the goal and the challenge of missions. "Culture becomes the key to unlocking the hearts of people all over the world. Studying it illuminates strategies ordained by God to reach people in their own setting" (Snead 2013:43). The power of the parable and oral communication can be the key to unlock the hearts of people around the world.

Jesus bridged the culture gap from God to man. He, himself was a cultural bridge, but he also used the parables as another bridge. Jesus described the indescribable with common every day terms. He created a picture of God that humans could grasp. He presented things in such a way that it would be sought after like a precious jewel.

For Living Communication

A young boy was marveling at a butterfly that he saw floating in the air, going from flower to flower. It moved effortlessly and had a beauty that was captivating. The brilliant colors of the wings were stunning; the fluid motion of its flight was magnificent. He longed to keep it and show it to his friends, so he caught it and took it apart. He took off the wings and put them in one pile, the legs in another pile, the antenna and the body in another pile so that he could show his friends; but in doing so, he killed the butterfly.

That story illustrates what we can do to the living, breathing narratives of the Bible. We dissect them into several parts in order to show our friends. A sermon on a parable is given a title, three points, sub points and a concluding application, but the living Word is killed. Where is the encounter with the story and all of its emotion, awe, and wonder? Where is the anticipation of the wedding, the buried treasure, the friend knocking on the door in the middle of the night, and the man lying half dead on the side of the road? Where is the longing father as he waits for his son and the tenants killing the son of the landowner? A parable communicates more than just information, it is an experience with God.

Jesus left lasting memories in the minds of the disciples and the ministry that has multiplied throughout the world is evidence of its effectiveness. Scholars have studied the parables of Jesus and come to various conclusions regarding how they should be understood and interpreted, but the beauty of the parable is its inherent life apart from dissection, categorization, or systemization. It is important to consider a detailed analysis of these teachings but it is also important to step back and look at the parables, simple as they are.

Gilles Gravelle published an article in *Orality Journal* on how the brain understands meaning. In it he highlights the fact that the process of communicating is more than deciphering a group of symbols into words, it is more than transferring those words into sounds that make up a language. Communication happens when meaning gets transferred from one person to another. This study addresses where meaning resides and how is it communicated.

Studies using MRI imaging suggest that meaning is made
in our minds through simulation. … Simulation involves
seeing. Our visual system sees non-present things in the
'mind's eye' in the same way it sees present things in the
world. So this means that thinking is performing. When
you are seeing it in the mind's eye, you are performing
it in your mind, too. When you hear language about
things, like the action of running, you use the same brain
pathways to visualize it as if you were actually doing it.
It's not just vague perception. You construct very detailed
meaning. You hear a sound in your mind. You see an action
happening. You imagine a result (Gravelle 2013:49-50).

In a parable or an oral story, meaning is transferred directly from
the one sharing to the one receiving. Instead of deciphering and processing
information, the mind can go directly to the meaning because it is simulating
the information that the person sharing is conveying. "If we use our brain
systems for perception and action to understand, then the processes of
meaning are dynamic and constructive. It's not about activating the right
symbol; it's about dynamically constructing the right experience" (Bergen
2012:16). The mental visualization is the meaning. Both oral processors
and print media processors mentally simulate the things that they hear or
read, according to Benjamin Bergen, (Gavelle 2013:52).

This means that Jesus' use of parables had a benefit beyond the goal
of relating to people or sharing stories that would be easy to remember. It
means that the parables gave the people the chance to experience the events
Jesus was telling them. The people were able to hear the information, but
they were also able to enter into the story, to see the events unfold, to feel
the emotion and respond as the people in the parable would respond. Oral
processing is an active dynamic transformational process.

For Transforming Lives

The gospel's own record describes an exciting response from the
recipients of Jesus and his teaching. Jesus was connecting with his hearers.
Their response reveals that he was getting their attention.

Matthew 7:35: "The crowds were amazed at his teaching."

Matthew 31:54: "they were amazed. 'Where did this man get this wisdom and these miraculous powers?' they asked."

Luke 4:22: "All spoke well of Him and were amazed at the gracious words that came from His lips."

Luke 4:32: "They were amazed at His teaching, because his message had authority."

It would make sense for them to be amazed at the miracles. We would expect their astonishment when the blind see, the lame walk, and the dead are raised to life, but repeatedly, the crowd is amazed at his teaching. Their descriptions include wisdom, gracious words, and authority. They were not just impressed with a polished orator. They could see that what Jesus said was right and good. His words reflected an insightful application, a compelling inviting tone in contrast to that of the Pharisees. Even the parables carried with them authority.

The images, objects, and settings from these stories made God's Word come alive. These down-to-earth illustrations communicated deep spiritual truths, and the people responded. The crowd represented the full range of people; children, farmers, fisherman, widows, soldiers, Pharisees, rich and poor together. The parables included the same characters. Jesus spoke to a diverse audience and his parables reflected the same diversity yet all of them were able to understand him. "It is of fundamental importance to remember that the parables of Jesus were spoken to ordinary folk. They were related to be understood by even the most simple person" (Scharlemann 1963:30).

The disciples responded to the parables by listening carefully and asking for clarification or explanation. Their desire for understanding shows that the Word was at work inside. They wanted and needed to know more. They were unwilling to leave the story until they understood.

The Pharisees also were affected by the parables but with a different response. Matthew 15:12 says, "Then the disciples came to Him and asked, 'Do you know that the Pharisees were offended when they heard this?'" In

Matthew 21:45-46 it says, "When the chief priests and the Pharisees heard Jesus' parables, they knew that he was talking about them. They looked for a way to arrest him" (Matthew 21:45-46, NIV).

There were many who followed Jesus who were transformed from their encounter with Jesus; Peter, Zacchaeus, Nicodemus, the woman at the well and the man born blind. The Bible does not directly connect the telling of parables to the changes in their lives except for the fact that it was the way that he communicated to the people. All of them had encountered Jesus and heard him speak to their hearts.

Summary

It is clear from looking at the parables of Jesus that they were an effective tool for him as he made disciples, taught the people, bridged the cultures, and transformed lives. What began with Jesus multiplied exponentially as those he trained passed on what they had learned to others. The recent return to the parables or oral training has the same potential for the modern mission movement and the church as a whole.

The parables are effective tools for passing on the knowledge of God, transforming the student's character, and invigorating the ministry life of those involved. They work because they include the doctrine, the emotions, and the real lives of real people. When all three aspects of discipleship are woven together, the result will be a well-rounded disciple.

In the parables, we see a reflection of who we are as well as a window into the things of God. Jesus used them to stir the interest of the crowds and from that many began to follow him. The disciples took these illustrations seriously and wanted to know more. For them, Jesus was able to reveal the kingdom of God, but the Pharisees hardened their hearts to Jesus and could not see the glory that was right before them. To the one group the love of God was shown, to the unbelieving, his wrath was made known.

Jesus had to break through the traditions of man in order to let the living Word of God get out into people's lives. The same may be needed today as people have grown accustomed to a certain form or method of training. Jesus also faced challenges and yet he was able to work with people from many backgrounds. This revolution of thought needs to take place in missions as well as in education generally.

It is important to consider how people understand meaning and how thoughts are transferred from one person to another. It seems that the parables actually enhance understanding by recreating the experience in the mind of the listener. The fact is, a large percent of the population prefers to learn by methods other than the written text and there are many that cannot learn by reading.

It is possible to consider the parables and be amazed in the same way that the crowds responded. The real question is whether you will be changed by them. Many people were followers. Few became disciples.

References Cited

Bergen, Benjamin K.
    2012   *Louder Than Words: The New Science of How the Mind Makes Meaning.* New York, NY: Basic Books.

Gravelle, Gilles
    2013   "More Than Words: Linguistics, Language and Meaning", *Orality Journal* 2, (2).

Kistemaker, Simon J.
    2002   *The Parables: Understanding the Stories Jesus Told.* Grand Rapids, MI: Baker Books.

Scharlemann, Martin H
    1963   *Proclaiming the Parables.* Saint Louis, MO: Concordia Publishing House.

Snead, Durwood
    2013   "Culture." *Orality Journal* 2, (2).

Terry, J. O.
    2009   *Basic Bible Storying: Preparing and Presenting Bible Stories for Evangelism, Discipleship, Training, and Ministry.* Fort Worth, TX: Church Starting Network.

Wiersbe, Warren
    1979   *Meet Yourself in the Parables.* Wheaton, IL: Victor Books.

Willis, Avery T. Jr., and Mark Snowden.
    2010   *Truth That Sticks: How to Communicate Velcro Truth in a Teflon World.* Colorado Springs, CO: NavPress.

Wilson, Musasizi
    2013   Interviewed by author, Jinja, Uganda, January 28, 2013.

APM

Theological Considerations for Mission Education

A Wesleyan Theology of Cultural Competency

ESTHER D. JADHAV

DOI: 10.7252/Paper. 000038

About the Author

Rev. Esther D. Jadhav, a United Methodist Church ordained elder of the Kentucky Annual Conference, is the Director of Intercultural Programs at Asbury University. Her call to ministry and mission began at a very early age. This involvement took her across the country of India (South Asia) and the continents of Africa (Uganda), South East Asia (Japan) and North America (United States of America). Positioning her to build bridges across cultures and serve persons of diverse backgrounds through preaching and teaching. Esther's academic pursuits are in Anthropology, Sociology and Theology. She has a Th.M and M.Div from Asbury Theological Seminary, Kentucky and a BA majoring in Anthropology and Sociology from the Mumbai University, India. She is currently working on a Ph.D.in Intercultural Studies through Asbury Theological Seminary exploring cultural competency development.

Introduction

Cultural competence has become an increasingly significant concern in Christian higher education. The Council for Christian Colleges and Universities has adopted two major themes for work over the next several years to emphasize racial harmony and diversity and to equip campuses to be more global in every respect. These themes have taken priority because employers are looking for persons who know how to work for and with people of increasingly diverse racial, ethnic, religious, and cultural backgrounds (Andringa 2002).

These themes have also gained importance because of the changing demographics in the classroom, and the society in general in North America and elsewhere. Increased numbers of students from non-Caucasian ethnic backgrounds demand educator versatility in knowledge and skills which will help equip students in American classrooms. Persons who come from Black, Hispanic and Asian ethnic backgrounds, although born and raised in North America, often bring cultural capital that is unique to them and their ethnic communities. Linguist Joshua Fishman argues:

> Ethnicity has always been experienced as a kinship phenomenon, continuity within the self and within those who share an intergenerational link to common ancestors. Ethnicity is partly experienced as being bone of their bone, flesh of their flesh and blood of their blood. It is crucial that we recognize ethnicity as a tangible, living reality that makes every human a link in an eternal bond from generation to generation – from past ancestors to those in the future (Fishman in Scupin 2003:76).

Ethnicity is a common experience shared by a group of individuals that lends itself to being both particular and universal in time and in place. It is particular in that members of an ethnic group will hold to certain values, beliefs, and norms particular to their group (recognizing that consensus among members of an ethnic group regarding these may not be present). It is universal to the extent that Christians from different ethnic groups across the world share a common experience through the values and beliefs held in regard to their faith.[1]

In this paper, theological resources offered by John Wesley will be explored to respond to the need for cultural competency in North America today. I will begin by exploring the meaning of cultural competency and present a working definition of the concept. Toward the end of the paper I will outline possible applications for constructing a Wesleyan theology of cultural competence.

Cultural Competence

This paper will work with the definition student affairs practitioners Pope, Reynolds, and Mueller provide. They define cultural competence as, "the awareness, knowledge, and skills needed to work with others who are culturally different from self in meaningful, relevant and productive ways," (2004:13). No individual is an exact replica of the other. While there are several characteristics such as personality and gender that make us unique from each other, another is coming from a different cultural and ethnic background. Cultural competence then is one's ability to engage with someone from another culture. It is said that cultural competence, understanding one's own culture and other cultures, can lead to more effective action across cultures (Kennedy 2013:5). The ability to engage and relate with one another comes from having an awareness of the differences and similarities amongst cultures, gaining knowledge by experiencing another culture and developing the skills in order to interact effectively.

Pope, Reynolds, and Mueller emphasize that cultural awareness, or the ability to be aware of different values, attitudes, and assumptions, is a significant aspect of cultural competence.

> Cultural knowledge consists of the content knowledge about various cultural groups. Cultural skills consist of those behaviors that allow us to effectively apply the cultural awareness and knowledge we have internalized. Central to those skills is the ability to communicate across cultures and understand how culture influences the content as well as the verbal and nonverbal aspects of communication. Without a foundation of cultural awareness and knowledge, it is difficult to make culturally sensitive and appropriate interventions (2004:15).

The above definition and explanation helps us understand what is implied by "they are looking for persons who know how to work for and work with people of increasingly diverse racial, ethnic, religious and cultural backgrounds" (Andringa 2002). Employers are looking for people who are able to communicate across cultures while understanding the implications of a person's cultural context. This concern, of course, is not limited to the employment sector of our society alone. The changing demographics of our societies require us to know how to communicate across cultures.

Student inquiries on addressing persons of different ethnicity, nationality, and race, and comments expressing a preference for one race over another suggest a limited knowledge of the Christian faith, compassion and communication. These questions have partly prompted this paper to explore questions of cultural competence and diversity through Wesleyan Theology.

How does one become culturally competent, equipped with awareness, knowledge, and skills to enable effective interaction in an ever increasing intercultural environment? How does one learn to relate effectively across cultures?

Christian Higher Education

Christian higher education is a place where faith and learning come together, where a purportedly biblical worldview becomes the lens for learning and understanding. Christian colleges and universities continue to be sought out today by students because of the unique dynamic of being able to integrate faith and learning. While there are challenges to this unique dynamic in the twenty-first century, places of Christian higher learning have persisted by finding ways to stay current.

The distinctive of the Christian college is not that it cultivates piety and religious commitment, for this could be done by church sponsored residence houses on secular campuses. Rather the Christian college is distinctive in that the Christian faith can touch the entire range of life and learning to which a liberal arts education exposes students. In principle Christian perspectives are all

redeeming and all transforming, and it is this which gives
rise to the idea of integrating faith with learning (Holmes
1975:45).

The Christian faith provides several significant theological tenets for an
all-redeeming and all-transforming education that can theoretically free
the mind and allow it to capture themes that liberate it from societal
statuses and prejudices that confine and limit.

The Protestant Reformation of the sixteenth century provided
a special impetus to Christian higher education. According to Mayers,
Richards, and Webber, the reformers "renewed the biblical concept of
humans and operated from the viewpoint of a unified reality (1972:15)."
It taught that humans are created in the image of God, while sin and
rebellion caused alienation; humanity's hope lies in God who provides
renewal through His grace. The sacred and the secular are realities that
both constitute the presence of God. All of life's activities are to be done
unto the glory of God. The significance of the Reformation, therefore,

> lies in the groundwork it laid down for a Christian view
> of the world and life. It called for a religion of the whole
> person involved in the whole of culture. Its demands
> were for a world under God, a Christian society, a people
> informed by a biblical point of view, serving and enjoying
> God in all of life. The genius of the Reformation – which
> also drew from other late-medieval developments – lay
> in the freedom of the individual under God, the world as
> the arena of humankind's religious activity, and God at
> the center of life, giving meaning to history and culture
> (Mayers, Richards, and Webber 1972:16).

The Protestant Reformation, of course, preceded the development
of Wesleyan thought. The Wesleyan quadrilateral of scripture, tradition,
reason, and experience, the emphasis on sanctification of the believer, and
the call to holy living and social holiness were not only the major motifs
of the Wesleyan tradition but proved to be major contributors to Christian
Higher Education. Many of the concepts developed in the Reformation
also find expression in the themes of Wesleyan thought, particularly the
call for a religion of the whole person involved in the whole of culture. "The
Wesleyan quadrilateral fostered a sense of theological charity, whereas the
emphasis on sanctification and holy living called for higher standards of
conduct. Social holiness demanded a concern for the poor and vulnerable

of society," (Hughes and Adrian 1997:323). The integration of faith and learning continues to be the hallmark of Christian higher education, creating a space for the integration of the whole person and the whole culture.

Christian higher education, then,

> is a process of involvement in a community of scholars who investigate the areas of human knowledge and experience from a [purportedly] Christian worldview. From an enlightened reason and regenerated love, students of Christian higher education will align themselves with the on-going responsibility of the Christian in modern society. The outcome will be participation in the social order as a mature Christian who has an active sense of spiritual responsibility for vocation, whatever that may be (Beebe and Kulaga 2003:140-141).

In a recent address former president of the Council of Christian Colleges and Universities, Robert Andringa, said this about the two major themes identified by the Council as its initiatives:

> We must be more global in our thinking, praying, planning and actions. With the partnership of affiliate campuses in 15 nations outside of North America, we have a chance to provide enrichment experiences for students beyond the capacity of most secular institutions. We hope to facilitate ideas of how to make our curricula more reflective of the global economy. Certainly God's kingdom knows no national boundaries, so Christian students need to be prepared to be thoughtful, informed citizens of the world... The second priority theme for Council staff is, again, such a natural for Christ followers--to be intentional and consistent about advancing racial harmony and diversity. The biblical mandate on this issue is without question (Andringa 2002).

While there is a lack of ethnic diversity on many Christian campuses, this is no excuse to developing cultural competence. In surveys, CCCU students have expressed a disappointment in the lack of diversity on their campuses (Andringa 2002). While a critical mass of persons from other ethnic backgrounds will definitely provide a more robust atmosphere on a college campus regarding issues of diversity, institutions of higher learning that do not have that critical mass can still strive to be more global in their thinking and in their actions, and can advance the cause of racial harmony and diversity through learning more about other cultures and ethnicities.

Wesleyan Resources

In John Wesley one can find themes that lend themselves towards a rich theology of cultural competence. While these themes don't directly address cultural competence per se, they are concerned with humanity and human life. Cultural competence is the awareness, knowledge, and skills needed to work with others who are culturally different from self in meaningful, relevant, and productive ways. John Wesley learned from many who were different from him both culturally and ethnically. While he may not have always agreed with the "other," he was open to listening and understanding his own thought better due to his interactions with persons different from himself. In his sermon on *A Caution Against Bigotry*, Wesley says,

> Take care, first, that you do not convict yourself of bigotry by your unreadiness to believe that any man does cast out devils who differs from you…Yea, if it could be supposed that I should see a Jew, a deist or a Turk doing the same, were I to forbid him either directly or indirectly I should be no better than a bigot still. O stand clear of this. Tis well we go thus far, but do not stop here. If you will avoid all bigotry, go on. In every instance of this kind, whatever the instrument may be, acknowledge the finger of God. And not only acknowledge but rejoice in his work, and praise his name with thanksgiving. Encourage whomsoever God is pleased to employ, to give himself wholly up thereto. Speak well of him wheresoever you are; defend his character and his mission. Enlarge as far as you can his sphere of action. Show him all kindness in word and in deed. And cease not to cry to God in his behalf, that he may save both himself and them that hear him (Outler and Heitzenrater 1991:297).

Philip Meadows says there is something hospitable, open and inclusive to be found in the theology of John Wesley, something that can make him optimistic about the activity of God in everyone (2000). John Wesley looked for God in every place he went and in everyone he related with, whether on land or on sea. It did not matter that the person was from another ethnic background or from another culture. On the one hand, he was prepared to affirm all those ways of life in and through which he perceived the grace of God at work, and, on the other hand, he criticized all that he perceived to be contrary to the test of holiness, or love for God and neighbor (Meadows 2000). John Wesley understood that God's grace and His gift of salvation were available for all those who believe. Wesley provides a caution in his sermon against racism and being racist. His famous – and perhaps overused - phrase, "I look upon all the world as my parish" is nonetheless suggestive of his global mindedness. His love of God opened him up to the world. He no longer was limited and confined to England but he traveled to the Americas as a missionary, during which he found himself inadequate. He realized that he came to convert, but he himself was not fully converted to God. His limitations became so glaringly difficult for him to live with that his time in Georgia rendered him desiring a deeper and a stronger faith in God, which would both transform him further and equip him for the cause of preaching Christ to others. Wesley was out of his "comfort zone" in America. He was able to see things in himself that he couldn't when in England. Being out of our "comfort zone" is an important part of becoming culturally competent—we are transformed in the process with the right support and resources. The more he understood who God was the more his understanding of humanity and the purpose of humanity changed. He saw humanity as made in the image of God, deserving the grace of God, saved and perfected by God's own love.

1) Image of God

A good place to begin reflection on a theology of cultural competence is with Wesley's understanding of humanity as made in the image of God. Men and women are made in the image of God, and thus we each reflect God. Although Wesley was not without his own ethnocentrism, he still believed that whether one was a Jew, a deist, or a Turk they were to be treated equally if found doing the work of God. He thoroughly cautioned against judging the instrument whatever it may be.

The Protestant Reformation affirmed that humans were created in the image of God, while sin and rebellion caused alienation; humanity's hope lies in God who allows renewal for people through his grace. Wesley maintained the tension between humanity's created and fallen nature; there is no overlooking sin and the alienation, guilt, and judgment that result from it.

> All have sinned and fall short of the glory of God. For Wesley, that is neither the last nor the first word. Sin is the defacing, but not the total loss, of the image of God. In every person, there is something worth saving and something that can be restored. There is capacity for good, for creativity, for self-giving love—even a capacity to make an everlasting contribution to the kingdom of God that only that person can make (Snyder 2011:75).

Dignity and worth of persons is hard to come by. The world does not easily provide such dignity and worth to persons. The poor are left to be poor, the abandoned are left abandoned, the abused are left abused, and the destroyed are left unattended in many instances. The biblical message calls us to assist in restoring the image of God that has been left poor, abandoned, abused and destroyed, regardless of the person's ethnic or racial status; the image of God must be restored. Part of this process of restoration invites us to relate to – and engage with – the other in meaningful, productive and relevant ways, (Pope *et al* 2004). Skills need to be developed in order to know how to work for and work with people of diverse racial, ethnic, religious, and cultural backgrounds in order to help restore the image of God in them.

What does it mean to be made in the image of God? What image are people being restored to? Christopher Wright states,

> Much theological ink has been spilled on trying to pin down exactly what it is about human beings that can be identified as the essence of the image of God in us. Is it our rationality, our moral consciousness, our capacity for relationship, our sense of responsibility to God? Even our upright posture and the expressiveness of the human face have been canvassed as the locus of the image of God in humankind. Since the Bible nowhere defines the term, it is probably futile to attempt to do so very precisely. In any case, we should not so much think of the image of God as an independent "thing" that we somehow possess. God

did not give to human beings the image of God. Rather, it is a dimension of our very creation. The expression, "in our image" is adverbial that is it describes the way God made us, not adjectival that is, as if it simply described a quality we possess. The image of God is not so much something we possess, as what we are. To be human is to be the image of God. It is not an extra feature added to our species; it is definitive of what it means to be human (Wright 2006:421).

So, if the Bible does not define the term for us, are we able to conclude the image we are to restore from understanding who God is and who we are in relation to Him? Genesis 1-3 affirms at least four significant truths about humanity; all human beings are addressable by God, all human beings are accountable to God, all human beings have dignity and equality, and the biblical gospel fits all (Wright 2006:424).

Student comments expressing a preference for one race over another undermine or deny biblical truth that we all embody the image of God. Whether we are Black or Hispanic, White, or Asian, Native American or Pacific Islander we are the image of God. We all in some sense reflect God. We all have similar dignity and equality in the eyes of God. And since institutions of Christian higher learning bring faith and culture together in their learning, we should explicitly and implicitly teach our students the biblical truth that is affirmed right down through the ages, from the Reformation to John Wesley, we are made in God's image. Wesley says,

Man was made in the image of God....He was, after the likeness of his Creator, endued with *understanding*, a capacity of apprehending whatever objects were brought before it, and of judging concerning them. He was endued with a *will*, exerting itself in various affections and passions; and lastly with *liberty*, or freedom to choice, without which all the rest would have been in vain, and he would have been no more capable of serving his Creator than a piece of earth or marble. He would have been as incapable of vice or virtue as any part of the inanimate creation. In these, in the power of self-motion, understanding, will and liberty, the natural image of God consisted (Outler 1985:439).

In his sermon, *The Image of God,* John Wesley further acknowledges that,

> there are those of our age and nation who greedily close with this old objection, and eagerly maintain that they were not made in the image of the living God, but of the beasts that perish; who heartily contend that it was not the divine but the brutal likeness in which they were created, and earnestly assert 'that they themselves are beasts' in a more literal sense. These consequently reject with scorn the account God has given of man, and affirm it to be contrary to reason and (to the account itself), as well as it is to their practice (Outler and Heitzenrater 1991:14).

Societies have often played a significant part in diminishing the image of God in persons by considering one ethnic or racial group to be superior to another. Biblically, however, in our essential humanity we are no less nor more than the other because we are all made in the image of God. The grace of God gives us the opportunity to renew our understanding, the understanding that is distorted and that refuses to acknowledge the image of God in the other. Wesley's theological anthropology constantly returned to the threefold social-historical interpretation of human existence: created in the image of God, fallen by its own volition, restored and reclaimed by God's mercy (Oden 1994:133). The image of God in humans was, as a result of the Fall, distorted but not eliminated.

2) Grace of God

The grace of God makes restoration of fallen men and women possible. Wesley understood grace as prevenient, justifying, and sanctifying.

> The threefold distinction describes the way people experience that grace and shows the depth and breadth of God's redemptive initiative. Through prevenient grace people are drawn to God—though most often they resist God's gracious love. If they respond positively, however—receiving God's "awakening"—then preceding grace becomes justifying grace. Justifying grace then is

immediately transformed into sanctifying grace as people
continue to open their lives to the work of God's Spirit
(Snyder 2011:76).

The grace of God is not determined by the situations we encounter in life
but is found in encountering God alone. John Wesley says, "There is no
person that is in a state of mere nature…that is wholly void of the grace
of God. No person is entirely destitute of what is vulgarly called 'natural
conscience.' But this is not natural; it is more properly termed 'preventing
grace," (Meadows 2000: 101-102). So the grace of God provides hope to
all persons everywhere for salvation from sin. As Philip Meadows puts it,
"grace has the effect of immediately including all people in God's plan of
salvation, not as those standing outside and waiting to get in, but already
indwelled by the transforming presence of the Spirit of God, simply by
virtue of being human," (102). Any person, anywhere can reach for the
grace of God; it is not out of their reach due to God's prior gracious action.

> Wesley affirms that some great truths, such as the being
> and attributes of God, and the difference between moral
> good and evil, were known, in some measure, to the
> "heathen" world. The traces of them are to be found in
> all nations: So that, in some sense, it may be said to every
> person, *He hath showed thee, O man, what is good: even to do
> justly, to love mercy and to walk humbly with thy God*. With
> this truth he has, in some measure, enlightened every one
> that cometh into the world (Meadows 2000: 103-104).

All people everywhere can potentially activate the life of God in them
through prevenient and justifying grace. Wesley emphasizes this gift. In
fact, as Collins puts it,

> the consequence of Wesley's soteriological intentionality
> as reflected in his practical divinity in general and his order
> of salvation in particular was to make the graces accessible
> to all people but especially to the poor, the very least of all.
> Invited to participate in a class meeting, the downtrodden
> came to know themselves not through the diminishing
> scripts prevalent in eighteenth–century British society,
> whereby they were mistakenly labeled as lazy and
> shiftless, but through the gospel narrative itself, whereby
> they were invited to receive the richest love and the most
> profound graces. The destitute were no longer alienated

but embraced, no longer dispossessed but empowered, no longer forgotten but cherished. Having been forgiven and renewed by God in Christ, having received the witness of the Holy Spirit that they indeed were the beloved of the Lord, the poor were gifted in so many ways that they had not hitherto imagined. Such graces created the bonds of fellowship and care that transcended the divisions of class and hateful pride. The poor thus received a different narrative through which they could come to know themselves in a new way, that is, as nothing less than the beloved of the Lord, as the children of the Most High (Collins 2007:329).

In our societies today we need to invite not only the poor, but also those who are the culturally and ethnically different to partake in "the richest love and most profound graces" as members of the kingdom of God. John Wesley invited the poor; he stepped out of his familiar place into an unfamiliar place and extended a hand of fellowship. Wesley did not shy away from interacting with those who were different from him or from those whom his English society deemed unworthy of interaction. The knowledge he gained from his study of the scriptures regarding humanity and his own experience compelled him to relate to the marginalized or socioeconomically different. The burden to see that others have the same liberty in Christ was so strong that he was moved to act. He was moved from awareness to action.

The grace of God goes before and after, and we are called to participate with God in the redemption of humankind and the restoration of the image of God through His grace. God is already active in all persons, cultures, and societies, even if in hidden ways. As Howard Snyder argues, "non-Christian religions are not in themselves means of grace, but God's grace to some degree works in them—if in no other way, at least to restrain evil," (Snyder 2011:77). The grace of God is unmerited and because God is love He extends the gift of grace to each one of us.

3) Saved by God

Salvation is the central theme in Wesley's theology. In Ephesians 2:8 we read, *by grace you are saved through faith.* Wesley writes in his sermon on *Salvation by Faith,*

> If then sinful man finds favor with God, it is grace upon grace. If God vouchsafe still to pour fresh blessing upon us, the greatest of all blessings, salvation—what can we say to these things but thanks be unto God for his unspeakable gift. And thus it is. Herein 'God commendeth his love toward us in that while we were yet sinners Christ died to save us.' By grace then we are saved through faith. Grace is the source, faith the condition of salvation (Outler and Heitzenrater 1991:40).

There is no sin that is beyond the ability of God to forgive. When we are saved we begin to be perfected in God's love. An important part of this process is the transformation that comes as a result of the renewing of our mind (Romans 12:2). As a result, our attitude towards ourselves as well as others must be transformed as well albeit over time. Our biases need to be reconstructed; we need to develop a bias towards the grace of God instead of remaining biased against others and ourselves. "For Wesley, the point of Christ's atonement is that human beings, and by extension their societies and cultures, can be healed from the terrible disease of sin," (Snyder 2011:79). Salvation is a gift for all of God's creation, accessible through faith in Christ Jesus and the work of the Holy Spirit.

Why is being saved important to cultural competence? Cultural competence has to do with interacting with others who are different from us. Persons inevitably take on the stereotypes and biases towards the culturally, ethnically, racially, and socioeconomically different. Regeneration allows us to *begin* the process of having these negative stereotypes and biases transformed. As we have noted in the previous sections under Image of God, and Grace of God, we find the affirmation in Wesleyan thought that we are all made in the image of God, and that the grace of God is available to all. There are no categories of persons who are allotted more favor than other categories of persons. The grace of God through salvation and sanctification should increase our capacity to relate positively with others.

4) Perfected By God

Perfection is often misunderstood as meaning being without flaws. However, Wesleyan thought teaches that we learn that our flaws are redeemed by the grace of God and we are renewed.

> Now let this perfection appear in its native form, and who can speak one word against it? Will any dare to speak against loving the Lord our God with all our heart, and our neighbor as ourselves? Against a renewal of heart, not only in part, but in the whole image of God? Who is he that will open his mouth against being cleansed from all pollution both of flesh and spirit; or against all the mind that was in Christ, and walking in all things as Christ walked? What man, who calls himself a Christian, has the hardiness to object to the devoting, not in part, but all our soul, body, and substance to God? What serious man would oppose the giving God all our heart, and the having one desire ruling all our tempers? I say again, let this Christian perfection appear in its own shape, and who will fight against it (Wesley 1966:118).

The complete giving of our heart and mind to Christ is significant in the scriptures and in Wesleyan thought. Wesley insists on the complete giving of our heart and mind to Christ in order to gain from Christ his virtues. For Wesley, Christian Perfection means we are becoming more like Christ, we more and more embody the attitudes of Christ. Our sinful and fallen nature is overcome by the life of Christ in us. The indwelling Holy Spirit, working in part through the Christian community, guides us and directs us as we daily strive to overcome our sinful selves. The goal of God's work in us is Christian perfection, or the maturing and perfecting of Christian character, so that we may perfectly love God and neighbor.

It is clear from his writings that by Christian perfection Wesley meant the Spirit-given ability to love God with all our heart, soul, strength, and mind and our neighbors as ourselves. Wesley repeatedly emphasized this. "The central issue is the work of the Spirit in transforming us personally and communally into the image of Christ; of forming in us the character of Christ," (Snyder 2011:81). This was a central Wesleyan emphasis. The power of the life of Christ in us is such that it transforms us. It transforms our mind, and it transforms our hearts. It transforms our mind in the sense that it changes our way of thinking and it transforms our heart in the sense that it transforms our actions.

Wesley's sermon on *Christian Perfection* outlines what Christian perfection is and what it is not. Christian perfection is being holy as Christ is holy. This holiness transforms us and transforms our behaviors. When students attend places of Christian higher education that exemplify such teachings and such a life, they learn to see themselves as part of a greater narrative, a greater reality that helps them understand and see life from a perspective they may have not heard or understood before. As a result of this renewing of their mind ,their lives can be set on a trajectory of freedom to attain greater understanding of the grander truth, the truth that we are all made in the image of God.

Implications of Wesleyan Theology for Cultural Competence

The aim of this paper has been to explore Wesleyan theology to identify a few key themes that provide sources for developing a Wesleyan theology of cultural competence. The themes addressed in this paper are Wesley's understanding of the image of God, the grace of God, the salvation of God, and Christian perfection. These four aspects of Wesley's theology provide a broad framework to begin developing a Wesleyan theology of cultural competence. As we have seen through Wesleyan thought, it is incumbent upon us to enter lives and communities which may be different from our own in order to share the saving knowledge of Jesus Christ.

While Wesley may not have dealt with the need for cultural competence as we have come to understand it today, it is important to recognize that his theology lays the foundation for the need to develop such competence. "What was it that people on the social margins found so compelling in the Methodist movement that offered no immediate release from entrenched positions of subordination (Hempton 2005:131)?" Many have emphasized the spiritual and cosmological syntheses of evangelical enthusiasm while others have maintained the social utility of the faith, offering personal assurance and communal identity to those in sore need of both," (Hempton 2005). Just as in Wesley's day, many of today's societies are marked by sociocultural divisions, which often lead to conflict. We tend to judge others (to borrow from Dr. Martin Luther King, Jr.) either by the color of their skin rather than the content of their character—or, as I have argued here, by the image of God – however distorted – that they possess. Our interactions with others should be based on the understanding gained through scripture, which Wesley emphasized in his theology. Our interactions with others should be based on the premise that we are created in the image of God, and the truth that the grace of God transforms us by his grace into his holy character.

1) Image of God: Understanding the concept helps to see every person in the image of God

The problem in intercultural encounters is that we often place a higher value on our own cultural beliefs and practices, viewing other ways of understanding the world as inferior or, more commonly, wrong. Anthropologists refer to this attitude as ethnocentrism, and it is part of our "natural state" as individuals brought up in particular societies and cultures; thus, it has to be unlearned. We must graduate from looking simply at external differences to internal differences, from physical features to values and beliefs that determine our interactions with one another. We can begin by recognizing that everyone, despite his or her physical or cultural differences, is created in the image of God.

2. Grace: The gift of God for everyone

The grace of God is unmerited favor. No one can earn it. It is given. The gift of this grace of God is not bound to one ethnic or cultural community. There is no boundary to this gift as it is freely given to all of us, and we must extend the same gift of grace to others from different ethnicities and cultures. There is a line in a familiar Christian song that says, "Freely, freely, you have received, freely, freely give. Go in My name, and because you believe, Others will know that I live," (*United Methodist Hymnal* 1989: 389). Grace does not belong to us; it belongs to God and hence it is a gift we must not withhold from others. But it is not enough to simply share it; we want to share it effectively. To do this we must have the cultural competency skills to present the Gospel in such a way that it makes sense to the culturally different other.

3. Salvation of God: Transforms Our Understanding

John Wesley once said, "I who went to America to convert others, was never myself converted to God," (Owens 2001: 34). He later had a heart-warming experience that transformed his life. Before this transformational experience he had the requisite knowledge, but this knowledge needed to be experienced and felt. When John Wesley felt the touch of God he was moved to action with understanding towards others. When we experience the love of God that transforms our understanding and moves us from our limited knowledge and limited abilities, we can then engage with awareness with others. When we see ourselves with our weaknesses, we recognize our insufficiency. We understand the need for Jesus Christ and it is through him and through Christian community that our self-image is restored. When we recognize that we are not better than a Jew, deist or a Turk we learn to engage others who are different from us with understanding. We do this because the grace of God has gone before us and continues to be with us and is even there long after we have left the scene.

4. Christian Perfection: Christ-like nature in our behavior

We are never without God. In Matthew 28:20 we read the words, "and lo I am with you always." God never leaves us. He is always with us through the presence of the Holy Spirit in our lives, working in us, preparing us to do his good will, to practice justice, mercy, and truth. When we love God with all of our minds and with all of our hearts we are with God and God is with us. And when we are with God we are able to share God and that which is God's specifically, love and grace with others. We are able to walk in love and grace. We are more willing to take the time to understand and to be present with people. This helps us as we grow in cultural competence, developing the necessary awareness, knowledge and skills for working with others. Working with people from different cultures can be demanding because there are so many different meanings associated with different cultural elements. As we are perfected into God's holy character we develop the fruit of the Spirit, which is, love, joy, peace, forbearance, kindness, goodness, faithfulness, gentleness and self-control. Against such things there is no law, says Galatians 5:22-23. As God continues to transform us and our attitudes and behaviors, we relate with understanding and appreciation of the other.

Conclusion

As the character of God grows within us we can grow in our cultural competence. While one may argue that we can be culturally competent without God, I wonder if we can truly be competent in the way Reynolds, Mueller, and Pope have defined cultural competence – "the awareness, knowledge, and skills needed to work with others who are culturally different from self in meaningful, relevant and productive ways," (2004: 13). Through what has been addressed in this paper we find some key aspects of Wesleyan theology that are necessary resources for developing a framework for cultural competence in order to work with others in a meaningful, relevant, and productive way as the character of God develops within us.

Notes

1. This is not to diminish the fact that local theologies and local expressions of worship are critical in the contextualization of the Gospel.

Works Cited

Andringa, Robert C.
    2014 "Opening Address, Forum 2001 of the Council of Christian Colleges and Universities. http://www.cccu.org/professional_development/resource_library/2002/prepared_text_of_speech_by_robert_c_andringa. Accessed 13 September 2014.

Beebe and Kulaga
    2003 *A Concept to Keep*. Spring Arbor, Michigan: Spring Arbor University Press.

Collins, Kenneth J.
    2007 *The Theology of John Wesley: Holy Love and the Shape of Grace*. Nashville: Abingdon Press.

Curnock, Nehemiah
    1951 *John Wesley's Journal*. Great Britain: Philosophical Library, Inc.

Hempton, David
    2005 *Methodism: Empire of the Spirit*. New Haven, London: Yale University Press.

Hughes, Richard T. and William B. Adrian
    1997 *Models For Christian Higher Education: Strategies for Success in the Twenty-First Century*. Grand Rapids, Michigan: Wm.B. Eerdmans Publishing Co.

Holmes, Arthur F.
    1975 *The Idea of a Christian College*. Grand Rapids, Michigan: William B. Eerdmans Publishing Company.

Kennedy, Thomas E.
    2013 *Building Trust Between Cultures: Ethnocentrism and Intercultural Competency*. D.Min Dissertation, Asbury Theological Seminary, Wilmore, KY.

Maddox, Randy L. and Jason E. Vickers
  2010 *The Cambridge Companion to John Wesley.* New York: Cambridge University Press.

Mayers, Marvin K. and Lawrence Richards and Robert Webber
  1972 *Reshaping Evangelical Higher Education.* Grand Rapids, Michigan: Zondervan Corporation.

Meadows, Philip R.
  2000 "Candidates for Heaven: Wesleyan Resources for a Theology of Religions." *Wesleyan Theological Journal*, 35 (1): 99-129.

Mudge, James
  1913 *Heart of Religion: As Described by John Wesley.* Cincinnati: Jennings and Graham.

Oden, Thomas C.
  1994 *John Wesley's Scriptural Christianity: A Plain Exposition of his Teaching on Christian Doctrine.* Grand Rapids, Michigan: Zondervan.

Outler, Albert C.
  1985 *The Works of John Wesley.* Nashville, Tennessee: Parthenon Press.

Outler. Albert C. and Richard P. Heitzenrater.
  1991 *John Wesley's Sermons: An Anthology.* Nashville: Abingdon Press.

Owens, Jody
  2001 "Restoring Faith and Practice? John Wesley's Missionary Journey to Georgia." *Stone-Campbell Journal* 4 (Spring).

Pope, Raechele L., Amy L. Reynolds, John A. Mueller
  2004 *Multicultural Competence in Student Affairs.* San Francisco, CA: Jossey-Bass.

Potts, James H.

    1891   *Living Thoughts of John Wesley: A Comprehensive Selection of the Living Thoughts of the Founder of Methodism as Contained in his Miscellaneous Works.* New York: Hunt & Eaton.

Scupin, Raymond

    2003   *Race and Ethnicity: An Anthropological Focus on the United States and the World.* New Jersey: Pearson Education Inc.

Snyder, Howard A.

    2011   *Yes In Christ.* Toronto, Canada: Clements Publishing Group Inc.

Snyder, Howard A.

    1980   *The Radical Wesley: And Patterns for Church Renewal.* Eugene, Oregon: Wipf and Stock Publishers.

Wesley, John

    1966   *A Plain Account of Christian Perfection.* Kansas City, Missouri: Beacon Hill Press.

Wood, J.A.

    1921   *Christian Perfection as Taught by John Wesley.* Chicago: Christian Witness Co.

Wright, Christopher J.H.

    2006   *The Mission Of God: Unlocking the Bible's Grand Narrative.* Downers Grove, Illinois: IVP Academic.

Engaging in Pneumatic Mission Praxis

ROBERT L. GALLAGHER

DOI: 10.7252/Paper.000036

About the Author

Robert L. Gallagher (Ph.D., Fuller Theological Seminary) is the department chair, director of the Master of Arts program in intercultural studies, and associate professor of intercultural studies at Wheaton College Graduate School in Chicago, where he has taught since 1998. He previously served as the president of the American Society of Missiology (2010-2011) and as an executive pastor in Australia (1979-90), as well as being involved in theological education in Papua New Guinea and the South Pacific since 1984. His publications include the co-editing of *Footprints of God: A Narrative Theology of Mission* (MARC 1999), *Mission in Acts: Ancient Narratives in Contemporary Contexts* (Orbis Books 2004), and *Landmark Essays in Mission and World Christianity* (Orbis Books 2009).

Introduction

The aim of this paper is to craft a philosophy and methodology of mission praxis. I will begin by securing my reflections in scripture and by carefully defining terms. I will then survey mission history and explore guidelines of Christian proclamation in local situations. This praxis involves movements of reflection and action always returning to the Word of God, reliant and impregnated with the illumination of the Holy Spirit outworking with a specific messenger, motivation, message, and method (see a missional example of the process in Gallagher 2006d: 127-132).

Before engaging in the journey of pneumatic mission praxis, it is important to emphasize the intertwining role of the Holy Spirit throughout the process. First a bold impeachment: I sometimes wonder if many Western Christians really believe in the Holy Spirit. Today's church may have a theology of the Holy Spirit, yet it has little awareness of his presence and power. The Spirit, however, played a vital role in the first-century church.

A reading of the book of Acts reveals two main categories. The Holy Spirit worked in the disciples of the early church to bring: joy in the midst of persecution (5:41), paradigm shifts from monocultural to cross-cultural perspective (1:6-8; 2:21; 3:25; 4:24; 8:14-25; 9:43; 10:44-48; 11:15-18; 15:6-11), boldness in preaching (4:29-31), contextualization of the message (2:14-40; 3:12-26; 13:16-41; 14:15-17; 17:22-31), selection and training of leadership (6:1-7; 13:1-4; 20:28), planning and development of the church (15:28; 16:6-7), and deep spirituality (1:14; 3:1; 4:31; 6:4; 8:15; 10:1; 13:3). On the other hand, the Spirit also worked in non-Christians through the gifts of the Spirit to empower the weak and lowly (1:13-14; 2:17-18; 9:32-42; 16:14-15, 25-34), as well as to create a sense of awe and wonder (2:6-7, 12; 3:10-11) through the fear of God (5:5, 11), and the joy of the Gospel (8:8) (Gallagher 1999: 208-209).

Samuel Chadwick proclaimed, "Theology without experience is like faith without works: dead" (1969: 12). The signs of contemporary death abound with lack of prayer and prophesying, and a focus on investigation and not in inspiration. The creative act of the Spirit of illumination has lost its hold on intellect and heart. J. Hudson Taylor concurred, "Since the days before Pentecost, has the whole church ever put aside every other work and waited upon him for ten days that [the Spirit's] power might be manifested? We give too much attention to method and machinery and resources, and too little to the source of power" (1930: 516). And again from Lesslie Newbigin,

> What I have called the Pentecostal Christian has the New Testament on his side when he demands first of all of any body of so-called Christians, "Do you have the Holy Spirit?" For without that all your creedal orthodoxy and all your historic succession avails you nothing. To quote again the blunt words of St. Paul: "If any man hath not the Spirit of Christ, he is none of his" (1954: 100-101).

In the Western church we need to repent of two closely related sins. We need to repent of underestimating that God's Spirit can speak and direct through his word, history, and any other means he chooses (see Gallagher 2006a: 17-33; Gallagher 2006c: 336-341). Second, we need to repent of overestimating our own importance in helping the engagement of mission praxis to grow and strengthen his kingdom. The real issue in these assumptions is that we think we are better able to determine the action of ministry than the Holy Spirit. The end result is a sense of dependency on human wisdom rather than the wisdom of the Spirit of God—the divine helper—and unfortunately, this is all too prevalent in many churches today. François Fénelon, the seventeenth-century mystic once said,

> It is certain from the Holy Scriptures (Rom. viii; John xiv) that the Spirit of God dwells within us, acts there, prays without ceasing, groans, desires, asks for us what we know not how to ask for ourselves, urges us on, animates us, speaks to us when we are silent, suggests to us all truth, and so unites us to him that we become one spirit (1 Cor. vi 17). This is the teaching of faith, and even those instructors who are farthest removed from the interior life, cannot avoid acknowledging so much (1853: 89).

The Holy Spirit is a person. He is not a power or energy. He has a will, intelligence, and knowledge. He has ability to love and see and think. The Holy Spirit is the teacher, a constant presence, which we cannot be. He is the one who leads us to God. In the words of John V. Taylor, "It is through worship that we constantly renew, by the activity of the Holy Spirit, our Abba relationship with the God of Jesus Christ," (1980: 296). David Platt warns:

> Let us not, then, be so foolish as to confine the work of the Spirit to one professional, speaking in one place, at one time of the week. Let us not be so unwise as to bank the spread of the gospel on a certain person at a certain place when all week long the Spirit of God is living in every single man and woman of God, empowering each of us to advance the kingdom of God for his glory (2011: 70).

Christ lives in people through the Spirit as a living presence. Christian faith reproduces Christ as our lives are sanctified, possessed, and transformed by the power of the Spirit through Christ living in us.

> Or think of it this way. It is as if the Spirit stands behind us, throwing light over our shoulder on to Jesus who stands facing us. The Spirit's message to us is never, "Look at me; listen to me; come to me; get to know me," but always, "Look at him, and see his glory; listen to him and hear his word; go to him and have life; get to know him and taste his gift of joy and peace." The Spirit, we might say, is the matchmaker, the celestial marriage broker, whose role it is to bring us and Christ together and ensure that we stay together (Packer 2005: 57).

We must always be dependent on the Holy Spirit through prayer (Gallagher 2006b: 19-20). The Spirit is the activity of our prayer as we pray *in* the Holy Spirit. And daily we can be used by God in the power of his Spirit (Gallagher 2004b: 21-33). "The pattern of the people of God praying and the filling of the Spirit propelling people into mission is a Lukan motif that begins at the baptism of Jesus and continues throughout Luke-Acts" (Gallagher 2004a, 54). As Pope Francis reiterates,

> In every activity of evangelization, the primacy always belongs to God, who has called us to cooperate with him and who leads us on by the power of his Spirit.

The real newness is the newness which God himself mysteriously brings about and inspires, provokes, guides, and accompanies in a thousand ways. God asks everything of us, yet at the same time he offers everything to us (2013:12).

The resources of the Church are supplied by the Spirit of God. The Spirit is more than the comforter. He reveals what Christ could not speak, and uses resources that were unavailable to the human Jesus. He is the Spirit of truth and revelation. The Church needs to be open and available to the reserves of the Holy Spirit. The abilities of the world and the Church are futile and inadequate. It is only the fullness of the Spirit who will give the Church of Jesus an abundance of wisdom and power (Gallagher 2012: 9-22).

A. Biblical Interpretation of Mission

Having established the significance of the role of the Holy Spirit in all of Christian life, and particularly in the engagement of mission praxis, the paper will now suggest an approach to growing in interpreting the Bible prayerfully and rightly; and obediently in community with the help of the Holy Spirit (see an example of the expanded methodology in Gallagher 2013: 3-22). There are different translations, strategies, and theologies in understanding the scripture, yet reading and studying should involve the contexts of responsibility, community, and mission. We will comment briefly on the first two settings before focusing on the mission context.

First, a follower of Christ needs to study the Bible in the context of a life-long commitment to Christ and his mission with a persisting method of steady and systematic study. Mariano Magrassi encourages diligence in our pursuit of understanding the scriptures, which will eventually lead to familiarity (1998: 64-69). He exhorts that the disciples of Jesus need not become expert biblical exegetes before studying the Bible. Instead, they are simply asked to feed daily on God's word and in doing so will mature in understanding (1998: viii-ix). Without a growing relationship with Jesus and his word, there is the risk of drifting towards contemporary relativism.

Eugene H. Peterson writes that the spiritually mature need to continue in rigorous exegesis, and "this is not a task from which we graduate" (2006: 53).

Second, the Bible needs to be considered in appropriate rhythms of individual and communal responsibility. The Protestant tendency towards individualism is only one way that God speaks through the Bible (Matthew 6: 4, 6, 18); as is the Catholic belief in the magisterium, the authority that lays down what is the authentic teaching of the Church. For the Catholic Church, "the task of interpreting the word of God authentically has been entrusted solely to the magisterium of the Church, that is, to the Pope and to the bishops in communion with him" (Ratzinger 1994: 100). As N.T. Wright proposes, however, if the mission of God is "to make the deep, life-changing, kingdom-advancing sense it is supposed to, it is vital that ordinary Christians read, encounter, and study scripture for themselves, in groups and individually" (2011: 133).[1] Followers of Christ need to seek both individual and communal interpretation of scripture.

Protestant scholars such as David R. Bauer and Robert A. Traina (2011: 57) and Lindsay Olesberg (2012: 40) emphasize the individual study of scripture in terms of process and conclusions arguing that the reader needs to be available to break from faith community conversations, which will increase private motivation and comprehension. The Catholic author, Henri J.M. Nouwen, also encourages individuals to cultivate a personal spirituality through reading the Bible. He contends that unless we protect our own "inner mystery" we will not be able to form community (1975:31). Furthermore, unless we nurture a genuine individual spirituality:

> Our relationships with others easily become needy and greedy, sticky and clinging, dependent and sentimental, exploitive and parasitic, because we cannot experience the others as different from ourselves, but only as people who can be used for the fulfillment of our own, often hidden needs (Nouwen 1975:44).

On the other hand, most of the books of the Bible were written to faith communities to collectively shape the followers of God. Thus it remains essential to read the sacred texts together in community since the church is called to advance God's kingdom and not individuals. This missional togetherness brings unity of purpose and action in addition to training and obedience, as well as enriching the interpretative process through dialogue and testing in the context of community (Arnold 1993:

19; Olesberg 2012: 41, 75-76, 80-82). Magrassi blends both dynamics as he claims, "God speaks not only to his people; he also addresses me personally" (1998: 7).

Lastly, we need to comprehend the Bible in the context of God's mission to redeem and restore all creation. The Bible is the Spirit's instrument to transform followers of Christ for the mission of God. In *Scripture and the Authority of God*, N.T. Wright commends reading the Bible within the larger context of the authority of God set by the biblical authors (2011: 26). God's authority stems from his sovereign power accomplishing his mission of redeeming and renewing the entire cosmos. For Wright, the authority of the Bible over the Church is shorthand for the authority of God exercised through scripture, which as an extension of God's authority over all creation, is made manifest in his mission (2011: 21, 24).

This is the central narrative of the scripture with its origin in the story of the people of God found in the Hebrew text. The climax of Israel's story came with the death and resurrection of Jesus, which served as the inauguration of the kingdom of God, and will come to full consummation in the future redemption and renewal of the cosmos (Wright 2011: 41). Empowered by the transformative agency of the Holy Spirit, the Church is God's vehicle for advancing his kingdom in the world. The early church believed that God accomplished his purposes "through the 'word'; the story of Israel now transmuted into God's call to his renewed people" (Wright 2011: 50). The Church is invited into and nurtured for this mission by the Bible. Followers of Christ, led by the Holy Spirit, gather in Christian community to be transformed by the word to advance the mission of God in the world (Wright 2011: 115-116).

Kevin J. Vanhoozer modifies Wright's approach of locating the Bible within the greater story of God by using theatrical language. He argues that theatre has occurred "when one or more persons 'present' themselves to others" (2009: 156). God has accomplished this dramatic task by presenting himself and his mission in the world on the stage of world history, as well as inviting people to participate in the drama, which becomes a theodrama (156-158). The audience does not merely view the divine play from the seats, but is invited to participate in the "dialogue in action." The Bible as the story of God is a drama in which readers join the encounter. Vanhoozer believes that the Church does not submit to a perfect book filled with perfect truths, but to God and his mission of redemption as revealed in the Bible (163). The scriptures direct our attention to the godly drama and invite our participation. People's lives are changed by retelling the story of God's mission, which carries genuine power and God's authority (156).

Although Jeffrey Arnold (1993), Bauer and Traina (2011), Gordon D. Fee and Douglas Stuart (1981), Bob Grahmann (2003), Olesberg (2012), Leland Ryken and James C. Wilhoit (2012), and Ruth Sun (1982) have all written Bible reading handbooks and agree in principle with Wright and Vanhoozer on the view of biblical authority, they appear negligent in implementing the foundational mission of God context in their interpretative methodologies. Instead they rely on a "principilizing" hermeneutic that emphasizes the identification of universal principles from a biblical passage so that readers can align their lives. Olesberg explains this principilizing message: "The word of God describes reality and shines light into our lives so that we can be aligned with what is true" (2012: 21). Further, Grahmann emphasizes, "A belief in the truth of the Bible and a desire to obey its precepts is a foundational value of evangelical Christianity" (2003: 28-29).

In other words, the disciple of Christ reads the Bible and learns the universal truths and commands found therein, which are then applied in contemporary situations bringing the authoritative truth into the world. The Bible is God's spoken revelation disclosing all the necessary truths of life, especially regarding the death and resurrection of Christ. The truth found within the scriptures carries the authority of God into the world. The "Word" is the Son of God, Jesus, messiah made flesh, and it is through his death and resurrection that the world's sins were paid and forgiven. An over-emphasis on principilizing, however, can separate the reader from the wider context of the Church and the kingdom of God. Accompanying this assumption is the notion that the Bible's authority comes from its essence as a perfect book, carrying perfect truths, and given by a perfect God.

Vanhoozer claims that this interpretative approach substitutes a cognitive "logic of redemption" for the "drama of redemption." This method "de-dramatizes" the Bible and thrusts the reader towards "the 'point' without the parable, the content without the form, the 'soul' without the body of the text" (2009: 158-159). Underlying principles and truths are only uncovered when they are extracted from a specific context in which they were initially planted. Yet, in the process of proper interpretation it is challenging to determine from these truths an application for today. The Bible's authority is founded in the theodrama—God's mission to the world that the Church is invited to join—and the reader should seek wisdom from how the biblical text portrays "concrete wisdom-in-act;" and not just extract principles from the text. Biblical understanding is more than an intellectual exercise since it requires participation in the story of God.

The Bible is not primarily a set of commands and doctrines, but a call to participate in the theodrama. Peterson states:

> The Bible does not present us with a moral code and tell us, "Live up to this;" nor does it set out a system of doctrine and say, "Think like this and you will live well." The biblical way is to tell a story and in the telling invite: "Live *into* this—this is what it looks like to be human in this God-made and God-ruled world; this is what is involved in becoming and maturing as a human being (2006: 43-44).

Followers of Jesus do not simply study the Bible, but their lives are changed in thinking and behavior as they demonstrate concrete acts of love and mission in God's world (Peterson 2006: 18).

Christopher J.H. Wright suggests that interpreting the Bible should find a healthy rhythm between a missional and principilizing hermeneutic since the two views are complementary. He maintains that the views of N.T. Wright and Vanhoozer need to address how obedience to the scriptures in today's world actually takes place. Thus some method of principilizing is necessary. Likewise, the principilizing hermeneutical approach needs the contribution of knowing the fullness of the biblical metanarrative (2009: 321-322). Christopher Wright maintains that it is important for readers to understand that the mission of God provides the authoritative context of the Bible, and allow that realization to permeate their reading methodology. The church participates in the mission of God, "and the only access that we have to that mission of God is given us in the Bible. This is the grand narrative that is unlocked when we turn the hermeneutical key of reading all the scriptures in the light of the mission of God" (Wright 2006: 534). At the same time, students of the Bible should desire to follow specific commands and truths in their daily lives.

B. Defining Missional Terms

The paper will now move to the third major focus of engaging in pneumatic mission praxis—after the function of the Holy Spirit and a biblical theology of mission—by defining key terms. The consequence of definitions may be shown in considering the approach of David J. Bosch in his influential tome, *Transforming Mission: Paradigm Shifts in Theology of Mission*. Bosch states concerning the meaning of the expression "mission:"

> [O]n the issue of mission we run into difficulties here, particularly if we adhere to the traditional understanding of mission as the sending of preachers to distant places (a definition which, in the course of this study, will be challenged in several ways). There is, in the Old Testament, no indication of the believers of the old covenant being sent by God to cross geographical, religious, and social frontiers in order to win others to faith in Yahweh (1991:19).

Bosch does not recognize any mission in the Hebrew scriptures based solely on the traditional definition of mission as "sending." His paradigm shifts in theology of mission thus begin with the Gospels of the New Testament; simply ignoring over eighty-five percent of the sacred word.

Yet, if you have the concept of mission defined as, "leading people in their life's journey across barriers towards repentance and faith in the one, true, living God," then the whole of the first testament is relevant to our discussion, since there are numerous examples that fit this definition. Ivan Illich reinforces this notion in his definition of missiology. "Missiology studies the growth of the Church into new peoples, the birth of the Church beyond its social boundaries; beyond the linguistic barriers within which she feels at home; beyond the poetical images in which she taught her children" (1974: 7).

When I ask my students the question, "Name the people of God in the Old Testament who have intercultural encounters," they respond with quite a list of names: Abraham and Sarah, Isaac and Jacob and their wives in Canaan, Joseph and the patriarchal family in Egypt, Moses in Egypt, etc. Perhaps a better question would be, "Name the people of Yahweh in the Hebrew Bible who are not in any connection with the other nations." The answer is resoundingly, "Not many." All of us have various descriptions of the phrase "mission" that serve as a lens to view the Bible missiologically: shaped by our theological tradition, personal journey, and mission context in ongoing hermeneutical spirals over time.

The importance of this awareness of definitions is not confined to the first testament only. The definition of "the Gospel" of Jesus Christ in the second testament also bears evidence of the need of careful understanding of first-century ideas embedded in words and phrases (see Mark 1:1). The expression, "the Gospel," was derived from the Greek word, *euangelion*, meaning "good message" or "glad tidings". This noun was used 27 times in the English New Testament. The verb, *euangelizo*, was used 55 times and means "to bring good news" or "announce glad tidings". The word, *euangelistes*, was found three times to describe the function of the office of an evangelist, especially in the letters of Paul (Ephesians 4:7-13). The content of the Good News has an apostolic and Christological formula, with the synthesis being the rule or reign of God. The LORD calls the church to communicate the Good News of God's victory over all that is wrong in humanity and the world, through the life, death, and resurrection of Jesus Christ.

These preliminary ideas regarding the significance of missional terms and phrases need to be further teased out. Bosch's "Evangelism: Theological Currents and Cross-currents Today" (1987: 98-103) is a survey of the various ways the terms "mission" and "evangelism" were understood and practiced by contemporary missiologists and theologians. At first, the terms "mission" and "evangelism" were used as synonyms even if technical definitions were different. They ranged from the narrowly evangelical to the broadly ecumenical. It is possible to identify six positions along this continuum.

> *Position 1:* Mission and evangelism (M/E) was seen as winning souls for eternity and saving people from hell so that they might go to heaven. This was the task of the church, and to be involved in anything else was a diversion from its ministry. Most theologians who took this approach were pre-millennialists.

Position 2: M/E conveyed a "softer" emphasis on soul winning. It was also good to be involved in some activities such as relief work and education. "Mission as soul-winning" viewed such efforts as distractions. Involvement in social reform was deemed optional.

Position 3: M/E was soul-winning, yet with service ministries (e.g. education, health care, and social uplift) important in bringing people to Christ. They were aids to mission, or buttresses to the Gospel.

Position 4: M/E focused on individuals being transformed through the proclamation of the gospel. That transformation, it was believed, led to their involvement in society. The church proclaims the Good News, and redeemed people change society.

Position 5: M/E were synonymous, yet the scope of activities expanded considerably beyond the proclamation of the Gospel. The people of God were to be involved in Christian ministry outside the church in ever-expanding ecumenical circles. In the 1960s and 70s the World Council of Churches used "mission," "witness," and "evangelism" somewhat interchangeably often with only a muted call to conversion (in the traditional evangelical sense) being present in their documents.

Position 6: M/E did not include a call to repentance and faith in Christ. Instead, the focus was solely to change the structures of society. M/E was understood in terms of interhuman categories with salvation involving only this world (Bosch1987: 98).

In addition to the synonymous use of the terms "mission" and "evangelism," it is also possible to identify four different ways that evangelism was distinguished from mission.

1. "Objects" of mission and evangelism were different. For instance, Johannes Verkuyl viewed evangelism as communicating the Christian faith in Western society; those being evangelized were no longer Christian or were only nominally so. Mission, by contrast, was

communicating the Gospel in the majority world to those who were not yet Christians. This view was held in Europe by Lutheran, Reformed churches, and Catholicism (1978: 9).

2. Some theologians omitted "mission" from their vocabulary. Evangelism became comprehensive and all-embracing. Catholics, in particular, objected to the colonial implications of the term "mission." Evangelization became the preferred term to refer to what the church was doing in the areas of human development, liberation, justice, and peace.

3. Both "mission" and "evangelism" were used, although "evangelism" was the wider term and "mission" was the narrower. Evangelism was an umbrella term for anything to do with the Gospel: proclamation, translation, dialogue, service, and presence. Mission became a theological concept used for the origin and motivation of the above activities.

4. "Mission" was the wider term and "evangelism" the narrower. Mission equals evangelism plus social action (two separate parts of mission). Further, there were three different ways that this notion was understood: a. John Stott and the Lausanne Covenant believed that in the church's mission, evangelism was primary. Stott stated that evangelism was more important than social involvement, and eternal salvation does not equal economic and/or political liberation. b. Both words were equally important, and we should not prioritize between the two since they were intertwined. c. Social involvement was more important than evangelism (Bosch 1987: 98-99).

In light of all of these variations of definition, what can one finally say about "evangelism?" Bosch spoke of eight unique dimensions (1987: 100-102):

1. The center, core, or heart of mission was evangelism. This involved proclaiming salvation through Jesus Christ to nonbelievers, announcing forgiveness of sins, calling people to repentance and faith in Christ, and inviting

them to join Christ's earthly community, living in the power of the Holy Spirit. This does not limit evangelism to soul-winning. The Bible always sees the human person as a living body-soul connected to their society. Evangelism was not just concerned with the inward/spiritual side of people. The Gospel was incarnational. Persons who adhered to this view of evangelism understood that calling people to faith and a new life was an essential activity.

2. Evangelism sought to bring people into the visible community of believers. It was not recruiting people to become members of a local church. Protestants saw evangelism as involving church expansion by transference: from the world to the church. Numerical church growth equaled the fruit of successful evangelism.

3. Evangelism involved witnessing to what God had done, is doing, and will do. The focus of attention was on God and not on us. Evangelism was telling what God had already done in Christ. This does not mean that evangelism was restricted to verbal witnessing. It consists of word and deed, proclamation and presence, explanation and example. Both our verbal and our visual need to match: our lips and our life. We should embody the Gospel in the midst of our culture.

4. Evangelism was an invitation: it did not involve coaxing or threats by playing on feelings of guilt, or the terror of hell. People should turn to God because they are drawn to him by his love and not because they are pushed to God through fear.

5. Evangelism was possible when the church radiated the life of Christ. If our message is faith, hope, and love, then we should manifest our message in real life (see Acts 2:42-47; 4:32-35). Hans Werner Gensichen, the German missiologist, mentions five characteristics of a church involved in evangelism: a. it lets outsiders feel at home; b. it was not merely an object of pastoral care with the pastor having the monopoly; c. its members were involved

in society; d. it was structurally flexible and adaptable; e. it did not defend the interests of any select group of people (1971:170-172).

6. Evangelism involved risk. You never know what the Gospel will do in a person's life; and evangelizing may change the messenger. Both Cornelius and Peter were converted (see Acts 10).

7. There was a concern to not view evangelism as purveying a guaranteed happiness for this life or the next. It was important to stress that evangelism not be seen as excessively individualistic, or as encouraging a consumer mentality. It was not simply to receive life that people are called to Christ, but rather to give life.

8. Evangelism was calling people to follow Christ and to continue his mission. It was not seen as a list of do's, don't's, or attainments.

In this essay, mission is regarded as the wider concept and evangelism as the narrower. Yet, there are problems with defining "mission" as equaling evangelism plus social action since this leads to the question of which one is more important. This could suggest that you can have evangelism without social action and the social component without evangelism. Then what is mission? In broad terms, I accept Bosch's wider definition of mission as being the total task that God has set the church for the salvation of the world. Mission is the church carrying God's message of salvation across all types of barriers: geographical, social, political, ethnic, cultural, religious, and ideological. Mission also involves the redemption of the universe and the glorification of God.

Additionally, evangelism may be defined as that dimension and activity of the church's mission which seeks to offer every person, everywhere, a valid opportunity to be directly challenged by the Gospel of explicit faith in Jesus Christ, with a view to embracing him as savior, becoming a living member of his community, and being enlisted in his service of reconciliation, peace, and justice on earth.

C. History of Christian Mission

Thus far this essay has discussed the role of prayer and the Holy Spirit, responsible scriptural reflection in the contexts of community and mission, and the value of carefully delineating terms such as mission and evangelism. The purpose of the next section is to outline seventeen movements in the expansion of the Christian church that I teach in my mission history course. This missiological reinterpretation of church history focuses on the dynamics of the expansion, and the implications for contemporary strategies of mission. Engaging in pneumatic praxis concerns itself with understanding the processes through which the Christian movement has expanded, and not merely in the recitation of dates and names. In the course I pay specific attention to the means of Holy Spirit renewal, structure of mission, role of leadership, and the relationship between the three. The movements will now be briefly considered in approximate chronological order starting with the Church of the East followed by Orthodox mission, early monasticism, and Celtic Christianity to Moravianism and Methodism, stopping short of William Carey, the so-called "father of modern mission" (who went to southern India in 1792).

Church of the East: How did Christianity come to China? So much of missions' history focuses on Europe and the Western church. Yet the expansion of the Christian faith is not the exclusive domain of the West. With such information so easily accessible, it is effortless to slide into the old routines of victorious Eurocentricism, and miss the amazing stories of the Church of the East (so-called Nestorianism) in Persia, India, Central Asia, China, and Japan. Exploring answers to the question posed above, unfolds the fascinating account of a missions' movement that originated in the East and pushed the borders of Christendom into unexplored territory (Brock 1996: 23-35; Moffett 1998: 169-184).

Orthodox Church: From the Celts of Europe's western tip to the east coast of Japan, God was also at work in his church during the Middle Ages. Exposure to Orthodox mission strategy involves examining case studies such as the missionaries Cyril and Methodius in what is now known as the Balkans, Stephen of Perm in Siberia, Herman of Alaska, and Nicholas Kassatkin in Japan, as well as gaining an overview of the two main eras of Orthodox mission—the Byzantine and Russian (Stamoolis 1986; Gallagher 2011).

Monasticism: The rise of early monasticism is traced from Egypt to southern France and Asia Minor. Key leaders such as Antony and Benedict (Benedictines) contributed to the renewal of the declining church, followed by other mission movements such as the Cistercians, Cluniacs, and the pillar saints (Latourette 1975: 221-235; Moreau, Corwin, and McGee 2004: 93-113; Gallagher 2005a: 87-106).

Celtic Christianity: The Irish mission movement began with Patrick in Ireland and expanded via Columba to Scotland and Columba to Bobbio, Italy. Also, English monks were encouraged towards mission by this radical Irish vision, such as Willibrord and Boniface who proclaimed the Gospel in Holland and Germany, respectively (Blocher and Blandenier 2013: 53-79).

Medieval Renewal: Before the Protestant reformation, Hussites, Lollards, and Waldensians challenged the church to return to the Gospel of Jesus and the scriptures. Among the more influential of these leaders were Jan Hus of Prague, John Wycliffe of Oxford, and Peter Waldo of Lyons. The lives of these men created a legacy for the church of today (Pierson 2009: 79-128).

Medieval Friars: Dominic and Francis were early thirteenth century lay leaders in the Catholic Church that began renewal movements, which spread throughout Europe. Two hundred years before the first Protestant missionaries, the Dominican and Franciscan friars took their message of Christian love and service to the outposts of the Middle East, North Africa, China, and the Americas (Bevans and Schroeder 2004: 137-170; Blocher and Blandenier 2013: 103-118).

Protestant Reformation: The historical and contextual conditions of early sixteenth century Germany laid the foundation for a European reformation of the church. The printing press allowed the influential writings of Martin Luther to be quickly distributed into the hands of the peasants. Many German princes of the Holy Roman Empire also turned from Catholicism, and became followers of Luther's teaching, along with the people of their provinces. Students from all over Europe joined

Luther at the University of Wittenberg, Saxony and later returned to their home country to share the Lutheran message of reformation, especially in Scandinavia (Shelley 1995: 237-310; Pierson 2009: 129-176).

Swiss Protestants, such as Huldreich Zwingli, expanded the reformation by calling for a return to biblical water baptism and church governance. This radical form of Protestantism created the Anabaptist movement, which in the midst of persecution spread to parts of Europe and the American colonies. Second generation reformers centered on Geneva, Switzerland and the ministry of the Frenchman, Jan Calvin. John Knox of Scotland, and other international students, attended Calvin's Academy in Geneva, and returned to their home countries to initiate Calvinism, another form of Protestant reformation (Gallagher 2005b: 107-127; Irvin and Sunquist 2012: 71-124).

Catholic Reformation: Only partially in response to the Protestant Reformation, Ignatius of Loyola led a reformation of his own in the Catholic Church. At the University of Paris, Loyola and six other students formed a Catholic teaching order known as the Society of Jesus or the Jesuits. This quasi-military group helped turn back the Protestant expansion, especially in Eastern Europe, and became a strong missionary force in Asia and Latin America with missionaries such as Francis Xavier and Pedro Claver, respectively (Bevans and Schroeder 2004: 171-205; Noll 2012: 189-214).

Protestant Mission: The Puritan movement in England called for a reformation of Anglicanism that would be more in line with scripture and less with the Catholic Church. The process of renewal switched back and forth from persecution to acceptance, depending on the religious affiliation of the English monarch. The Puritan, John Elliot, was one of the first missionaries to successfully minister among the Native Americans around present-day Boston (Bosch 1991: 255-261; González 2010: 193-210).

In the mid-seventeenth century, Philip Spener and August Franke became leaders of the Pietist movement in Germany. They sought for a renewal of the Lutheran church that emphasized a personal faith in Christ and small group meetings for discipleship. Halle University became the center of Pietism, and produced the first successful Protestant missionaries, sending its graduates to Greenland, Scandinavia, and India (Neill 1990: 194-204; Hartley 2007: 340-341).

The early eighteenth century saw the persecuted Bohemian Brethren seek refuge at the Herrnhut estate of Count Nikolaus Ludwig von Zinzendorf. After experiencing their own Holy Spirit Pentecost, this small group of believers formed one of the foremost missionary movements of modern history. Under Zinzendorf's leadership, the Moravians commissioned more missionaries in their first 20 years than the previous two hundred years of Protestantism. Within two decades they had missionaries in over twenty of the most difficult regions of the world (Gallagher 2008a: 237-244; Gallagher 2008b: 185-210).

Influenced by the Moravians, John and Charles Wesley experienced a personal awakening of the Holy Spirit that launched a revival in eighteenth century Britain. Along with George Whitefield, John Wesley preached in the open fields of Bristol, traveling extensively throughout the country, and influenced thousands to commit their lives to Christ. These new converts were then formed into discipleship bands, which became the seedbed of further revival and missionary activity around the world (Neill 1990: 207-272; Gallagher 2005c: 129-142).

More could also be revealed of key people and movements in the expansion of the Christian faith within the nineteenth and twentieth centuries, yet limitations of scope prevent us from further exploration (see Mellis 1976, Bebbington 1989, Poewe 1994, Yates 1994, Walls 1996, Carpenter 1997, Robert 1997, Synan 1997, Hastings 1999, Shenk 1999, Corten and Marshall-Faratani 2001, Freston 2001, Jenkins 2002, Walls 2002, Tucker 2004, and Robert 2009).

D. Missional Action in the Local Context

In crafting a philosophy and methodology of mission praxis, the final section of this essay will explore guidelines of Christian proclamation in the local context. In particular, the essay will explore how to share the Christian faith in a postmodern North American situation. In the first half of the twentieth century many North Americans were asking spiritual questions such as: Is Christianity rational? Is there a God? Is Christ God? Is he the only way to God? What is the evidence that Christ rose from the dead? Do science and scripture agree? How can miracles be possible? These questions were answered by Christian apologists such as C.S. Lewis. In 1945 Lewis reflected, "I am not sure that the ideal missionary team ought not to consist of one who argues and one who (in the fullest sense of the word) preaches. Put up your arguer first to undermine their intellectual prejudices; then let the evangelist proper launch his appeal. I have seen this done with great success" (1970: 99).

Most people today, however, are asking a different set of questions: Why are Christians imposing their beliefs and morality on others? How can Christians tell other people who they are? Why do I hurt? Why did my family break apart? Why is there so much hatred and violence in the world? Why should I trust the church, which has done so many terrible things? Does the Christian belief make any difference? Do I have to become Republican and right wing to be a Christian? The questions that contemporary seekers are asking have changed in the last fifty years.

In dealing with these hard questions, postmodern apologists often begin their response by first asking, "Why do you ask?" In developing a mission strategy in responding to questions of a postmodern generation, we should be mindful of addressing the trust issue that lies behind the tough questions. That is, identify with people as you ask them to tell their story. As you share your story, talk about how your questions received answers. Challenge them with the truth you had to face in your life. At that point you may want to generalize to truth for everyone, which speaks to the experience-centered person. Then ask them how they respond to what you have said.

We have already suggested that mission involves the people of God carrying Christ's message of salvation across all kinds of barriers; and in doing so, incorporates evangelism in offering people an opportunity to embrace the Gospel of faith in Jesus Christ as savior. These activities of the Church are not exclusively verbal declarations, but are correspondingly intertwined with proclamations of social activism. To focus our discussion, however, I will limit the guidelines of Christian decree to the spoken word. This missional approach towards a North American postmodern context is adapted from the Billy Graham Center for Evangelism at Wheaton College in Wheaton, Illinois. The remaining segment unfolds how to announce the Good News of Christ using the previous framework via the concepts of messenger, message, and method of mission.

Messenger: We are in the era of the messenger as an artist, and hence we must heighten our abilities. Western culture's expectation of communicators has risen in the digital age. Leonard Sweet affirms, "Just as the printing press revolutionized the world 500 years ago, the electronic media is re-defining today's society. The impact of visual communication is profound" (1993: 3). In our contemporary world, the messenger of the Gospel should deliver the word of God in simplicity and humor coupled with authenticity and passion.

> *Simplicity:* Simplicity is the ability to make truth clear, concise, and organized. Our goal is simplicity on the other side of complexity. Educational research is calling for fewer ideas in greater depth. Simplicity requires presenting one idea, and demands translation of technical language in clear logical transitions.

> *Humor:* Humor is the ability to laugh, bring laughter, and allow for emotional and mental rest. The best humor comes out of a spontaneous interjection rather than planned jokes. For those who have little skill or lack an innate sense of timing, however, good clean jokes are acceptable. Humor accomplishes several things: creates relevance and affinity; emphasizes a point with subtle power; and relaxes an audience.

> *Authenticity:* Authenticity is the most compelling trait in communication since it creates a sense of presence. Preaching demands this capacity for it is truth through personality. Moreover, effective communication is truth through a true person. What you say must be true for who you are. Preaching is a most self-revealing activity as you expose your inner being.

> *Passion:* Passion is the ability to communicate with a full commitment and sense of urgency. Biblical passion is fueled by a love for those separated from God (Matthew 9:35-39). People easily manifest felt needs; yet have insoluble longings for justice, relationships, beauty, spirituality, and freedom.

Finally, there are a number of cautions for the messenger to effectively communicate. For example, avoid the trap of only entertaining without explaining. Stories are not enough since there is a need of substance. There is also the danger of too little Bible with inadequate theological interpretation. Paul wrote, "Unlike so many, we do not peddle the word of God for profit. On the contrary, in Christ we speak before God with sincerity, as those sent from God. . . . We do not use deception, nor do we distort the word of God. On the contrary, by setting forth the truth plainly we commend ourselves to everyone's conscience in the sight of God" (2 Corinthians 2:17; 4:2).

Message: The messenger delivering the word of God with simplicity, humor, authenticity, and passion likewise needs to be conscious of the substance of the message. The central point of Christianity is that sin is the breaking of God's shalom: God's full blessing for humanity. Any deed, word, desire, or emotion contrary to God's will is displeasing to him and deserves blame. The scripture refers to this problem as the wrath of God— God's holiness reacting to evil—the unavoidable progression of cause and effect in an ethical universe. The wrath of God towards sin establishes the stage for the doctrine of the atonement.

Forgiveness is a problem for God. How can God forgive and still be consistent in his revulsion of evil? The love of God must not be seen apart from the wrath of God, or the cross is no more than an emotionally excessive action. Similarly, the wrath of God must not be seen apart from the love of God, or God is a tyrant. Our relationship to God through the Holy Spirit dissolves all our imperfections. All our debts and evil ways were taken and paid for on the cross by the blood of Christ. Through faith in the work of Christ Jesus, we become children of God born of the Father's love. This is the Good News of the atonement. Lewis confirms, "The central Christian belief is that Christ's death has somehow put us right with God and given us a fresh start" (1952: 57).

Method: Having established the importance of the trained communicator and the centrality of the cross in responding to a postmodern generation, this essay will now move to the last of our guiderails: mission method. More than one-third of scripture and ninety per cent of the material contained in the Gospels was narrative. Listen to Peterson's version of how Jesus used story. "With many stories like these, he presented his message to them, fitting the stories to their experience and maturity. He was never without a story when he spoke. When he was alone with his disciples, he went over everything, sorting out the tangles, untying the knots" (Mark

4:33-34, *The Message*). And again in Matthew 13:34-35: "All Jesus did that day was tell stories—a long storytelling afternoon. His storytelling fulfilled the prophecy: 'I will open my mouth and tell stories; I will bring out into the open things hidden since the world's first day'" (*The Message*).

Why should modern speakers major in the use of story as a method of communication? Stories are compelling. People love stories. They were the dominant biblical genre of God's messengers, and the major type of transmission in the Gospels. Stories relate truth visually to the whole person: emotions, intellect, memory, commonality, and community. Because of this, stories make the truth easier to remember. They also ignite vision and beliefs, as well as solidifying our identity and security. Since our lives become stories they have the power to redeem. Stories bridge the gap between the biblical and present-day world as a most effective tool of persuasion in an anti-authoritarian age.

In this final section of the paper, we have explored how to share the Christian faith to a postmodern generation by emphasizing the importance of the prepared communicator who has the message of the centrality of the cross interwoven with personal story as the prime method of communication.

Conclusion

It is well to remember that this whole journey involves rhythms of contemplation and engagement, together with the accumulated awareness of the following practices: spiritual disciplines to hear and obey the voice of the Holy Spirit; proper biblical hermeneutics in the contexts of commitment, community, and mission; purposeful treatment of defining fundamental terms; and an appreciation of the historic progress of the Christian faith. After the resulting missional action (taking into account the messenger, message, and method), the reflection again returns to the scripture for further enlightenment. In this manner we are always prayerfully reliant on the revelation of the Holy Spirit, as we reexamine each step of our engagement in pneumatic mission praxis.

Notes

1. My intent is not to draw an extreme or perfect contrast between what N.T. Wright and Joseph Ratzinger have noted. The Roman Catholic magisterium also encourages faithful Catholics to read and study Holy Scripture. Ratzinger's concern is for the Catholic Church to maintain more strict oversight (at least officially) over *how* scripture is interpreted. Generally, Protestants do not have as strict of controls in this regard.

Works Cited

Arnold, Jeffrey
    1993   *Discovering the Bible for Yourself.* Downers Grove, IL: InterVarsity Press.

Bauer, David R. and Robert A. Traina
    2011   *Inductive Bible Study: A Comprehensive Guide to the Practice of Hermeneutics.* Grand Rapids, MI: Baker Academic.

Bebbington, David W.
    1989   *Evangelicalism in Modern Britain.* New York, NY: Routledge.

Bevans, Stephen B. and Roger P. Schroeder
    2004   *Constants in Context: A Theology of Mission for Today.* American Society of Missiology series, No. 30. Maryknoll, NY: Orbis Books.

Blocher, Jacques A. and Jacques Blandenier
    2013   *The Evangelization of the World: A History of Christian Mission.* Michael Parker, trans. Pasadena, CA: William Carey Library.

Brock, Sebastian
    1996   "The 'Nestorian' Church: A Lamentable Misnomer." *Bulletin of the John Rylands Library* 78/3: 23-35.

Bosch, David J.
    1987   "Evangelism: Theological Currents and Cross-currents Today." *International Bulletin of Missionary Research* 11/3: 98-103.

    1991   *Transforming Mission: Paradigm Shifts in Theology of Mission.* American Society of Missiology series, No. 16. Maryknoll, NY: Orbis Books.

Carpenter, Joel A.
    1997   *Revive Us Again: The Reawakening of American Fundamentalism.* Oxford, England: Oxford University Press.

Chadwick, Samuel
    1969   *The Way To Pentecost.* Fort Washington, PA: Christian Literature Crusade.

Chidester, David
    2000   *Christianity: A Global History.* New York, NY: HarperOne Publications.

Corten, Andre and Ruth Marshall-Faratani
    2001   *Between Babel and Pentecost: Transnational Pentecostalism in Africa and Latin America.* Bloomington, IN: Indiana University Press.

Costas, Orlando E.
    2009   "Captivity and Liberation in the Modern Missionary Movement." In *Landmark Essays in Mission and World Christianity*, Robert L. Gallagher and Paul Hertig, eds. American Society of Missiology series, No. 43. Maryknoll, NY: Orbis Books, 33-45.

Fee, Gordon D. and Douglas Stuart
    1981   *How to Study the Bible for All Its Worth: A Guide to Understanding the Bible.* 3rd ed. Grand Rapids, MI: Zondervan.

Fénelon, François
    1853   *Christian Counsel, Spiritual Progress: or Instructions in the Divine Life of the Soul,* James W. Metcalf, ed. New York, NY: M.W. Dodd.

Freston, Paul
    2001   *Evangelicals and Politics in Asia, Africa, and Latin America.* Cambridge, England: Cambridge University Press.

Gallagher, Robert L

2013   "Missi.onary Methods: St. Paul's, St. Roland's, or Ours?" In *Missionary Methods: Research, Reflections and Realities*, Craig Ott and J.D. Payne, eds. Pasadena, CA: William Carey Library, 3-22.

2012   "Mission from the Inside Out: An Integrative Analysis of Selected Latin American Protestant 'Writings' in Spirituality and Mission." In *Missiology: An International Review* 40/1: 9-22.

2011   "Figourovsky, Innocent," Vol. 2, 938-939; "Gloukharev, Macarius," Vol. 2, 1040-1041; "Herman of Alaska," Vol. 2, 1124-1125; "Ilminski, Nicholas," Vol. 2, 1181-1182; "Ivanovsky, Paul," Vol. 2, 1217-1218; "Kassatkin, Nicholas," Vol. 2, 1267-1268; "Stephen of Perm," Vol. 4, 2262-2263; and "Veniaminov, Innocent," Vol. 4, 2453-2454. In *The Encyclopedia of Christian Civilization*, George Thomas Kurian, ed. Chichester, West Sussex, United Kingdom: Wiley-Blackwell.

2008a   "Zinzendorf and the Early Moravians: Pioneers in Leadership Selection and Training." In *Missiology: An International Review* 36/2: 237-244.

2008b   "The Integration of Mission Theology and Practice: Zinzendorf and the Early Moravians." In *Mission Studies: Journal of the International Association for Mission Studies* 25/2: 185-210.

2006a   "The Holy Spirit in the World: In Non-Christians, Creation, and Other Religions." In *Asian Journal of Pentecostal Studies* 9/1: 17-33.

2006b   "Praying for Mission." In *The Pneuma Review* 9/1: 19-20.

2006c   "Spirit-Guided Mission." In *Evangelical Missions Quarterly* 42/3: 336-341.

2006d   "'Me and God, We'd Be Mates:' Towards an Aussie Contextualized Gospel." In *International Bulletin of Missionary Research* 30/3: 127-132.

2005a   "a World Perspective (I): From Pentecost to Protestantism."
         In *Changing Worlds*, Nathan Bettcher, Robert L. Gallagher,
         and Bill Vasilakis, eds. Adelaide, South Australia: CRC
         Churches International, 87-106.

2005b   "A World Perspective (II): From Protestantism to the
         Present." In *Changing Worlds*, Nathan Bettcher, Robert
         L. Gallagher, and Bill Vasilakis, eds. Adelaide, South
         Australia: CRC Churches International, 107-127.

2005c   "A World Perspective (III): From the Present to Potential
         Prospect." In *Changing Worlds*, Nathan Bettcher, Robert
         L. Gallagher, and Bill Vasilakis, eds. Adelaide, South
         Australia: CRC Churches International, 129-142.

2004a   "From 'Doingness' to 'Beingness:' A Missiological
         Interpretation of Acts 4:23-31." In *Mission in Acts: Ancient
         Narratives in Contemporary Context*, Robert L. Gallagher
         and Paul Hertig, eds. American Society of Missiology
         series, No. 34. Maryknoll, NY: Orbis Books, 45-58.

2004b   "Receiving the Holy Spirit's Power for Missions." *Stulos
         Theological Journal* 12/1: 21-33.

1999   "The Forgotten Factor: The Holy Spirit and Mission in
         Protestant Missiological Writings from 1945-95." In
         Footprints of God: A Narrative Theology of Mission, Charles
         Van Engen, Nancy Thomas, and Robert L. Gallagher, eds.
         Monrovia, CA: MARC, 199-214.

Gensichen, Hans Werner
1971   *Glaube für die Welt*. Buchverlage, Gütersloh: Gerd
         Mohn.

González, Justo L
2010   *The Story of Christianity: The Reformation to the Present
         Day*. Vol. 2. Rev. ed. New York, NY: HarperCollins.

Grahmann, Bob
2003   *Transforming Bible Study: Understanding God's Word
         Like You've Never Read It Before*. Downers Grove, IL:
         InterVarsity Press.

Hartley, Benjamin L.
    2007   "Pietism." In *Encyclopedia of Missions and Missionaries*, Jonathan J. Bonk, ed. Routledge Religion and Society series. Vol. 9. New York, NY: Routledge.

Hastings, Adrian
    1999   *A World History of Christianity*. Grand Rapids, MI: Eerdmans.

Illich, Ivan
    1970   *Mission and Midwifery: Essays on Missionary Formation*. Mambo Occasional Papers: Missio-Pastoral series No. 4. Gwelo, Rhodesia: Mambo Press.

Irvin, Dale T. and Scott W. Sunquist
    2012   *History of the World Christian Movement: Modern Christianity from 1454-1800*. Vol. 2. Maryknoll, NY: Orbis Books.

Jenkins, Philip
    2002   *The Next Christendom: The Coming of Global Christianity*. New York, NY: Oxford University Press.

Latourette, Kenneth Scott
    1975   *A History of Christianity: to A.D. 1500*. Vol. 1. Rev. ed. San Francisco, CA: Harper San Francisco.

Lewis, C.S.
    1952   *Mere Christianity*. New York, NY: Macmillan.

    1970   "Christian Apologetics." In *God in the Dock: Essays on Theology and Ethics*, Walter Hooper, ed. Grand Rapids, MI: Eerdmans.

Magrassi, Mariano
    1998   *Praying the Bible: An Introduction to Lectio Divina*. Collegeville, MN: Liturgical Press.

Mellis, Charles J.
    1976   *Committed Communities: Fresh Streams for World Missions*. Pasadena, CA: William Carey Library.

Moffett, Samuel.
    1998   *History of Christianity in Asia: Beginnings to 1500.* Vol. 1.
            Rev. ed. San Francisco, CA: HarperCollins.

Moreau, A. Scott, Gary R. Corwin, and Gary B. McGee
    2004   *Introducing World Missions: A Biblical, Historical, and
            Practical Survey.* Grand Rapids, MI: Baker Academic.

Neill, Stephen
    1990   *A History of Christian Missions.* 2nd ed. London, England:
            Penguin Books.

Newbigin, Lesslie
    1954   *The Household of God.* London, England: SCM Press and
            New York, NY: Friendship Press.

Noll, Mark A.
    2012   *Turning Points: Decisive Moments in the History of
            Christianity.* 3rd ed. Grand Rapids, MI: Baker Academic.

Nouwen, Henri J.M.
    1975   *Reaching Out: The Three Movements of the Spiritual Life.*
            New York, NY: Image Books-Doubleday.

Olesberg, Lindsay
    2012   *The Bible Study Handbook: A Comprehensive Guide to an
            Essential Practice.* Downers Grove, IL: InterVarsity Press.

Packer, J.I.
    2005   *Keep In Touch With The Spirit: Finding Fullness In Our
            Walk With God.* Grand Rapids, MI: Baker Books.

Peterson, Eugene H.
    2006   *Eat This Book: A Conversation in the Art of Spiritual
            Reading.* Grand Rapids, MI: Eerdmans.

Pierson, Paul E.
    2009   *The Dynamics of Christian Mission: History through a
            Missiological Perspective.* Pasadena, CA: William Carey
            International University Press.

Platt, David
    2011   *Radical Together: Unleashing the People of God for the Purpose of God*. Colorado Springs, CO: Multnomah Books.

Poewe, Karla, ed.
    1994   *Charismatic Christianity as a Global Culture*. Columbia, SC: University of South Carolina Press.

Pope Francis
    2013   *Evangelii Gaudium*. Rome: Vatican Press, 12.

Ratzinger, Joseph
    1994   *Catechism of the Catholic Church*. 2nd ed. Citta del Vaticano: Libreria Editrice Vaticana.

Robert, Dana L.
    1997   *American Women in Mission*. Macon, GA: Mercer University Press.

    2009   "Shifting Southward: Global Christianity since 1945." In *Landmark Essays in Mission and World Christianity*. Robert L. Gallagher and Paul Hertig, eds. American Society of Missiology series, No. 43. Maryknoll, NY: Orbis Books, 46-60.

Ryken, Leland and James C. Wilhoit
    2012   *Effective Bible Teaching*. 2nd ed. Grand Rapids, MI: Baker Publishing Group.

Shelley, Bruce L.
    1995   *Church History in Plain Language*. 2nd ed. Nashville, TN: Thomas Nelson Publishers.

Shenk, Wilbert R.
    1999   *Changing Frontiers in Mission*. American Society of Missiology series, No. 28. Maryknoll, NY: Orbis Books.

Stamoolis, James J.
    1986   *Eastern Orthodox Mission Theology Today*. American Society of Missiology series, No. 10. Maryknoll, NY: Orbis Books.

Sun, Ruth
    1982   *Personal Bible Study: A How-To*. Chicago, IL: Moody Press.

Sweet, Leonard
    1993   *Current Thoughts* (June): 3.

Synan, Vinson
    1997   *The Holiness-Pentecostal Tradition*. Grand Rapids, MI: Eerdmans.

Taylor, J. Hudson
    1930   "The Source of Power for Christian Missions." In *The Missionary Review of the World*. Vol. 53. New York, NY: Missionary Review Publishing, 516.

Taylor, John V.
    1980   "The Lord's Prayer: The Church Witnesses to the Kingdom." In *International Review of Mission* 69/275: 295-297.

Tucker, Ruth A.
    1983   *From Jerusalem to Irian Jaya: A Biographical History of Christian Missions*. Grand Rapids, MI: Zondervan.

Vanhoozer, Kevin J.
    2009   "A Drama-Of-Redemption Model." In *Moving Beyond the Bible to Theology*, Stanley N. Gundry and Gary T. Meadors, eds. Grand Rapids, MI: Zondervan, 151-199.

Verkuyl, Johannes
    1978   *Contemporary Missiology: An Introduction*. Grand Rapids, MI: Eerdmans.

Walls, Andrew F.
    1996   *The Missionary Movement in Christian History: Studies in the Transmission of Faith*. Maryknoll, NY: Orbis Books and Edinburgh, Scotland: T & T Clark.

    2002   *The Cross-Cultural Process in Christian History: Studies in the Transmission and Appropriation of Faith*. Maryknoll, NY: Orbis Books and Edinburgh, Scotland: T & T Clark.

2009   "The Gospel as Prisoner and Liberator of Culture: Is There a 'Historic Christian Faith?'" In *Landmark Essays in Mission and World Christianity*. Robert L. Gallagher and Paul Hertig, eds. American Society of Missiology series, No. 43. Maryknoll, NY: Orbis Books, 133-145.

Wright, Christopher J.H.
    2006   *The Mission of God: Unlocking the Bible's Grand Narrative.* Downers Grove, IL: IVP Academic.

    2009   "Reflections on Moving Beyond the Bible to Theology." In *Moving Beyond the Bible to Theology*, Stanley N. Gundry and Gary T. Meadors, eds. Grand Rapids, MI: Zondervan, 320-346.

Wright, N.T.
    2011   *Scripture and the Authority of God: How to Read the Bible Today.* Rev. ed. New York, NY: HarperOne.

Yates, Timothy
    1994   *Christian Mission in the Twentieth Century.* Cambridge, England: Cambridge University Press.

APM

Rethinking
the Mission
Curriculum

Redesigning Missiological Education for the Twenty-First Century

International Joint Degrees in Development Studies and Missiology Through Institutional Partnerships in the Americas

KEVIN BOOK-SATTERLEE

DOI: 10.7252/Paper. 000039

About the Author

Kevin Book-Satterlee is field dean for William Carey International University and academic coordinator for Avance, a training program of United World Mission in Mexico City.

Abstract

It is time to design twenty-first century models for theological higher education to replace the nineteenth-century models. Missiological education ought to be a forerunner in this era of globalized and internationalized education, and the idea of international joint-degrees in development and missiology is a groundbreaking start for future collaboration. While joint degree programs are not uncommon in higher education, their inclusion in higher theological education is rare. This is especially true regarding joint missiological degrees, and to do so through international partnerships is even more rare. This paper reviews Schreiter's third-wave mission and opportunities for globalizing missiological education through joint degree partnerships to engage the changing context of mission. A key emphasis for missiological joint degrees is a hybridization of cultural contexts for andragogical glocation. I also conduct a content survey of missiological curricular course offerings at the master's level among institutions in the Americas to determine course and curriculum similarities and differences. This content survey provides an initial way to begin to look for joint degrees, and one can draw potential suggestions from the survey for other schools to consider modeling.

As global studies and mission scholars, why is it that we are behind in global academic collaboration? Why are more and more specialize degrees popping up in our schools therefore creating in some cases, unhealthy competition among institutions?[1] Why are we continuing to play an "us and them" game between U.S. institutions and those of our companions throughout the globe? Missionaries and missiologists, by and large, have pushed for global theological education, contextualization, and the study of world Christianity, yet our missiological programs are perhaps the least reflective of shared equity in the missiological education of our world, recruiting foreign nationals to study in U.S. institutions, yet providing little to encourage potential students to study abroad for any significant length of time.

The future of missiological education will be through global collaboration.[2] Tennent (2012) remarks, "We must have greater bi-lateral exchanges based on relationships and shared vision… [the notion that] all 'real' education takes place in the West must be replaced by a new era of mutuality and shared vision with seminaries and training institutes around the world." Creating a solid network or system of international schools would be ideal, but the establishment of joint degrees to formulate and cement an internationalization commitment among institutions is also a way forward. While international joint degree programs are not uncommon in higher education, their inclusion in higher theological education is rare. This is especially true regarding missiological joint degrees. Neo liberal capitalist models are characterized by an increasing global competition, with an ethos that only the fittest survive. Most seminaries, reacting to this, are protectionist and scrambling to keep their institutions in order. This is not only evident in the United States, but similarly oresent among institutions in Latin American, and elsewhere. For some, a caution to be labeled colonialist adds to the reservation of joining with others, especially cross-global institutions. No institution is now ignorant of the global growth of Christianity. In light of this, Walls (1991) describes the academic state with historical reference to the 15th century:

> The discovery of America did not mean that people threw their maps away and got new ones; still less did it mean that learned people abandoned ideas about humanity and society that were the product of European ignorance of the world beyond their own. In fact, the new discoveries were intellectually threatening, requiring the abandonment of too many certainties, the acquisition of too many new ideas and skills, the modification of too many maxims,

the sudden irrelevance of too many accepted authorities. It was easier to ignore them and carry on with the old intellectual maps...even while accepting the fact of the discovery and profiting from the economic effects (149).

Perhaps, despite Walls' (1991) call for restructuring mission studies to reflect the growth and input of those from the growing church, "the rule of the palefaces over the academic world [still] is untroubled," (152). The above quote is fitting regarding the state of protectionism and the neoliberal competitive response. Yet, the fittest seem to survive this global competition, not through protectionist isolation and commoditized education, but through networked collaboration.

This paper continues the theme of last year's APM conference, educating for justice, and fits this year's theme by offering frameworks for thinking about global collaboration in missiological education for the globalized world. I propose that global institutions should form missiologically-based joint degrees with an emphasis in international development in response to challenges of globalization and missiological education and as a starting point for long-term, mutual collaboration. To do so, I begin this paper discussing globalization and mission by drawing from Schreiter's (2005, 2012) observations about the "third wave" of globalization and "third wave" mission. I specifically highlight the dynamics of deterritorialization and hybridization and their effects on mission education. Schreiter emphasizes the importance of mission as reconciliation (2005: 86), for which the inclusion of development and justice guided by missiology is crucial. In the second part of this paper I conduct a content survey of missiological curriculum offerings at Latin American and U.S. evangelical seminaries and universities in order to explore opportunities for constructing joint degrees. I further discuss how the collaborative efforts of joint degrees in missiology are important for Schreiter's "third wave" mission and how collaborative degrees have andragogical benefits for the student of mission. I end this paper with concluding thoughts based on my research and the potential to shape such collaborative efforts via joint degree partnership.

Globalization and Mission

There would be no reason to propose new models of missiological education if globalization did not change the context of mission. In this section I will summarize Schreiter's observations of the changing context of mission due to third wave of globalization (2012: Kindle location 901) focusing on deterritorialization and hybridization. In response to this changing context of mission Schreiter coined "third wave mission," (ASM 2014). I will close this section by mentioning Schreiter's fifth task of mission – mission as reconciliation – added to the list of four tasks developed at the 1981 SEDOS conference, and the importance of international development to engage in this task.

Schreiter (2005, 2013) highlights three points about the changing context of mission due to current or third wave of globalization (2005: 76, or 2013: Kindle location 914). This new context of mission stems from the characteristics of modern globalization: the compression of time and space due to technological advances; economic consumption for some and economic exclusion for others due to neo-liberal capitalism, political privatization, and the degrading of civic imaginary in favor of the individualist consumer.

Two significant consequences of globalization for mission are deterritorialization and hybridization. Where once culture was considered static and concrete, the postmodern understanding of culture shows it to be dynamic and ever-changing (Arbuckle 2010:17). This is not lost on Christian mission, yet the complexities of both deterritorialization and hybridization make culture and mission within culture considerably more complicated.

Kennedy (2010), drawing from Welsch (1999) writes:

> ...so profound have been the changes brought by cultural flows and scapes that we need to jettison the idea of interculturality and multiculturality since both presume we still live in a world of separate and internally coherent cultural 'islands or spheres'. Instead, there is transculturality characterized by overlapping and interconnecting of

> cultures through 'external networking'…With fragments
> of every culture implanted everywhere, hybridization also
> becomes inevitable and commonplace," (33).

In light of this statement, especially with regard to interculturality, the intercultural studies titles of many of our missiologically-based degrees may need rethinking. Yet, Kennedy's statement makes the assumption of synthesis in hybridization that overstates the situation, and in so doing makes the global situation less complicated. Networks and overlap are not constructed neatly. In some cases they are planned, but in most cases such overlapping occurs unconsciously, without a driving center. Perhaps one may find familiar cultural anchors or viral narratives creating recognizable hegemony, but hybridization does not negate the art of culture-crossing. The gospel may be transcultural (Moreau: 2012:61) and not territorial, but people are the opposite. People create place and boundaries, even if porous ones. Escobar (2001) writes: "Places concatenate with each other to form regions, which suggests that porosity of boundaries is essential to place, as it is to local constructions and exchange. Locality, in this way becomes marked by the interplay between position, place and region; by the porosity of boundaries; and by the role of the lived body between enculturation and emplacement…," (144).

While hybridization and deterritorialization do complicate dynamic and consistent cultural change, mission *ad gentes* (Schreiter 2012) or *to the people* still requires the education of ministering to and ultimately *with* the people (Gutzler 2013:Kindle location 1079) who are networked, mobile, yet continue to create pliable boundaries. We may or may not need to change the titles of our degrees, but they must expand the ability to navigate networks, cultural change, and overlapping glocality if we want our students to truly engage in third-wave mission.

Schreiter reemphasizes the tasks of mission developed from the 1981 SEDOS seminar as proclamation, interreligious dialogue, inculturation, and liberation of the poor. In light of neo-liberal globalization, he adds the fifth task of mission as reconciliation (2005:86). He states: "Because so much of the work of mission is done on behalf of the poor people of the world, missionaries who call the world's attention to what is happening in their locales play a significant role in countering the worst aspects of globalization," (Schreiter 2005:78). This is echoed in another of his works, where he reimagines mission as "mission *ad vulnera*" or mission to the wounds. He explains (2012) that "[t]his kind of mission would focus itself on locating the breaches and wounds in the contemporary world…Considering wounds – the wounds of our world and the wounds of Christ…might provide the stimulus to imagination needed to help reshape mission in the twenty-first century," (Kindle location 996). While mission as reconciliation is not particularly new, the new context of mission advertises the need in the context of global and cultural change.

In order to be effective in third wave mission, missiological education must encompass all five of Schreiter's noted tasks of mission *with* people. To accomplish this in missiological education I advocate for international residential joint degrees focused on international development and justice with missional principles as a core basis among evangelical schools. I do so in light of Schreiter's suggestion for the fifth task as reconciliation, combined with liberation of the poor; in light of the changing missional motivation of evangelical seminary students (Slimbach 2010:190); in light of student-driven consumer demands to add new emphases to missiological education; and in light of the consequential opportunities in mission thanks to deterritorialization and hybridization and third wave mission.

Missiological Education and International Development as Ministry of Reconciliation

Before moving into my research survey of evangelical missiology programs in the Americas and opportunities to generate missiological joint degrees in international development, it is important to understand how international development fits into missiological education as a response to Schreiter's fourth and specifically fifth tasks of mission. Development is a broad category with as many variations of definitions as there are definitions.[3] This is both debilitating and freeing when it comes to the ministry of reconciliation that Schreiter mentions. It is debilitating in that there is no set standard and even little agreement on best practices. It is freeing in that it is holistic. *Integral Mission* author Yamamori (2000) proposes that, "Development is a process of qualitative change of life in which a person's total maturity (social, physical, and spiritual, as well as in understanding) as an individual or as a person-in-community" occurs

(12, translation mine). Bryant Myers's (1999) idea of "transformational development," reflects Yamamori's emphasis. Transformational development seeks "positive change in the whole of human life, materially, socially, and spiritually," (Myers 1999:1). Development in its broadest sense is holistic as well as integrative.

Development as holistic is manifested in many forms, (Hoekbergen 2012:60). Church-life, and theological education as it continues to inform the practice of the church, is essentially a piece of the wide range of missional and transformational development in that it recognizably covers the spiritual dimension mentioned by Myers. But the church need not just occupy itself with spiritual components of people, as transformational development is not so easily partitioned. Yamamori (2000) notes that the holistic local church directs and focuses individuals and communities to obey the commands of Christ to love God and neighbor (13). He also states that the local church helps its leaders and members grow like Jesus (14). These two key functions of the local church – to love God and neighbor – popularly interpreted with greater spiritual emphasis, reinforces the concept of segregating development. Yamamori's third key function of the local church also requires recognizing the overall needs – spiritual, as well as physical and emotional needs – of individuals and the community and respond with wisdom to those needs (14).

As globalization continues to complicate those needs, seminary educators need wisdom and understanding to integrate international development alongside traditional missiological education. While *one* of the principal tasks of mission is proclamation, Schreiter's tasks of poverty alleviation and reconciling the wounds caused by globalization and other factors are also critical.

Course Survey for the Basis of Joint Degree Opportunities

Seminaries in the United States are beginning to recognize poverty alleviation and a ministry of reconciliation to globalization's wounds as key aspects to address in degree and course offerings. Most institutions have incorporated these into traditional missiological degree programs or created new programs such as the Master of Arts of Global Development and Justice at Multnomah University and the Master of Arts of Justice and Mission at Denver Seminary.[4] These degrees are important in addressing the need for and growing interest in Christian international development, especially when incorporated alongside other traditional seminary offerings. For thirty years Eastern University's School of Leadership and Development has offered an MBA in Economic Development with a focus on developing countries. Students may also combine this degree with a Master of Divinity degree at Eastern University's Palmer Theological Seminary.[5] Many other programs have courses in international development as electives or concentrations for their missiological degrees.

Added degrees and courses in international development may move towards an unhelpful partitioning of missiological tasks set out by Schreiter. Seminaries in Latin America are also influenced by poverty alleviation and international development. These categories are often described as *mission integral* (Bullón 2013:234). Alcántara Mejía (2001) echoes Myers's perception of the term "transformational" from a context of *misión integral*. He writes, "'transformation' has synthesized for me what the Good News of the cross does in the person, and by him or her, in society and its structures," (88). Here development and mission are more intricately entwined and reflect an integration of Schreiter's five tasks of mission.

To understand points of collaboration based on the strengths of degree programs in the U.S. and Latin America, I conducted a content survey to look for possible joint degree collaborations. I do not offer any specific prototype that can be implemented as "already packaged." Partnerships do not work that way (Spencer-Oatey 2012). Instead, I offer recommendations based on the surveyed content to demonstrate possible collaboration. For this research I have conducted a content survey of degree and course offerings in order to explore the possibilities and opportunities for partnership through a joint missiological degree in international development. I will explain the parameters of my content survey, summarize the data, and outline three possible joint degree collaborations based on the data.

Parameters and Data Observation

There are many seminaries and mission training programs scattered throughout the globe which are too numerous to survey with too many variables to produce helpful data for this paper. I have therefore set my parameters to survey master's level missiology and international development degrees at evangelical institutions (seminaries or universities) in the United States and Latin America. My choice for incorporating institutions from the United States is most relevant for this conference, since many participants in the Association of Professors of Mission are representatives of one or more of these institutions. My choice to include Latin America builds from my other curricular surveys among Latin American evangelical theological education including course offerings, descriptions, and course syllabi.[6]

In a technologized world people turn to the internet for quick, cursory information. I begin choosing my data-set in the same way that a person might begin to investigate their potential degree, via searches on the Internet to look for possible programs in Latin America and the United States.[7] To narrow the search initially, I omitted any programs which were not tied to an expressly academic institution. Even with this initial filter my survey resulted in hundreds of potential degrees from both regions.

One observable difference between many Latin American institutions and those from the United States was the academic entry level for missiological education. Latin American students tend to enter their missiological education at a certificate or associate's level, completing their missiological degree as a second degree, and have been involved in formal ministry or mission prior to entering. By contrast, U.S. students tend to enter their missiological education at the master's level, with varying levels of prior formal ministerial and mission experience. Since joint degrees work best administratively when coursework is conducted at the same academic level and the typical entry point for U.S. students of missiology is at the master's level, I narrowed my survey parameters to postgraduate certificates and master's degrees.

The number of master's degrees in missiology or intercultural studies in the U.S. is numerous, so I limited my list of U.S. institutions to those with international development or justice degrees in order to find manageable possibilities of partnering in the area of international development. This resulted in eight master's programs in development or justice among six institutions. Some other international development programs were contained within the business and management departments of their institutions, which, for the purposes of missiological collaboration I removed from the final list. I also did a second search for Latin American evangelical schools for post-graduate work with a similar focus in international development.[8] This resulted in including two more programs, and the final list includes ten Latin American missiology and development post-graduate programs among nine schools (Appendix A). Neither of the lists are likely to be exhaustive, however they provide a good example of the kind of content that students in both regions will find in an internet search.

Because I conducted a content survey rather than completing a full content analysis I did not investigate the constantly changing syllabi of each course within the programs. In order to keep language consistency for Latin American institutions I chose only institutions offering degrees in Spanish. This removed global mission giant Brazil (Center for the Study of Global Christianity 2013: 76), as well as French or English-dominant countries. It also eliminated programs designed to be completed in indigenous languages. Each of these omitted options would warrant similar surveys to gain a more complete picture of degree and course offerings in Latin America. Despite language similarity, I also did not look into North American Spanish-based missiological education, although this too would produce interesting findings. Future surveys might also include content of non-academic programs, as well as a survey of comparative content for technical, undergraduate, and doctoral degrees.

Survey Observations

Generally, I found that justice and development master's programs in the U.S. are few and relatively new. Their recent addition to seminaries reflect the growing interest in global development issues and justice from the church, and especially younger students termed "New Evangelicals" (Slimbach 2010:193). Each of these programs contain some classical seminary courses to provide adequate biblical, theological, historical, and missiological foundation, yet firmly address development studies. With the exception of one program, at least one-third of each degree required development and justice courses. Among these programs, most have a generalist curriculum, however some have specific foci, such as Fuller Seminary's children-at-risk or Eastern University's urban studies with community development.[9] U.S. institutions tend to offer more electives and provide greater student flexibility in their degree programming.

Despite decades of influence from the *Fraternidad Teologica Latinoamericana* and *misión integral* among evangelical circles and seminaries throughout Latin America (Bullón 2013), there are still few courses or missiological emphases geared directly towards development studies. *Seminario Teológico de Puerto Rico* (STDPR) incorporated development courses for one-eighth of its program. *Seminario Sudamericano's* (SEMISUD) children-at-risk program does not dedicate much of its curriculum to the development category described above, only one course, however seventy percent of its courses fall into counseling and social work. Interestingly, this program at SEMISUD included no courses in theological, biblical, or missiological formation. I kept it in the list because the degree was offered directly in a seminary, as opposed to the development programs offered from business and management schools. Apart from the programs at STDPR and SEMISUD, no other surveyed program in Latin America listed coursework in development. Instead, program emphases varied between ministerial leadership or missiology categories. That said, a number of programs required at least one course of *misión integral*. Further analysis of each course syllabi will help to determine the influence of development as *misión integral* within each course.

When analyzing both data sets, a significant content complication can arise in the discrepancy with regard to number of hours, credits, units, classes, etc. (Michael and Balraj 2003:138) required by each institution surveyed. This diversity in degree lengths will make collaboration difficult, but not impossible. As long as the core concerns for each partner are met, the remainder of classes, while important, can be negotiated to some extent. Stand-alone creations, however, especially those borrowing from, but not as an extension of, existing programs may help in this process as degree lengths will be consistent with already existing degrees at both (all) institutions. Despite the requirement variations in institutions, a key similarity for constructing joint degrees is that most programs in both Latin America and the United States require some sort of practicum and cross-cultural experience. This suggests that there is a common value placed on experiential learning, an important component to the andragogical formation of students.

Many factors must be considered with regard to possible pairings for institutional collaboration. Based on the content survey I have done, I propose three partnerships for offering residential joint degrees of missiology and international development as examples of immediate potential opportunities. The first collaborative partnership is a SEMISUD-Fuller Seminary partnership around children at risk; the second is a partnership between *Seminario Teológico Centroamericano* (SETECA) and Denver Seminary in urban ministry and justice; and finally a three-way collaboration could include SETECA, Eastern University, and Fuller Seminary in urban mission.

SEMISUD's program with an emphasis in working with children-at-risk emphasizes counseling and social work a great deal with only two courses in development studies. This particular program requires no courses in Bible, theology, or missiology. The missing theological, biblical, and missiological foundation can be buttressed by partnering with Fuller Seminary's Master of Arts of Intercultural Studies with a children-at-risk emphasis.[10] Based on an already existing partnership, courses from SETECA may transfer to either Denver Seminary or Dallas Theological Seminary and vice versa.[11] SETECA and Denver Seminary could build a collaborative joint-degree around urban ministry and justice. And, since the relationship already exists and classes have already gained recognition between the schools, two major hurdles in collaboration have already been met. Not wanting to complicate matters by increasing too many collaborative options for SETECA, the Guatemalan school could, by course-load, collaborate in an urban mission joint degree with both Fuller Seminary and/or Eastern University. A three-institution collaboration could be tricky administratively, but it could also provide a rich model for deeper collaboration. The difference in proposals with SETECA form around one specific concept "justice" which Denver Seminary already has as a degree where Fuller and Eastern seminaries do not have a specific focus on "justice" as a degree *per se*. In all proposals, I would suggest offering each institution a rotating directorship or leadership (Michael and Balraj 2003:143) so as to not alienate one institution or the other.

These three examples of joint degree possibilities between SEMISUD and Fuller Seminary, SETECA and Denver Seminary, and the three-way collaboration between SETECA, Fuller Seminary, and

Eastern University, are only possibilities. Much would have to be worked out beyond curricular collaboration. Many other partnerships could also be developed given this content survey data. Even cursory surveys can find potential connections to begin to develop joint degrees, thus globalizing missiological education and adding to a collaborative andragogy in the preparation of students of mission to alleviate poverty and be ministers of reconciliation. Similar content surveys within missiology around disciplines other than development would also be valuable for collaboration to meet the changes of the third wave of globalization and prepare for participation in third-wave mission.

The Case for Joint Degrees and Andragogical Collaboration in Mission

Schreiter reminds us of our task to work with the poor as ministers of reconciliation. In order to do so God's people must engage in international transformative development. But should seminaries add degrees in development and justice at all? Could not these degrees be found outside of the seminary and in secular institutions? Seminaries certainly do not have a monopoly on training for all the ways Christians engage in the world, so perhaps they should just work to engage Schreiter's first three tasks of mission: proclamation, interreligious dialogue, and inculturation, and leave the final two – liberation of the poor and a ministry of reconciliation – to non-seminary programs. I contend that seminaries must begin to look to all the tasks of mission, not to monopolize, but to be adequately holistic as institutions in the education, training, and mobilization of mission. From this perspective, U.S. institutions may have a great deal to learn from the inclusion of *misión integral* into their programs, just as Latin American schools might look to U.S. schools for specific development courses. This mutual learning is why I have proposed the creation of joint degrees between the two regions. In this section I will define joint degrees and why I choose such collaboration over other options like dual degrees, as well as highlight the andragogical benefits of residential joint degrees.

Joint Degrees

Institutional collaboration in the form of joint or dual degrees is the way of the future of higher education. Joint degrees and dual degrees represent similar but different levels of collaboration in education. Obst, Kuder, and Banks (2011) define joint degrees as follows:

> International joint degree programs are study programs collaboratively offered by two (or more) higher education institutions located in different countries. They typically feature a jointly developed and integrated curriculum and agreed-on credit recognition. Students typically study at the two (or more) partnering higher education institutions. Upon completion of the study program, students are awarded a single degree certificate issued and signed jointly by all institutions involved in the program (9).[12]

The difference between joint degree and dual/double degrees is subtle, in that with joint degrees, "[u]pon completion of the study program, students receive degree certificates issued *separately* by each of the institutions involved in the program," (9).

87% of the U.S. institutions surveyed by the Institute of International Education and Freie Universität Berlin in 2009 (Obst and Kuder 2009) plan on developing more relationships to enhance internationalization (32). Globally, dual degrees tend to be more popular among institutions (6) for a number of factors. In comparing the two, dual degrees provide a broader range of flexibility for institutions, not the least of which is greater autonomy and even independence. Distinct programs may share as little as a few elective courses to be able to confer a dual degree, requiring little coordination or interdependence. The onus is on the student and not on the well-working collaboration between institutions or departments.

It is because of the very limited nature of interdependence in dual degrees that I recommend joint degrees instead, pushing for greater collaboration. In contrast to dual degrees, joint degrees require a high level of interdependence and attentiveness of two (or more) partnering authorities (Michael and Balraj 2003: 137). Such interdependence is complicated. The institutions must come together creatively (Spencer-Oatey 2012: 258) in mutually deferential partnership to ensure adequate curriculum development and to be accountable to each other in administration and in the delivery of their respective portions to the curriculum. Most joint degrees are created as stand-alone degrees rather than as add-ons to existing programs in most institutions (Obst, Kuder, and Banks 2011: 12). Because of this, more groundbreaking work is necessary to maintain standardization (20). Complications are exacerbated among differing cultural contexts, and even more so when done in multi-lingual collaborations.

It is precisely this kind of complication that makes such collaboration less attractive, and yet the overall missiological benefits are abundant. The rise in the number of global Christian higher education institutions, including seminaries (Carpenter 2008), and their increased recognition further accentuates the importance of collaboration. This is obvious, but what deterritorialization and hybridization have taught theological and missiological education is that we cannot function as independent islands. It is time that our "glocal" institutions begin to break impervious shells and interdependently influence one another. There has been a historic West-to-the-Rest hegemony, but this is tempered as non-Western institutions have inserted their much-needed voices. Tennent (2012) says, "We are clearly beyond the day when Western scholarship is viewed as the only non-hyphenated theology... We must engage in a new level of partnership which is fully bi-directional."

The difficulty of interdependence without intentionally difficult arrangements such as joint degrees means that institutions will naturally err in more independent ways, losing the collaborative effort. As Sweeting (2012) has noted, seminary leaders must strive to find ways of connecting educational institutions. He provides a number of suggestions from library sharing, cross faculty exchange, projects, and collaborative research – all good things – but nothing so sticky and binding as considering joint degrees.

Unfortunately, in degree creation, dual degrees are likely to continue to be the more common due to the effort of joint degrees that must occur to make them successful and healthy (Obst, Kuder, and Banks

2011:35). A telling factor of such a trend is that the primary motivation for partnerships seems to stem from international recognition (Obst and Kuder 2009:6; Obst, Kuder, and Banks 2011:27) and institutional financial survival (Rizvi and Lingaard 2010:169). Sadly, there is little mention of the andragogical benefits of internationalization on the part of the institutions. It is the focus on recognition and finances over andragogical benefits that make the independence of dual degrees more attractive than joint degrees.

In the updated survey report from Obst, Kuder, and Banks (2011), student interest, research collaboration, and broadening educational offerings increased the motivation for institutions to collaborate on dual or joint degrees among surveyed institutions. Student interest stems from the desire for broader experiences, pride in multiple institutions, and access to the resources of those institutions (Michael and Balraj, 2003:135). Still, it appears that internationalization of higher education is more of a gimmick for competition in the global knowledge economy (Rizvi and Lingaard:173) rather than a "best practice" of collaboration. Such self-preserving motivation deepens the drive for competition and plays into a survival of the fittest, neo liberal, imaginary. It also fosters an economic attitude that makes it easy to "cut and run" when partnerships get complicated.

Another telling trend that may stunt international collaboration from the United States (despite planned increases of internationalization) is that U.S. students are less likely than their European counterparts to participate in such collaborative programs (Obst and Kuder 2009:5). One possible reason for this is that U.S. institutions and students do not seem to value the study abroad experience as highly as others in the world (27). While U.S. institutions do intend to expand their joint and dual degree programs, more than half of the survey respondents plan to *only* increase dual degree offerings, (Obst, Kuder, and Banks 2011:35). Latin America as a region seems to value internationalization even less (Gacel-Ávila 2011), with little student or faculty interest. As institutions plan for increasing their joint and dual degree offerings, such low interest across the Americas has dramatic impact on the actual establishment of complicated formal joint degree programs in higher education in both regions. Until these degrees are understood beyond their potential for competition, and for true global collaboration, it is likely that such degrees will remain only gimmicks for institutional survival in a neo liberal globalization context.

Yet, seminaries the world over can be prophetic and seek to promote the collaborative benefits of joint degrees. As institutions claiming to engage the world, it is precisely for this reason that mission programs must undertake the task of pursuing joint degrees and prophetically lead the academy in true global collaboration. Many of our missiological students are earnestly hoping to work in cross-cultural contexts, and as such an internationalized education is all the more appropriate for them. However, our programs might reflect this in theory but often do not in practice. This gap between intentions and practice provides a "hidden curriculum" of institutional superiority for U.S. institutions. Joint degrees, however, can move beyond the imperialistic hidden curriculum to advocate for new collaborative models and post-colonial deference in mission.

Andragogical Benefits

Aside from being prophetic, there are practical andragogical benefits to joint degrees. I intentionally choose the word andragogy here rather than pedagogy, because, in many conceptual ways andragogy is the opposite of pedagogy (see Table 1 of Taylor and Kroth 2009:47). They are not dichotomistic, but spectral, as pedagogy is more teacher-oriented by knowledge transmission whereas andragogy is learner-oriented through knowledge facilitation. The distinction between andragogy and pedagogy remains contested (Reichman 2005), but I favor a definition of missiological education that emphasizes facilitating or liberating rather than one that is transmitting or "banking" (Freire 2004) in nature. A key component of andragogy is the student's self-directed, autonomous, and independent drive for learning (Chan 2010:27), but I would advocate that true andragogy in a globalized world moves beyond the dependence-independence or oppressive-liberating dichotomies towards truly learning *inter*dependence and collaboration (Banks 1999: Kindle location 320).

Christian mission has a stained colonial history with regard to dependency (Kollman 2011) as does international development (Gunder Frank 1969/2007; Cardoso 1972/2007). Preferring program design around definitions and paradigms of andragogy rather than pedagogy promotes postures of collaboration and interdependence. If we are educating adult-learners to be reflective around collaboration and interdependence, specifically those who might serve in foreign, multi-, or cross-cultural contexts, we must also allow space for education to truly happen in contexts other than those directly familiar to the student and under the tutelage of education facilitators immersed in those contexts. Slibach (2010) writes, "Such an imposed distance from normative life...creates a state of liminality, moments out of ordinary time and place, wherein rules about old structures and identities are broken in order to create new ways of looking at reality," (35).

The benefit to andragogical learning for students stems from a temporal residential cross-cultural exchange between partnering schools. I suggest here mandatory residency requirements in and around each of the partnered institutions, further improving the student's cross-cultural sensitivities, interdependency, and contextual learning. Zielinski (2007) concludes that "Longer term study abroad may provide the levels of exposure needed to develop higher levels of cross-cultural adaptability, while shorter experiences may not be enough to broaden the horizons of students," (44). Hoksbergen (2011) states, "When asked what advice development professionals would give young people, an oft-repeated suggestion was, 'tell them to get as much overseas experience as possible, to go on as many study abroad programs as they can," (138). The same can be said by many career missionaries, and such residency requirements add value to the degree program by sheer experience in local realities and increased perceptual acuity (Zielinski 2007:43). Students can complete their practicum requirements in the "foreign" institution while simultaneously taking necessary classes to complete the joint degree from that culture. Andragogically this is of key importance, and I suggest that students complete their practicum during *each* residential location to broaden their andragogical benefit.

Students prepared for collaboration must understand the complexities of place in the deterritorialized, hybridized, and glocal reality because place always influences discourse of movement and change (Escobar 2001:150). To understand the importance of place they must understand the disruption of place through migration, even if for a short period. In this way students come to realize the true influence that place holds in the development of missiological theory and practice. No student can "know" every place, especially places that are constantly in flux. However, through good andragogical practice one may help students to experience and reflect upon how a certain place influences mission and how development provides praxiological tools that can be carried into other "glocal" contexts. Such an opportunity allows students from the U.S. to come under the educative authority of those from other cultural contexts with different forms of thinking. They can be removed, to some extent, from their hegemonic heritage through learning and collaborating with peers in another culture. For Latin American students, some of the and ragogical benefit is reversed. Rather than comply with a western missiological hegemony, they may take courses from their context and from Latin American scholars, but will also be able to critically incorporate external reflections on their own context when living and taking courses in the U.S. context.

Joint degrees require some level of praxis – action - reflection – and curricular integration. How missional education appropriates the action-reflection cycle and integration of curriculum is of great concern for Banks (1999), who writes:

> Our thinking should be embodied, experiential, and contextual, not abstract, objective, and universal. The principle characteristics of such praxis are accountability to minority groups, collaborative reflection, lives-in-relation as an epistemological starting point, cultural diversity, and shared commitment to the work of justice" (Kindle location 320) .

Such action-reflection in multiple "glocal" contexts, under the direction of multiple institutions, will inevitably prepare the student for greater collaboration and interdependence.

Concluding Reflections

Admittedly, this paper does not deviate far from the hegemonic principles that I chastised in my introduction. My proposal, considering my audience in the Association of Professors of Mission, inherently assumes initiation from U.S. seminaries. Missiology and development may also be perceived by some as hegemonic terms unhelpfully constructed and partitioned in the academy (Kollman 2011; Bullón 2013: 55). Yet we must begin, and have begun, to take steps towards minimizing U.S.-centric hegemony in mission. As U.S. educators, we come from within a specific system. Our own locale influences the way we pursue mission education. True collaboration is a process, but it takes intentionality to take strides towards that collaborative process. As mostly representatives from U.S.-based institutions, what we might have to offer are already developed coursework in development studies and global justice. This does not mean that we dominate or monopolize the subject. However, these are resources for the formation of the student to engage in Schreiter's missional tasks of poverty alleviation and reconciliation. Pushing for opportunities in developing joint degree programs based on one-sided perception of value would negate true collaboration. However, it is nonetheless important to promote an assumption of value in these programs to explore collaborative institutional connections which may arise. Such initiation, if done with utter humility and respect for global partners, will produce positive outcomes not perceived at the outset. Such a posture of humility leaves room for collaboration that will truly educate the student in the context of third-wave of globalization, third-wave mission, and the responsibility of mission as reconciliation.

This study's restriction of masters-level degree programs immediately places a recognized U.S.-centric construct in the programs I assess. One might argue that such a restriction promotes a hegemonic imposition in my survey, interpreting education by constructs developed in U.S. education systems. Herein lays an administrative challenge for partnership and one not easily navigated. That seminaries in Latin America are recently adding master's degrees demonstrates their participation in globalization trends in educational systems. Administratively, for U.S. institutions conforming to accreditation, this need to focus on master's programs is difficult to overcome. Nonetheless, Caldwell and Wan (2012) remind us that, "[s]eminaries must especially resist the temptation to do everything in light of accrediting bodies and government regulations. If necessary, [they should] develop a separate Center that is linked to the existing training institution but still has its own relevant...program," (114). Such a discussion of accreditation concerns, however, goes beyond the scope of this paper.

An overall content survey of the Latin American seminaries reveals that mission programs provide the most emphasis in either the proclamation or interreligious dialogue tasks, and veer away from the tasks of poverty alleviation and a ministry of reconciliation. However, as mentioned above, some programs require courses in *misión integral*. Bullón (2013) writes the important, *El pensamiento social protestante y el debate latinoamericano sobre el desarrollo*. In it, he remarks how the Seoul Declaration of 1982 (Seoul Declaration 1982) was influenced by and influenced much of the thinking of early *misión integral* thinkers (Bullón

2013: 236). The declaration states: "Theology will have to give priority to problems related to justice and peace..." (Seoul Declaration 1982: 493). This led *misión integral* proponents to state that theology in Latin America must be based out of praxis, but that "this practice is linked to a primary obedience, a response to a call, that comes from the Word proclaimed to the believer," (Bullón 2013: 239, translation mine). It is perhaps here that development is best reflected in the Latin American evangelical curriculum and is not so easily divorced from theological reflection. Alcántara Mejía (2001), writes, "A holistic Christian higher education must include a space of reflection on a person's spiritual being, but it must also be pertinent, relevant, and adequate to the reality that a professional confronts..." (105, translation mine). This is key to the posture of *misión integral* courses in the curriculum. However, do the minimal amount of courses specifically titled to *misión integral* among the Latin American institutions actually help to produce professionals who can "constructively help the development of our peoples and be recognized for doing so?" (Bullón 2001: 197, translation mine). Is there not room for the inclusion of development specific courses alongside *misión integral* courses in our degrees?

Joint degrees in international development and mission are not *the only* answer, but are opportunities to take steps in global collaboration among seminaries to initiate mutual collaboration. Joint degrees bring together multiple locales, multiple places, to influence the education of mission for our students. They provide students a model for a hybridized, deterritorialized, praxiological andragogy that addresses third wave mission.

We have the technology and both the virtual and physical infrastructure, yet our programs do not sufficiently enable multi-contextual missional arenas and learning environments. We are content to either train future missionaries, sending them out as representative alumni of our institution; or perhaps, with online education, we allow missionaries to remain in their ministry contexts but drive a thoroughly U.S.-centric education, thus tempting students to not interact with missiology student peers that are studying at seminaries physically located in the context in which our distance-learning students are working. Timothy Tennent (2012) concludes his opening address to the Lausanne Convention of the 2012 consultation of global theological education by stating, "As theological educators we stand at the vanguard of a whole new day in helping to form, shape, and direct the future of the theological education of the church. To do so we must become more globally astute, more culturally savvy, more theologically nuanced, and more missionally driven." I would also argue here that we must become more educationally creative. Joint degrees are administratively complicated, but Caldwell and Wan (2012), emphasize that: "…institutions – whether majority world or North American – must resist the urge to conform uncritically to nineteenth-century faculty, courses, and curricula, as well as to standards that are simply not appropriate for twenty-first century…ministry" (114). Seminaries should not be content with mission education models of the nineteenth-century that are not adequate or applicable in light of the changing context of mission brought on by third-wave globalization. Joint degrees, when lifted from the shackles of protectionist ideals provide new models of collaboration for the twenty-first century. Our institutions are at stake, but more so than that, at stake is the pursuit of excellence in third wave mission as a response to third wave globalization.

Notes

1.   There is something to be said for competition improving quality of education from both institutional output and student input, however, the rapidly growing number of nuanced degrees in a short period of time provides more options without time-tested and evaluated programs. This especially seems to be the case in the number of online and hybrid lower-credit master's degrees that appear to be truncated generalist degrees compared to their more lengthy counterparts. There is, however, some creation of nuanced degrees with targeted specialization whose curriculum is unique in the Christian higher education field.

2.   I contend here that such collaboration will also breed an appropriate competition for quality academics benefiting students and institutions.

3.   It is beyond the scope of this paper to review how the field of development studies has changed in recent decades or to review the variation which continues to exist in development studies programs in the U.S., the UK, or in Latin America. As a general rule, however, it is helpful to describe development studies as a field which primarily draws on the social sciences. Economics (and especially Agricultural Economics), Sociology, and (increasingly) Anthropology are some of the fields which influence all sectors of development studies.

4.   For more information about Multnomah University's program see http://www.multnomah.edu/programs/graduate/ma-in-global-development-and-justice/. For more information about Denver Seminary's program see http://www.denverseminary.edu/academics/master-of-arts/justice-mission/. Accessed on 13 September, 2014.

5.   Eastern University began offering an MA in International Development as well beginning in 2006. For more information on Eastern University's program, see - http://www.eastern.edu/3/

academics/programs/school-leadership-and-development/ma-international-development-global-or-urban. Accessed on 13 September, 2014.

6.   Content surveys can be conducted in this manner similarly for other geographic regions, for denominational institutions, different degree types, etc.

7.   Key words include: "misiología," "seminario," "universidad cristiana," "estudios interculturales," "Americalatina" "missiology," "seminary," "Christian university," and "intercultural studies."

8.   For these searches, I combined the following search terms: "desarrollo internacional," "maestría," "seminario," "desarrollo comunitario," for the Latin American programs, and "international development," "seminary," "master's degree," and "community development" for the U.S. programs.

9.   Eastern University has multiple programs in its School of Leadership and Development. Some of these focus on the United States' urban context while others focus on developing countries.

10.   SEMISUD already has a working relationship with Lee University. See http://www.semisud.edu.ec/index.php?option=com_content&view=article&id=67&Itemid=90 (accessed 1 June,, 2014). Adding Fuller Seminary as another institution may complicate matters. Such collaboration between SEMISUD and Lee University should be applauded. However, there is not a specific intention for a joint degree between SEMISUD and Lee, which therefore loses much of the and ragogical benefits discussed previously. In fact, upon first look, SEMISUD's collaboration with Lee appears to create a dependency on Lee's accreditation. The arrangement between SEMISUD and Lee need not negate a relationship between SEMISUD and Fuller regarding a missiological joint master's degree with an emphasis on working with children-at-risk, but in this specific case, careful diligence must be done so as to truly collaborate rather than compete – especially in the case for Lee and Fuller – and mutually benefit all institutions.

11.   For more information about Denver Seminary's programs in this regard see http://www.denverseminary.edu/about/who-we-are/missional-commitments/ Accessed on 1 June 2014).

12.   Michael and Balraj (2013) make an important distinction about collaborative degrees. They write, "While all joint degrees are collaborative in nature, not all collaborative degrees are joint degrees," (133). For instance a university-business partnership may be collaborative, but only one institution can confer the degree.

Appendix A: List of U.S. and Latin American Institutions

Latin American Institutions

Institution Name	Postgraduate Degrees in Research
SEMISUD	Maestría en Desarrollo Integral y Niños en Riesgo
Seminario Teológico de Puerto Rico (STDPR)	Maestría en Estudios Profesionales en Ministerios Cristianos con concentración en Misiones
Universidad Evangélica de las Américas (UNELA)	Maestría con Ciencias de la Religión con mención en Misiología
Programas de Maestría en Estudios Teológicos Accesibles (ProMETA)	Certificado en Misionología
Centro Evangélico de Misiología Andino-Amazónica (CEMAA)	Maestría en Misiología
Facultad Teológica Latinoamericana (FATELA)	Maestría en Misiones Transculturales Maestría en Teología Práctica con énfasis en Estudios Pastorales
FIET Instituto Teológico	Especialización en Teología y Misión
Recursos Estratégicos Globales (REG)[1]	Maestría de Misionologia
Seminario Teológico Centroamericano (SETECA)	Maestría en Ministerio con Énfasis en Misión Urbana

United States Institutions

Institution Name	Postgraduate Degrees in Research
Fuller Seminary	Master of Arts in Cross-Cutural Studies with an emphasis in Urban and International Development Master of Arts in Cross-Cultural Studies with an emphasis in Children at Risk
Multnomah University	Master of Arts in Global Development and Justice
Denver Seminary	Master of Arts in Justice and Mission
Carson-Newman College	Master of Arts in Applied Social Justice
Eastern University	Master of Arts or Master of Divinity in International Development Master of Arts in Urban Studies with a concentration in Community Development
Northern Seminary	Master of Arts or Master of Divinity in Christian Ministry with an emphasis on Christian Community Development

1.   REG curriculum is housed in *Seminario Biblico de Puebla* – Mexico, *Seminario Teológico de la Igelsia de Dios* – Paraguay, *Seminario Bautista* – Cuba, *Instituto Biblico Ibero Americano* – Chile, and *Programa de Entrenamiento Biocupacional y Ministerial* – Argentina.

Works Cited

American Society of Missiology
    2014   "Call for papers," 2014 Meeting of American Society of Missiology.

Alcántara Mejía, J. R.
    2001. "'Sean transformados mediante la renovación de su mente': El reto cristiano en la encrucijada de la educación cristiana superior en Latinoamérica." *Presencia cristiana en el mundo académico.* S. Rooy (Ed.). Buenos Aires: Ediciones Kairos.

Arbuckle, G. A.
    2010. *Culture, inculturation, and theologians: A postmodern critique.* Collegeville, MN: Liturgical Press.

Banks, R.
    1999 *Reinvisioning theological education: Exploring a missional alternative to current models.* Grand Rapids: Eerdmans.

Bullón, H. F.
    2001 "El docente cristiano y las ciencias económicas y sociales en el proceso de la transformación latinoamericano." *Presencia cristiana en el mundo académico.* S. Rooy (Ed.). Buenos Aires: Ediciones Kairos.

Bullón, H. F.
    2013 *El pensamiento social protestante y el debate latinoamericano sobre el desarrollo.* Grand Rapids, MI: Libros Desafío.

Cadwell, L. W. & Wan, E.
    2012 "Riots in the city: Replacing nineteenth-century urban training models with relevant "urbanized" training models for the twenty-first century." In *Reaching the city: Reflections on urban mission for the twenty-first century.* G. Fujino, T. R. Sisk, & T. C. Casiño (Eds.). Pasadena, CA: William Carey Library.

Cardoso, F. H.
    1972/2007   "Dependency and development in Latin America."
                In *The globalization and development reader: Perspectives on
                development and global change*. J. Timmons & A. B. Hite
                (Eds.). Malden, MA: Blackwell Publishing.

Carpenter, J.
    2008   "Christian higher education as a worldwide movement."
                Journal of Latin American Theology, 3 (1): 71-98.

Center for the Study of Global Christianity
    2013 *Christianity in its global context, 1970–2020: Society, religion,
        and mission*. Retrieved from http://wwwgordonconwell.
        com/netcommunity/CSGCResources/Christianityinits
        GlobalContext.pdf.

Chan, S.
    2010   "Applications of andragogy in multi-disciplined teaching
                and learning." *Journal of Adult Education*, 39 (2): 25-35.

Escobar, A.
    2001   Culture sits in places: Reflections on globalism and
                subaltern strategies of localization. *Political Geography*, 20:
                139-174.

Freire, P.
    2004   *Pedagogy of the oppressed*, 30th Anniversary Edition, New
                York: Continuum International Publishing Group Inc.

Gacel-Ávila, J.
    2011   "Comprehensive internationalization in Latin America."
                Trends and insights for international education leaders.
                http://www.nafsa.org/_/File/_/ti_latin_america.pdf.
                Accessed on 7 October 2014.

Gunder Frank, A.
    1969/2007   "The development of underdevelopment." In *The
                globalization and development reader: Perspectives on
                development and global change*. J. Timmons & A. B. Hite
                (Eds.). Malden, MA: Blackwell Publishing.

Gutzler, A.
    2013   "Response to Robert Schreiter." In *The gift of mission yesterday, today, tomorrow* (Kindle edition). J. H. Kroeger (Ed.). Maryknoll, NY: Orbis.

Hoksbergen, R.
    2012   *Serving God globally: Finding your place in international development.* Grand Rapids, MI: Baker Academic.

Kennedy, P.
    2010   *Local lives and global transformations: Towards world society.* New York: Palgrave Macmillan.

Kollman, P.
    2011   "At the origins of mission and missiology: A study in the dynamics of religious language." *Journal of the American Academy of Religion*, 79 (2): 425-458.

Michael, S. O. & Balraj, L.
    2003   "Higher education institutional collaborations: An analysis of models of joint degree programs." *Journal of Higher Education Policy and Management*, 25 (2): 131-145.

Moreau, A. S.
    2012   *Contextualization in world missions: Mapping and assessing evangelical models.* Grand Rapids, MI: Kregel Publications.

Myers, B. L.
    1999   *Walking with the poor: Principles and practices of transformational development.* Maryknoll, NY: Orbis Books.

Obst, D. & Kuder, M.
    2009   "Joint and double degree programs in the transatlantic context: A survey report." http://www.iie.org/en/research-and-publications/publications-and-reports/iie-bookstore/joint-degree-survey-report-2009. Accessed on 6 October 2014.

Obst, D., Kuder, M. & Banks, C.
    2011   "Joint and double degree programs in the global context:
            Report on an international survey." http://www.iie.org/
            Research-and-Publications/Publications-and-Reports/
            IIE-Bookstore/Joint-Degree-Survey-Report-2011.
            Accessed on 6 October 2014.Reichman, J.

    2008   "Andragogy." In *The Routledge International Encyclopedia
            of Education*. New York: Routledge, pages 23-24.

Rizvi, F. & Lingard, B.
    2010   *Globalizing education policy*. London: Routledge.

Slimbach, R.
    2010   "Learning from the slums. Transformations at the edge of
            the world." In *Forming global Christians through the study
            abroad experience*. R. J. Morgan & C. Thoms Smedley
            (Eds.). Abilene, TX: Abilene Christian University Press.

Seoul Declaration
    1982   The Seoul Declaration: Toward an evangelical theology
            for the third world. *Missiology*, 10, 490-494.

Schreiter, R. J.
    2005   The changed context of mission forty years after the
            council. *Verbum SVD*, 46 (1): 75-88.

Schreiter, R. J.
    2013   "The future of missions *ad gentes* in a global context." *The
            gift of mission yesterday, today, tomorrow* (Kindle edition). J.
            H. Kroeger (Ed.). Maryknoll, NY: Orbis.

Spencer-Oatey, H.
    2012   "Maximizing the benefits of international education
            collaborations: Managing interaction processes." *Journal
            of Studies in International Education*, 17 (3): 244-261.

Sweeting, D.
  2012   "The changing role of American seminaries in global theological education." Lausanne Consultation on Global Theological Education 2012, Gordon Conwell Theological Seminary, (Boston, MA). http://www.lausanne.org/en/multimedia/videos/theological-education-videos.html. Accessed June 2014.

Taylor, B. & Kroth, M.
  2009   "A single conversation with a wise man is better than ten years of study: A model for testing methodologies for pedagogy or andragogy." *Journal of the Scholarship of Teaching and Learning*, 9 (2): 42-56.

Tennent, T.
  2012   "Theological education in the context of world Christianity." Lausanne Consultation on Global Theological Education 2012, Gordon Conwell Seminary, (Boston, MA). http://www.lausanne.org/en/multimedia/videos/theological-education-videos.html. Accessed June 2014.

Walls, A.
  1991   "Structural problems in mission studies." *International Bulletin of Missionary Research*, 15 (4): 146-155.

Yamamori, T.
  2000   "Introduction." *El proyecto de Dios y las necesidades humanas.* C. R. Padilla & T. Yamamori (Eds.). Buenos Aires: Ediciones Kairos.

Zielinski, B. A. Z.
  2007   Study abroad length of program influence on cross-cultural adaptability. (Masters Thesis). http://scholar.lib.vt.edu/theses/available/etd-04302007-105204/. Accessed 6 October 2014.

Analysis of Spiritual Formation Practices in DMiss Cohorts

ELIZABETH "BETSY" GLANVILLE

DOI: 10.7252/Paper.000035

About the Author

Elizabeth "Betsy" Glanville is Assistant Professor of Leadership, and core faculty for the Doctor of Missiology program at Fuller Theological Seminary, School of Intercultural Studies

Spiritual Formation is an important part of who we are at Fuller Theological Seminary—at least we say it is. But we have struggled with how to measure it, how to determine what, and if, it is happening. What is the role of a seminary? What is the role of the church? Most professors regularly have some kind of devotion or prayer at the beginning of class, but how is this forming students? Do we know if this makes any kind of difference in the lives of our students? While these questions have been asked and discussed often, we seem to have few answers.

This study is an attempt to examine spiritual formation practices in one specific program only. Information has been gathered from thirteen current cohorts from the Doctor of Missiology Program (DMiss) at Fuller Theological Seminary, School of Intercultural Studies. The goal has been to do an initial assessment of our best practices and identify some key areas for improvement. The impetus for the study came from WASC (our accrediting body) who has required us to evaluate and report on our spiritual formation practices and outcomes in our various degree programs.

One of the biggest challenges, historically, in our doctoral programs has been the integration of our academic journeys with our spiritual journeys, bringing them together so they "speak" to one another and are not two separate pieces of our lives. My interest in this topic started when I was Director of our Doctoral Programs, PhD and DMiss, and came from talking with students about the loneliness of the academic journey as a doctoral student and the impact that had on their spiritual vitality. Now I am working with DMiss students in a cohort-based program. Students are on campus for two weeks each year for the first three years, and a single week the fourth year. During the remainder of the nine month term, students interact with each other and with the professors online, while doing their research, focused on their individual projects. The focus of this study is primarily on the spiritual formation practices and experiences during the two week intensives when students are gathered together on campus with potential implications for the rest of their nine-month term.

Value of Spiritual Formation

Studies have shown that one of the key reasons pastors leave the ministry or fail in ministry is due to the lack of intimacy with God, combined with the lack of accountability for personal life issues. Frequently these are related to the lack of balance between spiritual practices and disciplines with the overload of work and lack of attention to family and recreation. J. Robert Clinton's work on Leadership Emergence Theory has shown that Christian leaders who finish well are those that have established habits of intimacy with God and have had significant mentors in their lives (2012: 210-215). Spiritual formation is a key process of development over the life of a leader, not something that happens early in life and then lasts for the rest of life. Randy Reese and Robert Loane's work on mentoring has shown that the intentional relationships of accountability and mentoring one-on-one or in small groups increase the ability of a leader to be effective and maintain vitality in life and ministry (2013). Clinton (2012), Reese and Loane (2013), and Wilson and Hoffman (2007) all point to the need for intentionality throughout a life to develop healthy practices of spirituality and formation. For us, in the DMiss program, this raises the questions of what and how are we doing in guiding students along this journey? While there are skills that can be learned, what are we doing to encourage the practice of the skills for the future?

Research

The primary findings reported in this study are from two surveys, one with faculty and one with students. Selected responses to a question about spiritual formation on student course evaluations have also been included. The faculty survey was sent to twelve key faculty who have taught in two or more intensive courses in one or more cohorts. The student survey was sent to 94 students who had attended one to four module intensives. Forty-nine students responded to the survey, with a relatively balanced percentage representing the completion of the 1-4 modules (see Table 1). Each category, except those completing only Module 1, shows a greater than 50% response rate. Because of the timing of the survey in relation to the timing of module intensives, the results reflect greater numerical responses from those who had completed only Module 1 or all four modules than those who had completed just Modules 1 and 2, or just Modules 1 through 3.

Table 1: Student Respondents to Survey

Students who competed	Responses	Number of Cohorts	Total students who have completed each set:	Percent of responses
Module 1	16	4	42	38%
Modules 1 & 2	10	2	16	63%
Modules 1, 2, & 3	7	2	10	70%
Modules 1, 2, 3, & 4	14	5	26	54%

Faculty and students were asked to give a value to each of the different spiritual formation practices that have been used in different cohorts, and then to rank what they felt were the top five best practices. In addition they were asked to give an example of one of the best practices, and a practice that didn't work as well with suggestions for improvement. Respondents also indicated which practices they had not used or experienced.

Value Rating Selected Practices

While the number of respondents is not sufficient to guarantee a high degree of accuracy, the responses do provide information about some trends of what both students and faculty experience as valuable. While the exact order differs slightly between the students and the faculty, the practices seem to fall into three similar groupings in both surveys. (See Tables 2 and 3).

The first group relates to devotions led by faculty or students and prayer times that were either planned or spontaneous. The second group included times of praise and worship and the half-day retreats. The lowest ranking group included the personal rule of life and the community rule of life. The comments add to the significance of each of these categories.

While these values are only suggestive, the additional comments (discussed below) added further significance to the various choices.

Table 2: Student Value Rating of Selected Practices

	Rank of value 1-3	Based on # responses (out of 49)
1. Professor led devotions	2.79	47
2. Regular prayer for one another	2.74	39
3. Spontaneous prayer times as need arose	2.65	43
4. Student led devotions	2.60	48
5. Praise and worship times	2.48	35
6. Half-day retreat	2.43	28
7. Personal Rule of Life	2.10	42
8. Community Rule of Life	1.93	42
Other practices: time spent in fellowship over meals with students and professors together.		

Table 3: Faculty Value Rating of Selected Practices

	Rank of value 1-3	Based on # responses (out of 8)
1. Student led devotions	2.63	8
2. Professor led devotions	2.49	7
3. Half-day retreats	2.40	5
4. Spontaneous prayer times as need arose	2.38	8
5. Regular prayer for one another	2.29	7
6. Praise and worship	2.18	7
7. Personal Rule of Life	2.00	4
8. Community Rule of Life	1.50	6
Other practices noted included: simulation exercises, sharing personal life/spiritual journeys, Lectio Divina, Bible study exercises, sharing passions and experiences.		

Ranking of the Spiritual Practices

The respondents were also asked to rank their top five out of ten different practices. The results fall into two groups based on the number of people who rated each one in the top five. For students, the division was basically the same as the way they valued the different practices: Prayer times and devotions were ranked in the top five by 34 or more of the students, while the other four were ranked in the top five by less than 20 respondents, (see Table 4).

The responses of faculty were similar. Six or seven out of eight ranked devotions, spontaneous prayer times and praise and worship in the top five, only one or two ranked the remaining four in the top five. Interestingly, the faculty rated the devotional times significantly higher than the prayer times, while the students ranked the prayer times higher, (see Table 5).

Table 4: The Top Five of Ten Practices as Rated by Students (Weighted rankings)

	Ranking 1-5 (highest)	# ranked in top 5 (out of 49)
Ranked by 34 or more students		
1. Regular prayer for one another	3.15	34
2. Spontaneous prayer times as need arose	3.06	36
3. Professor led devotions	3.00	41
4. Student led devotions	2.87	40

	Ranking 1-5 (highest)	# ranked in top 5 (out of 49)
Ranked by less than 20 students		
5. Praise and worship times	3.32	19
6. Personal Rule of Life	2.75	16
7. Half-day retreat	2.53	19
8. Community Rule of Life	2.46	15

Table 5: The Top Five of Ten Practices as Rated by Faculty

	Ranking 1-5 (highest)	# ranked in top 5 (out of 8)
Ranked by 6 or 7 Professors		
1. Professor led devotions	4.8	6
2. Student led devotions	4.0	7
3, Spontaneous prayer times as need arose	2.1	7
4. Praise and worship times	2.1	7
Ranked by only 1 or 2 Professors		
5. Regular prayer for one another	2.2	2
6. Personal Rule of Life	2.5	2
7. Half-day retreat	1.6	2
8. Community Rule of Life	3.0	1

Examples of Best Practices

The responses of value ratings and ranking of the practices are just numbers. However, when responses to examples of best practices are considered, these numbers take on new significance. This section includes a number of examples that demonstrate the significance of different practices.

Students gave examples of praying together and for one another (10 examples), times of fellowship and sharing meals with professors and students together (10 examples); dedicated time alone with the Lord about their research program either on a half-day retreat, an overnight retreat, or a limited 90 minute reflection time (9 examples); experiencing the diversity of traditions, backgrounds, and cultures (9 examples), and the value of sharing personal journeys either in devotional times or in fellowship gatherings (8 examples).

The fact that students gave a number of examples of praying together and for one another was not surprising given their value ratings of these practices. However, the times of fellowship and sharing meals was a surprise in that it was not included in the initial choices, but very clearly emerged in the comments from the students. This kind of relational connection on an informal basis built significant bonds, provided encouragement, and support for the students. The personal connection with the lives of professors and one another in a casual context seemed to be key.

Likewise, the practices that led to times of retreat emerged as much more significant when combined with the three different types of practices among different cohorts that all led to the same result: half-day retreats, overnight retreat, and 90 minute mini-retreats were all identified as valuable times set aside to listen to God and what God might say about their course of study and research. Students felt that the intentional time set aside to seek God's guidance was essential. As one student said, "this was an important time, as God spoke to me [about my project]." Another commented that they had seldom had "such concentrated, personal listening-to-God time," and found that valuable. From personal observation, I almost always have students report that the Lord spoke to them either to affirm what they were planning, or to provide significant re-direction they had not anticipated when they got quiet and listened.

Several students noted the value of praying for peers after they led a time of devotions or when they shared their personal spiritual journeys. This became a time of affirmation for a student and sometimes a confirmation of what they had already been hearing from the Lord. Students commented on the value of experiencing the diversity of backgrounds and perspectives which gave them a deeper appreciation for differences among cohort members. A significant number of students named examples of times of fellowship and informal interaction over meals, including praying for one another and with peers and professors, saying these were times that built community and strengthened friendships. Some of the practices seem somewhat fluid, such as prayer for one another, in that it occurred in intentional times of devotion, moments when needs arise, times of retreat, or times of informal fellowship with faculty and peers. The fact that this appears in a variety of contexts suggests that an atmosphere of prayer does emerge in the context of the gathered cohorts.

One example that illustrates the value and importance of being open to a spontaneous response to a student need came when a student received a message about a crisis in his ministry. The entire cohort gathered around the student and spent about fifteen minutes in prayer with him. The student commented later that this had been a transformative experience in his relationship with the cohort as he had joined this cohort in Module 2 and had not been part of the initial formative experiences of Module 1. This experience in Module 3 affirmed to him that he really did belong to this cohort.

The creating of a Personal Rule of Life, and a Community Rule of Life definitely got mixed responses. Some professors have used these exercises very successfully. However, from student responses, it appears that others have not followed up on them when the cohorts are gathered, so the feeling is that these are just exercises without any intentional follow-up or accountability. One student noted that by Module 4, the Rule of Life had "fallen off the radar." This is definitely an area that we need to pursue further as faculty to see if and how we can better include these activities with the cohort. The Community Rule of Life seemed more problematic to students in that students are not closely connected with one another except during the intensives. They all have other "communities" they are connected to and more committed to than the cohort, so the Community

Rule of Life needs to consider this reality. Perhaps what is necessary is the connectedness to some community not necessarily the cohort community, and the cohort community rule of life would be simpler. At the same time one professor noted that a community of practice had emerged over the four years and was obvious in the commitment, of students to one another and their various projects. Each one was significantly invested in the work of their peers, and this arose naturally out of the ongoing relationships of working together and critiquing one another's work.

Conclusion

In conclusion, these findings suggest areas for growth and development as we move forward. They also reveal that spiritual formation is taking place, from students' perspectives, based on current practices and perhaps even in spite of what we are doing. In this section I want to look at practices we want to keep as they are, those we want to keep and perhaps change, and then suggest those things that we might want to stop or others we might want to consider adding.

First, times of devotions and prayer were significant to many students and faculty. Students commented on devotions that integrated with the topics being discussed, both in general and in reference to a specific devotion that had led to key insights for growth and perspective. Prayer times, both planned and spontaneous were highly valued by students. In addition, from their comments, they valued the informal times together with professors and peers. What professors live and model in their spiritual walk with God is important to students. These practices we want to continue including in intentional ways, though the specifics will vary with each professor. At the same time we need to encourage openness to the spontaneous opportunities that arise from time to time.

Second, as professors, we need to consider developing further how to make best use of the Personal Rule of Life. From studies done on the failure of leaders in ministry, practices of self-care, spiritual development, and accountability seem to be key elements to both thriving (thus not failing) and recovery from failure or burnout. Our use of these has been inconsistent and will require discussion among key faculty to think through ways to incorporate this practice with accountability into the cohort process. The biggest challenge seems to be the vision for follow through and means for accountability.

In addition, we need to look at a variety of ways to use the different forms of retreat and reflection. For example, in a recent cohort, Module 1, we took the students on a two and a half day retreat which included times of solitude, group interaction, and reflection, and some introductory teaching the doctoral study process. In the course evaluations, the students clearly valued this time because it created a space to separate from the business of their ministries, allowed them to build community and relationships with one another, and to seek God for his direction in life and studies. On the other hand, taking this time from the normal classroom schedule created pressure on how to best cover the required material for the cohort—a challenge that needs further discussion.

Third, I would suggest that we may want to consider dropping the requirement for the Community Rule of Life and in its place look at developing Communities of Practice, allowing them to emerge over the course of the program. Identifying this process would allow students to understand and value the relationships that are being built over the course of the entire program and not just one module.

Fourth, a number of suggestions appeared in the comments that have potential for inclusion in future cohorts, but need to be discussed among faculty. Perhaps the most significant to emerge is the importance of the informal gatherings of professors and students. While this seems to be emerging naturally, highlighting the significance of these interactions is important. In addition, a number of suggestions were mentioned only once, but have broader potential if available to all faculty. These might include such things as: Lectio Divina, simulation activities, a list of Ways God Speaks, sharing spiritual journeys, intentional conversations about the integration of spiritual journey and academic journey, a time of prayer and consecration at the beginning and end of intensives. Each one of these activities seem to be practices of one, or maybe two, professors that the rest of us could learn from for future cohorts.

In conclusion, these basic surveys have revealed that spiritual formation is happening, which is encouraging. At the same time, we can see areas where we can grow and be more intentional about practices in our cohorts that will enhance the spiritual development and leadership of our students.

Notes

1. See Clinton's work on finishing well (2012: 208-210), Wilson and Hoffmann on *Preventing Ministry Failure* (2007: 26-27)

2. See also Chuck Miller (2007), Leonard Doohan (2007), Ruth Haley Barton (2006), Reggie McNeal (2000), and Bill Thrall, Bruce McNicol, and Ken McElrath (1999).

3. Responses from those who did not use or experience a given practice were excluded from the calculations. I also discarded findings where fewer than twenty-five people responded as the weighted responses were skewed because of the lack of numbers, and they were practices used in only one or two cohorts. Only the same eight practices are included in the additional tables as well.

Works Cited

Barton, Ruth Haley
> 2006   *Sacred Rhythms: Aranging Our Lives for Spiritual Transformation.* Downers Grove, IL: IVP.

Clinton, J. Robert
> 2012   *The Making of a Leader: Recognizing the Lessons and Stages of Leadership Development.* 2nd ed. Colorado Springs, CO: NavPress.

Doohan, Leonard
> 2007   *Spiritual Leadership: The Quest for Integrity.* New York: Paulist Press.

McNeal, Reggie
> 2000   *A Work of Heart.* San Francisco, CA: Jossey-Bass Publishers.

Miller, Chuck
> 2007   *The Spiritual Formation of Leaders: Integrating Spiritual Formation and Leadership Development.* Longwood, FL: Xulon Press.

Reese, Randy, and Robert Loane
> 2013   *Deep Mentoring: Guiding Others on Their Leadership Journey.* Downers Grove, IL: IVP.

Thrall, Bill, Bruce McNicol, and Ken McElrath
> 1999   *The Ascent of a Leader.* San Franscisco, CA: Jossey-Bass Publishers.

Wilson, Michael Todd, and Brad Hoffman
> 2007   *Preventing Ministry Failure: A Shepherdcare Guide for Pastors, Ministers and Other Caregivers.* Downers Grove, IL: IVP.

Cultural Bias in Missionary Education

The Unintentional Dynamic of Trained Incapacity

BIRGIT HERPPICH

DOI: 10.7252/Paper.000033

About the Author

Birgit Herppich (Ph.D. and M.A. Intercultural Studies, Fuller Theological Seminary, B.A. Biblical and Cross-cultural Studies, All Nations Christian College, UK, B.A. Education, University of Bayreuth, Germany) worked eight years in Ghana with WEC International in children's ministry, leadership training and advising new missionaries in language and culture learning. Her publications include *Trained Incapacity: A Critical Examination of Basel Missionary Preparation and Early Engagement in Ghana (1828-1840)*, (2013), and *Immigrant Communities in America—Objects of Mission or Missional Agents? The Case of the Church of Pentecost (Ghana) in Urban America*, (2012). Her research interests include missionary preparation, missiology and contextualization studies, the history of World Christianity, in particular African Christianity, African missionary engagement and migration.

Introduction

Let me state at the outset that I am an educator with a passion. I believe in the need for innovative educational theory and practice to increase effectiveness in teaching and learning for Christian intercultural engagement. Looking for such educational insights I began researching the historical case study of missionary preparation that revealed the dynamic I am going to describe in this article. Since my eyes are opened, however, I see "trained incapacity" almost everywhere—maybe also a case of (cultural) bias.

Secondly, it is important to emphasize the unintentionality of this dynamic. Nobody sets out to train for incapacity. Consequently, this paper is not accusing missionary educators that they should know better. It is the character of trained incapacity that it is typically hidden to the people experiencing it. They just feel confusion about an apparent lack of success in cross-cultural mission which then is usually explained by the "hard field", the unresponsive people, the difficult situation, or other factors outside one's own cultural bias.

Cultural Competence and Intercultural Christian Mission

The goal of missionary education is the preparation of men and women for intercultural Christian missionary engagement. Today there is generally awareness that cultural competence is necessary for the communication and demonstration of the Gospel across different contexts and literature abounds on the theme.

Typically, the concept of culture employed is anthropological, emphasizing different basic values among ethnic groups which direct "the total way of life of a group of people that is learned, adaptive, shared and integrated" (Howell and Paris 2011:36). Sociologists and scholars of intercultural communication further highlight that cultural groups are formed within and across ethnic, racial, or sociolinguistic contexts "on the basis of nationality, ethnicity, gender, profession, geography, organization, physical ability or disability, community, type of relationship, or other factors" (Samovar, Porter, and McDaniel 2006:54). Groups create "cultures" based on various areas of commonality. This is not contingent on common ancestry and upbringing but reflects sociological and organizational allegiances. Cultural groups are constituted by a set of shared attitudes, values, goals and practices that characterizes an institution, organization or informal group and its language. This definition includes one important category which is surprisingly ignored by most authors, the significant and pervasive culture of religious groups and organizations.

The Need for Cultural Competency in Christian Mission

The capacity to engage people from a different background with cultural competence is crucial in Christian mission because of the character of the gospel. As Andrew Walls and Lamin Sanneh pointed out, the spread of the Christian movement is inseparable from the translatable quality of the Christian message which derives from the incarnation (Sanneh 1989; Walls 1996, 2002). In Christ "the Word became flesh" as a person "in a particular locality and in a particular ethnic group, at a particular place and time;" and so "[d]ivinity was translated into humanity" and this "first divine act of translation…gave rise to a constant succession of new translations" (Walls 1996: 27). When the Gospel moves from one cultural context to another the Christian faith is periodically transformed as it is incarnated in new cultures. "Mission by *translation*" then assumes "a relativized status for the culture of the message bearer" (Sanneh 1989: 29). Thus Christian mission involves a tension between the *indigenization principle* and the *pilgrim principle* (Walls 1996:7-9). Indigenization is the desire "to live as a Christian and yet as a member of one's own society" which makes all churches cultural churches, shaped by the culture and history of their context. On the other hand, the *pilgrim principle* entails a warning that there will be "rubs and frictions—not from the adoption of a new culture but from the transformation of the mind towards that of Christ." The tension between these two principles—between the particularity and the universality of the gospel—presents a considerable challenge for Christian missionaries as they attempt to facilitate the appropriation of the gospel in new cultural settings.

Today we recognize the need for contextualization. The message of God's saving grace in Jesus Christ can only be meaningful and elicit a response of faith if it makes sense in the mental frameworks of the people who hear it and addresses their felt needs. The establishment of new communities of believers will always involve the translation of the gospel into their language and cultural frameworks and the expression of faith and worship through their cultural concepts and forms. These facts about Christian mission imply the need for missionaries to develop cultural competence.

Theories of Cultural Competence

Since the 1960s the expressions *Cultural Competence* and *Cultural Intelligence* have come into use to depict the ability to understand diverse cultural behaviors and values and to accommodate cultural differences in various professional and political contexts. As a multicultural society, America has to engage with intercultural relationships in schools, commerce, social services, the judicial and the health system. These situations and international charitable and business endeavors have triggered substantial research. Consequently the fields employed in these studies are as diverse as education, sociology, psychology, business, and communication.

The terms *cross-cultural* and *intercultural* are often used interchangeably. However, communication scholars distinguish between the comparative study of communication processes in different cultures— *cross-cultural communication*—and face-to-face communication between people from different cultures—*intercultural communication* (Gudykunst 2003). By that definition, Christian mission always engages in *intercultural communication* to which *cross-cultural communication* is a prerequisite. Even though the terms are often used without clear distinction, significantly, in mission contexts the typical term is *cross-cultural* (For example: Elmer 2002, Lingenfelter and Mayers 2003, Kraft 2005). The implication is a uni-directional movement which is quite problematic because it assumes the transplanting of what the missionary brings into another cultural context with the agent remaining more or less unchanged in the process. The missionary adapts to cultural behaviors, learns the language, and frames the message in local concepts, but maintains a utilitarian attitude to the other culture that aims at a positive response to the presumed universal concepts, truths, facts, and best practices. These attitudes prevail in many contexts despite lip service to mutuality and partnership.

Cultural competence requires *intercultural* communication between people from different cultures. In this process other cultures are perceived as equally valid solutions to life's realities. There is an exchange and both parties are transformed. It is defined as the "ability to understand, communicate with, and effectively interact with people across cultures" and typically four components are identified: (a) awareness of one's own cultural worldview, (b) Attitude towards cultural differences, (c) knowledge of different cultural practices and worldviews, and (d) cross-cultural skills (Martin and Vaughn 2007). A "synthesis model" based on an overview of the diverse literature identifies the "iterative process of becoming culturally competent" and poses the desire to engage as a pre-condition (Balcazar, Suarez-Balcazar, and Taylor-Ritzler 2009). In addition to critical self-awareness of "biases towards people who are in any way different from us", cultural knowledge of "other's characteristics, history, values, belief systems and behaviors," skills development and practical application of all these in a particular context, Balcazar *et al.* highlight the importance of organizational and systemic factors in the ability to implement cultural competence.

Notwithstanding the commendable effort to improve competence to engage with clients, patients and business partners from a wide variety of cultural backgrounds, there is an important concern. This literature generally ignores that the goals and assumptions of professions and programs have *in themselves* the capacity to prevent true engagement with others on their cultural terms. Cultural competence is sought in an effort to increase the effectiveness of practitioners to achieve the goals of the profession, organization or service provider; but assumptions, values, goals and standards of the profession are taken for granted. Consequently, cultural competence becomes a tool to encourage compliance with standards the profession regards as universally valid.

In contrast to the cultural competence literature, the term *cultural intelligence* has been applied to Christian mission, notably by David Livermore (Livermore 2006, 2009). First articulated in 2003, the concept originates in studies of organizational psychology, builds on Gardner's *Multiple Intelligence Theory* and Goleman's *Emotional Intelligence,* proposes to measure people's *cultural intelligence quotient* (CQ) and is used dominantly in organizational, business and government related contexts (Earley and

Ang 2003, Peterson 2004, Dight 2004, Gardner 1993, Goleman, Boyatzis, and McKee 2002, Livermore 2010). Earley and Ang outline three "facets" of Cultural Intelligence: (1) *cognitive and metacognitive* abilities which include knowledge of self and social environment as well as flexibility in inductive and analogical reasoning, (2) *motivational* aspects including self-enhancement (personal felt needs and wants), self-efficacy (confidence in social discourse), and self-consistency (the desire for coherence in experiences and cognitions) and (3) the need to acquire and execute appropriate *behaviors* for different cultural situations (Earley and Ang 2003:59-92). This framework draws attention to the need for cognitive engagement, not only with facts about other cultures but also processing experience, emotions, and various perspectives. Furthermore, the importance of motivational factors it highlights cannot be overestimated.

David Livermore, building on the earlier studies, distinguishes two cognitive aspects, namely, acquisition of factual knowledge about cultures and meta-cognition or "Interpretive CQ." His emphasis on willingness and perseverance to truly engage other cultures also adds an important angle to the motivational facet. Livermore adopts a particular Christian perspective on "inward transformation" and "expressing love cross-culturally" in two books, but his website and most publications target primarily the management and business community. He identifies "four capabilities that consistently emerge among individuals who are effective in culturally diverse situations" as four components of *Cultural Intelligence* (Livermore 2010:23-31): Drive (showing interest, confidence, and drive to adapt cross-culturally), Knowledge (understanding cross-cultural issues and differences), Strategy (strategizing and making sense of culturally diverse experiences), and Action (changing verbal and nonverbal actions appropriately when interacting cross-culturally).

From theories on cultural competence it can be derived that effective missiological engagement or "capacity" in intercultural Christian mission entails the willingness and ability to adjust to life, build relationships, and communicate the gospel of Jesus Christ meaningfully with people of another culture in order to initiate and foster the development of culturally relevant and missionally engaged communities of believers. While such communities are ultimately dependent on indigenous agency and appropriation of the Christian message, cross-cultural missionaries play an important initial catalyzing role that can foster or hinder their development. A few Christian authors apply the insights from these scholars (for example Stallter 2009, Rah 2010) but generally missionary preparation tends to build on educational theories.

Training for Cultural Competence

Intercultural competencies are not easily acquired because enculturation makes humans naturally ethnocentric, i.e. convinced that their own culture is superior and their ways inherently better than others. Earley and Ang comment:

> Competence in cross-cultural functioning means learning new patterns of behavior and effectively applying them in appropriate settings. This kind of sophisticated cultural competence does not come naturally and it requires a high level of professionalism and knowledge. Cultural competence is also not static and requires frequent relearning and unlearning about cultural diversity (Earley and Ang 2003:263).

Knowing this, it is surprising how brief most educational interventions are. Kohls, for example, found that "Training, Orientation and Briefing" of business managers and executives range from ten minutes to a few weeks (Kohls 1987) and Whiteman's survey of training offered by missionary organizations averages 3.5 weeks with the shortest seven days and the longest about two months (Whiteman 2008: 8).

Often the focus is on deliberate educational efforts including the criteria and procedures for selection of candidates, goals, curriculum, instructional design, and specific methods of the training. But they form only part of the overall dynamic because a wide range of factors influence persons in training. The participants of any educational effort are shaped by dynamics of informal socialization before and during formally designed training. The context of origin, i.e. the cultural, socio-economic, intellectual, and religious background of missionaries, as well as the wider historical context shape their attitudes and missionary engagement. In addition, the term *hidden curriculum* was coined by Philip Jackson to highlight the influence of latent values and assumptions built into the social expectations and procedures of the school environment which are at least as powerful, if not more so, as the stated curriculum (Jackson 1968).

Acknowledging these dynamics, scholars agree about the need to adopt a holistic or integral approach to preparing people for intercultural engagement. Earley and Ang emphasize their "integrative motive and propensity [that] seeks to integrate the cognitive, the motivational, as well as the behavioral components of...developing cultural intelligence." They critique "the two extremes of cross-cultural training" in many organizations today: (1) the 'sponge' method, focused on 'thought'...in which trainees "absorb or acquire cultural knowledge and facts by attending lectures, briefings and information sessions" and (2) the 'hands-on' training method, focused on "action" in which people "learn how to display culturally appropriate behaviors" (Earley and Ang 2003: 260-261). They conclude it is "fairly well established that informational training and experiential training work best in tandem" and suggest "that effective cross-cultural training programs need to adopt a multifaceted and integrated approach" (Earley and Ang 2003:270-303).

In missionary training too, integrated approaches are championed and an additional spirituality and character dimension is seen as crucial.[1] As Christian intercultural engagement involves the demonstration and communication of the gospel, missionaries need the biblical knowledge and theological understanding to articulate this good news, personal spirituality and character qualities that represent the life of God's people. Arguably the most popular framework in missionary education is a tripartite approach that identifies knowledge and understanding (cognitive, "Head"), practical ministry skills (behavioral, "Hands"), and spirituality, character and attitudes (affective, "Heart") needed by cross-cultural missionaries (for example Elliston 1996, Harley 1995, McKinney 1991, Brynjolfson and Lewis 2006, Ferris 1995, 2000, Taylor 1991). Often, community learning, interactive teaching and field experience are emphasized, which is why educational theories that highlight the context and social character of learning have gained popularity; one example is *Communities of Practice* (Lave and Wenger 1991, Wenger 1998, Wenger, McDermott, and Snyder 2002).

Educationally, integrative approaches are regarded as very effective. They use behavioral theories, draw on insights about how individuals— in particular adults—learn and on experiential learning theory, and a community design utilizes the social dimension of learning (Fenwick

2003, Merriam and Caffarella 1999, Illeris 2002). While this effectiveness is acknowledged, potential concerns with such missionary training need to be critically examined.

Potential Concerns

Those who decide which learning outcomes are desirable typically constitute fairly homogenous groups, churches, or organizations. Consequently, they are likely to promote emphases, theological tenets, and religious ideals and practices which reflect their particular sub-culture. Even where cross-cultural sensitivity and skills are among the defined outcomes, the character formation and spirituality which are encouraged typically reflect the constituency's theological values and social practices. The fact that these are shaped by a particular culture, context, and history tends to remain hidden to conscious reflection and therefore unacknowledged. This creates a potential for lack of cultural competence in the cross-cultural encounter where flexibility, adjustment to another cultural framework, and a new appropriation of the gospel are paramount. Missionaries thus trained can be oblivious to how significantly their theological emphases, social values and religious practices are shaped by the cultural bias of their context of origin. Missionary education then serves primarily to reinforce the cultural perspectives of a particular constituency. The sociological framework of *trained incapacity* provides a helpful tool to highlight this—typically unconscious—dynamic.

Trained Incapacity

The term *trained incapacity* was coined in sociological studies to indicate a situation in which education, training, and experience establish mental frameworks and practices so thoroughly in people that they are unable to adjust appropriately to changed circumstances. Robert Merton (1910–2003) defined *trained incapacity* in 1949 as,

...that state of affairs in which one's abilities function as inadequacies or blind spots. Actions based upon training and skills that have been successfully applied in the past may result in inappropriate responses *under changed conditions* [emphasis in original]. An inadequate flexibility in the application of skills, will, in a changing milieu, result in more or less serious maladjustments (Merton 1957:197-200).

He applies the concept to the "Dysfunctions of Bureaucracy." In order to function, bureaucracy needs discipline in highly streamlined processes that demand exactness and consistency in the application of rules and regulations. Office workers are trained to follow processes with rigidity, so much so that it can lead to *trained incapacity*, the inability to flexibly adjust to changed conditions and different circumstances. Discipline becomes so engrained that exact application of regulations becomes a goal in itself. The effect is what is experienced as "red tape" and has the potential to defeat the purposes of the organization the bureaucratic apparatus was set up to serve. Thus, *trained incapacity* describes a condition where training, education, and experience produce mental predispositions, attitudes, values, and behaviors in people in such a way that their capacities become potential impediments; they lack flexibility to adjust attitudes and actions to different contexts.

The term was coined by Thorstein Veblen (1857-1929) in 1914 to describe the proclivity of businessmen and workers to evaluate their actions solely from the perspective of financial gain. He posed that this proclivity originated in the experience and education of the business world and was particularly concerned about the negative effects on workers, organizations and society at large through powerful businessmen with such *trained incapacity* to consider wider implications of their decisions. The tendency—induced by training and experience—to measure actions only by the money that can be made leads to incapacity to see the negative social outcomes and wider repercussions of business behavior. Veblen continued to explore how the perception of success purely in pecuniary parameters leads to seeing those as successful who deceive many people into paying them more than their services and goods are worth, thereby taking advantage of society (Veblen 1914:343-350; Wais 2005).[2]

In 1935, Kenneth Burke (1897-1993) identified similarities between Veblen's concept of *trained incapacity* and John Dewey's *occupational psychosis* in his deliberations on "Permanence and Change" (Burke 1954:7-

11, 38-47; Dewey 1931). Interestingly, Dewey's notion of *occupational psychosis* was in his time a revolutionary, much more comprehensive, and positive analysis of non-Western cultures than customary, which attempted to explain cultural practices in terms of people's prevalent occupations in their environment. Burke contemplated how both concepts can help to identify mental patterns that may have become obsolete and proposed the need for changed thinking and possibly very different approaches to life during the Great Depression. He claimed that attitudes, behaviors and ways of thinking—acquired through experience and education—that served well in the past, may lead to serious maladjustments under the new and changed conditions and lead to actions which ultimately were detrimental to people's wellbeing and survival.

The Potential of Trained Incapacity in Missionary Training

The latent pitfalls of integral, community-focused missionary training become apparent when it is examined through the lens of this sociological concept. Informal learning in intentional community for character development, spiritual, and ministerial formation fosters specific theological and practical emphases. Communities that are composed of people who essentially share commonly agreed theological convictions, norms of ethical behavior, preferences of social organization, values, attitudes, and perceptions of Christian mission establish specific traditions that reflect their cultural and historical context. Such communities have the potential to foster ideas and practices that are generally regarded as best to the exclusion of concepts which come from outside. Their missionary training aims to preserve and establish the religious and socio-ethical values, emphases, and practices of a particular constituency which potentially prevents the cultural competence (flexibility to adjust and work in other cultural contexts) that should be its aim.

Effectiveness is broadly defined as the ability to achieve desired goals. However, the effectiveness of educational efforts has the inbuilt potential of undesired effects in intercultural training. Learning communities are limited by the composition of their participants. Culturally homogeneous groups create communities which—typically unconscious and unacknowledged—champion their culturally shaped beliefs and practices. This can even be the case in interdenominational and international groups when theological convictions and practical socio-ethical emphases are shared by members and supporters of an organization. That whole movements can share limitations of perspective is illustrated by John Howard Yoder's incisive analysis of how the evangelical roots of the majority of Anglo-Saxon missionaries have predisposed them "to trust binary patterns of analysis which specifically tend to relegate matters of ethical concern to secondary or derivative status" (Yoder 1983:449-450). The outcome of missionary training designed by such homogenous groups is that the educational process raises the cultural bias of a specific group to the universal standard. Graduates perfect the convictions and practices of their constituency and become inflexible in their application in different cultural contexts. They developed *trained incapacity* for intercultural engagement.

In this way education functions as the transmission of culture; the more successful the learning process, the more completely the culture is transmitted and its continuation ensured. The very educational strength of communal, integrated training models is their potential weakness. When largely homogenous groups embark on communal education processes, culturally shaped assumptions, theological perspectives and socio-ethical practices are typically reinforced and standardized which results in *trained incapacity* in the very competencies intercultural training desires to develop in people.

True contextualization remains an elusive ideal as long as ecclesiastical constituencies prioritize what in their context is regarded as biblical and theological norms. If the selection of faculty ensures basic like-mindedness in a school, if supporting constituencies push for particular Christian forms and expressions, theological and ethical emphases and positions, if students originate in similar groups within a limited spectrum of the Christian family, if faculty and staff share theological convictions and students' spiritual and character formation is aimed at specific spiritual practices and ethical behaviors, indications are for a high potential of trained incapacity for intercultural engagement.

When missionaries so trained engage interculturally, the cultural bias of their home constituency, which by training and experience has become a universal standard, creates all kinds of difficulties and frictions. Attempts to impose meet with resistance, and the by-now-generally-discredited replication model of mission persists in numerous contexts, and Christianity continues to be perceived as Western, American, or "white man's" religion. Trained incapacity thus provides an explanatory framework for the difficulties and tensions encountered by missionaries and those they engage with in cross-cultural contexts.

Discovering Trained Incapacity: The Basel Mission Historical Case Study as Illustration

My own thinking started with the desire to transform teaching for mission by improving educational theory and practice. Researching educational theories, however, I concluded that the need is not for new educational models, but for implementation of available insights and for research into the long-term effects of missionary education. This led me to investigating a historical case study of missionary preparation and engagement (Herppich 2013).

The Basel Mission, founded in 1815, began and always prioritized systematic missionary training. Its Basel Missionary Training Institute (BMTI) became the model for later institutions in Britain and sent many graduates to other missionary societies into the middle of the nineteenth century (Piggin 1984; Walls 1996).[3] The primary constituency that influenced the proceedings at the BMTI were South German Pietist groups.

Despite considerable differences in social standing, ecclesiastical background, and geographical origin, all participants of the BMTI community shared for the most part theological convictions, practical emphases of Christian life and ideas of missionary work. Education at the BMTI was designed as a tightly knit community that fostered the specific attitudes and behaviors and taught the theological positions prioritized by this constituency. They included clear authority structures in relationships, values of frugality, cleanliness, and hard work, a quietist contemplative spirituality, and a morality condemning any excesses in joyful expression and emphasizing humility in a way that bordered humiliation. These emphases reflected Pietist groups in the rural background of missionary candidates and teachers as well as the worldview of the Basel based leaders of the organization.

When the missionaries who had received this preparation engaged the African context, they found it contrary and offensive to their values and their worst ideas of the "dark continent" confirmed. Many difficulties and tensions ensued as they set about to implement their visions of missionary work by attempting to plant an environment and a church that replicated their home experience.

Basel Mission authority structures made them incapable to function as a team when oversight was removed by distance and slow communication (Herppich 2013:239-246). It also made them incapable of making important decisions, as they "hunkered down" until directions arrived from Europe. This is the context in which the sociologist of religion Jon Miller uses the term *trained incapacity* in a footnoted remark in his insightful analysis of the Basel Mission that highlights issues of class collaboration, social control, and organizational contradictions. He states that trained incapacity contributed to the lack of "quick intelligence and flexibility," initiative, and creativity demanded by the ever changing challenges of the African context (Miller 2003:123-159).

Moral evaluations and practices fostered by the BMTI preparation lead Basel missionaries to adopt a rather judgmental attitude towards everybody else and even among each other. The results were constant frictions in missionary teams, a wholesale condemnation of African traditions that precluded contextualization, evaluations of political leaders that created numerous problems, and the inability to work together with others who did not share their moral code.

Basel missionaries' trained theological convictions and particular spirituality also made them incapable of collaborating with other missionaries because of the perceived diversion from biblical truth, eccentricity, and "strange practices" of other ecclesiastical traditions (Schlatter 1916:12).[4] The resulting rivalry and denominationalism of such attitudes is among the most strongly critiqued legacies of the Western missionary movement in Africa (Avery 1980:108-109, 116; Ekechi 1972; Tasie 1978: 202-234).[5] Europeans brought Christianity as a divided religion. At the least this was and is confusing to those who hear the gospel; many find it repelling, and it prevents translation of the faith into local cultures. The issues that divide Western denominations originated in past historical contexts that are irrelevant in other regions of the globe and even have become obsolete at home as the young generations often question the old divisions.

That this is not an issue of the past is clear. In 1997 Whiteman observed that "ecclesiastical hegemony—a carryover from colonial and political domination, and a close cousin of economic domination today—is one of the major obstacles to contextualization" (Whiteman 1997). His article highlights the gap between the contextualization studies of missiologists and the practice of denominational extension prevalent around the globe. He thus confirms that the trained incapacity fostered by ecclesiastical parochialism that can be observed in the Basel Mission is still present in Christian mission.

Much more could be said. Eventually, the historical context favored the Basel missionaries' attempts to replicate their European ideals and so-called "Christian villages" were built all over Ghana. They still constitute centers of the Presbyterian Church of Ghana that developed out of their work. Basel missionaries also prioritized language learning and Bible translation. For this work and the indigenous appropriation of Christianity it eventually facilitated, the Basel Mission is held in high regard today. Nevertheless, the effect of their missionary education was a trained incapacity to act with cultural competence in many areas of their engagement.

Conclusion

The historical study of the Basel missionary education and engagement in Africa reveals how cultural biases influence missionary education in ways which are typically hidden to the persons and groups holding them. Holistic training with strong emphasis on community and experiential learning can unintentionally reinforce culturally shaped theological convictions, social conventions, and ethical practices, especially when groups engaging in missionary education are essentially homogeneous in terms of their religious and socio-ethical emphases. The influence of the background and context of missionary constituencies on the goals and designs of educational processes creates a propensity to establish inflexible theological assumptions and social ideals that are potentially detrimental to cultural competence. The concept of trained incapacity thereby provides an explanatory framework for at least some of the difficulties and tensions encountered in intercultural Christian mission.

Notes

1. Whiteman for example describes "a well-trained missionary" as one who "has confidence in the gospel he or she is proclaiming and living out," who "knows the biblical story," and "has a godly character" as well as "skills to discover the deeper causes of cultural differences," "interpersonal skills…, a sufficiently healthy self-concept", and "resilience in the face of adversity and disappointment" (Whiteman 2008).

2. Erin Wais refutes the claim that the phrase does not appear in the works of Thorstein Veblen and provides a helpful discussion of Veblen's original use of the term and Kenneth Burke's adaptation and expansion of its meaning.

3. Andrew Walls highlights the fact that German Pietist circles both provided the first missionaries for the Protestant missionary societies and developed seminaries and systems for training of missionaries. The point that British training institutes reflect the BMTI is made in Piggin's detailed analysis of approaches to training missionaries by British societies.

4. Schlatter, writing in 1915, comments on the inability of the Basel missionaries in Liberia in 1828 to join forces with Baptists and "to endure the eccentricity of the Methodists" that affected their emotional and spiritual health. Rosine Widmann, a missionary in Ghana, expressed her discomfort with "the clapping of hands and generally strange" behaviors at a Wesleyan meeting she attended in London (BMA, D-10.4,9 "Diary Rosine Widmann", 26, entry October 26, 1846).

5. African historians criticize the "fragmentation of Christianity in Africa" as a consequence of "denominational rivalries" between European missionaries, and several scholars discuss specific examples in detail, especially in Nigeria and Sierra Leone. Njoku observes that "the theological and doctrinal voices were decidedly plural, and the various missionary groups came to Africa with a strong feeling of intolerant rivalry and mutual suspicion" (Njoku

2007: 195). Ajayi further highlights the change in attitudes in the last quarter of the nineteenth century as a result of the "scramble" of European nations "to stake out claims and secure possessions in Africa" (Ajayi 1965: 8, 233-273).

Works Cited

Ajayi, J. F. Ade
    1965   *Christian Missions in Nigeria, 1841-1891: The Making of a New Elite.* Ibadan History Series. Evanston, IL: Northwestern University Press.

Avery, W. L.
    1980   "Christianity in Sierra Leone." In *History of Christianity in West Africa*, Ogbu Kalu, ed. Pp. 103-121. New York: Longman.

Balcazar, Fabricio E., Yolanda Suarez-Balcazar, and Tina Taylor-Ritzler
    2009   "Cultural Competence: Development of a Conceptual Framework." *Disability & Rehabilitation,* 31 (14): 1153-1160.

Brynjolfson, Robert, and Jonathan Lewis, eds.
    2006   *Integral Ministry Training: Design and Evaluation.* Pasadena, CA: William Carey Library.

Burke, Kenneth
    1954   *Permanence and Change. An Anatomy of Purpose.* 2nd rev. ed. Los Altos, CA: Hermes Publications.

Dewey, John
    1931   "Understanding the Savage Mind." In *Philosophy and Civilization.* Pp. 173-187. Gloucester, MA: Peter Smith. Reprint, 1968.

Dight, Clare
    2004   "Trend Watch: Cultural Intelligence." *The Times.* http://business.timesonline.co.uk/tol/business/career_and_jobs/graduate_management/article397535.ece [accessed July 6, 2011].

Earley, P. Christopher, and Soon Ang
    2003   *Cultural Intelligence: Individual Interactions across Cultures.* Stanford, CA: Stanford University Press.

Ekechi, Felix K.
    1972   *Missionary Enterprise and Rivalry in Igboland, 1857-1914.* Cass Library of African studies. No. 119. London: Cass.

Elliston, Edgar J.
    1996   "Moving Forward from Where We Are in Missiological Education." In *Missiological Education for the Twenty-First Century: The Book, the Circle, and the Sandals: Essays in Honor of Paul E Pierson,* J. Dudley Woodberry, Charles Edward Van Engen and Edgar J. Elliston, eds. Pp. 232-256. American Society of Missiology Series. Maryknoll, NY: Orbis Books.

Elmer, Duane
    2002   *Cross-Cultural Connections. Stepping Out and Fitting In Around the World.* Downers Grove, IL: InterVarsity Press.

Fenwick, Tara J.
    2003   *Learning Through Experience: Troubling Orthodoxies and Intersecting Questions.* Malabar, FL: Krieger.

Ferris, Robert W., ed.
    1995   *Establishing Ministry Training. A Manual for Programme Developers.* Pasadena, CA: William Carey Library.

Ferris, Robert W.
    2000   "Standards of Excellence in Missionary Training Centers." *Training for Cross-Cultural Ministries,* 1:1-4.

Gardner, Howard
    1993   *Frames of Mind: The Theory of Multiple Intelligences.* 10th anniversary ed., Edited by Gardner Howard. New York: BasicBooks.

Goleman, Daniel, Richard Boyatzis, and Annie McKee
    2002   *Primal Leadership: Realizing the Power of Emotional Intelligence.* Boston, MA: Harvard Business School Press.

Gudykunst, William B.
    2003   *Cross-Cultural and Intercultural Communication*. Thousand Oaks, CA: Sage Publications.

Harley, C. David
    1995   *Preparing to Serve. Training for Cross-Cultural Mission*. Pasadena, CA: William Carey Library.

Herppich, Birgit
    2013   "Trained Incapacity: A Critical Examination of Basel Missionary Preparation and Early Engagement in Ghana (1828-1840)." Fuller Theological Seminary, School of Intercultural Studies, Pasadena, CA.

Hesselgrave, David J., and Earl J. Blomberg
    1980   *Planting Churches Cross-Culturally: A Guide for Home and Foreign Missions*. Grand Rapids, MI: Baker Book House.

Howell, Brian M. , and Jenell Williams Paris
    2011   *Introducing Cultural Anthropology: A Christian Perspective*. Grand Rapids, MI: Baker Academic.

Illeris, Knud
    2002   *The Three Dimensions of Learning*. Malabar, FL: Krieger.

Jackson, Philip W.
    1968   *Life in Classrooms*. New York: Holt, Rinehart and Winston.

Kohls, L. Robert
    1987   "Four Traditional Approaches to Developing Cross-Cultural Preparedness in Adults." *International Journal of Intercultural Relations*, 11 (1): 89-106.

Kraft, Charles H.
    2005   *Christianity in Culture: A Study in Dynamic Biblical Theologizing in Crosscultural Perspective*. Rev. 25th anniversary ed. Maryknoll, NY: Orbis Books.

Lave, Jean, and Etienne Wenger
    1991   *Situated Learning: Legitimate Peripheral Participation*. Cambridge: Cambridge University Press.

Lingenfelter, Sherwood G., and Marvin Keene Mayers
2003   *Ministering Cross-Culturally: An Incarnational Model for Personal Relationships.* 2nd ed. Grand Rapids, MI: Baker Academic.

Livermore, David A.
2006   *Serving with Eyes Wide Open: Doing Short-Term Missions with Cultural Intelligence.* Grand Rapids, MI: Baker Books.

Livermore, David A.
2009   *Cultural Intelligence: Improving Your CQ to Engage Our Multicultural World.* Youth, family, and culture series, Edited by Chap Clark. Grand Rapids, MI: Baker Academic.

Livermore, David A.
2010   *Leading with Cultural Intelligence: The New Secret to Success.* New York: American Management Association.

Martin, Mercedes, and Billy Vaughn.
2007   *Strategic Diversity & Inclusion Management.* San Francisco, CA: DTUI Publications Division,. http://www.dtui.com/ [accessed July 5, 2011].

McKinney, Lois
1991   "New Directions in Missionary Education." In *Internationalizing Missionary Training: A Global Perspective,* William David Taylor, ed. Pp. 241-250. Grand Rapids, MI: Baker Book House.

Merriam, Sharan B., and Rosemary S. Caffarella
1999   *Learning in Adulthood: A Comprehensive Guide.* 2nd ed. Jossey-Bass higher and adult education series. San Francisco, CA: Jossey-Bass Publishers.

Merton, Robert King
1957 *Social Theory and Social Structure.* Rev. and enl. ed. Glencoe, IL: Free Press.

Miller, Jon
    2003   *Missionary Zeal and Institutional Control: Organizational Contradictions in the Basel Mission on the Gold Coast, 1828-1917.* Studies in the History of Christian Missions. Grand Rapids, MI: Eerdmans.

Njoku, Chukwudi A.
    2007   "The Missionary Factor in African Christianity, 1884-1914." In *African Christianity: An African Story*, Ogbu U. Kalu, ed. Pp. 191-223. Perspectives on Christianity 5. Trenton, NJ: Africa World Press.

Peterson, Brooks
    2004   *Cultural Intelligence: A Guide to Working with People from Other Cultures.* Yarmouth, ME: Intercultural Press.

Piggin, Stuart
    1984   *Making Evangelical Missionaries 1789-1858: The Social Background, Motives and Training of the British Protestant Missionaries to India.* Abingdon, Oxfordshire: Sutton Courtenay Press.

Rah, Soong-Chan
    2010   *Many Colors: Cultural Intelligence for a Changing Church.* Chicago, IL: Moody Publishers.

Samovar, Larry A., Richard E. Porter, and Edwin R. McDaniel
    2006   *Intercultural Communication: A Reader.* 11th ed. Belmont, CA: Thomson Wadsworth.

Sanneh, Lamin O.
    1989   *Translating the Message: The Missionary Impact on Culture.* American Society of Missiology Series, no.13. Maryknoll, NY: Orbis Books.

Schlatter, Wilhelm
    1916   *Geschichte der Basler Mission 1815-1915: Mit besonderer Berücksichtigung der ungedruckten Quellen 3. Band: Die Geschichte der Basler Mission in Afrika.* Vol. 3 of 5 vols. Basel: Verlag der Missionsbuchhandlung.

Stallter, Tom
2009 "Cultural Intelligence. A Model for Cross-Cultural Problem Solving." *Evangelical Missions Quarterly,* 37 (4): 543-554.

Tasie, G. O. M.
1978 *Christian Missionary Enterprise in the Niger Delta 1864-1918.* Studies on Religion in Africa. Leiden: Brill.

Taylor, William David, ed.
1991 *Internationalizing Missionary Training: A Global Perspective.* Grand Rapids, MI: Baker Book House.

Veblen, Thorstein
1914 *The Instinct of Workmanship and the State of the Industrial Arts. With an Introduction by Joseph Dorfman.* Reprints of economic classics. New York: A. M. Kelley. Reprint, 1964.

Wais, Erin
2005 "Trained Incapacity: Thorstein Veblen and Kenneth Burke." *K.B. Journal* 2 (1): http://www.kbjournal.org/node/103 [accessed February 7, 2010].

Walls, Andrew F.
1996 *The Missionary Movement in Christian History: Studies in the Transmission of Faith.* Maryknoll, NY: Orbis Books.

Walls, Andrew F.
1996 "Missionary Vocation and the Ministry. The First Generation." In *The Missionary Movement in Christian History. Studies in the Transmission of Faith,* Andrew F. Walls, ed. Pp. 160-172. Maryknoll, NY: Orbis Books.

Walls, Andrew F.
2002 *The Cross-Cultural Process in Christian History: Studies in the Transmission and Appropriation of Faith.* Maryknoll, NY: Orbis Books.

Wenger, Etienne
1998 *Communities of Practice: Learning, Meaning, and Identity.* Learning in Doing. Cambridge: Cambridge University Press.

Wenger, Etienne, Richard McDermott, and William M. Snyder
   2002   *A Guide to Managing Knowledge: Cultivating Communities of Practice*. Boston, MA: Harvard Business School Press.

Whiteman, Darrel L.
   1997   "Contextualization: The Theory, the Gap, the Challenge." *International Bulleting of Missionary Research*, 21 (1): 2-7.

Whiteman, Darrell L.
   2008   "Integral Training for Cross-Cultural Mission." *Missiology: An International Review*, 36 (1): 5-16.

Yoder, John Howard
   1983   "The Experiential Etiology of Evangelical Dualism." *Missiology: An International Review*, 11 (4): 449-459.

APM

Anthropological/ Sociological Considerations in Mission Education

Transforming Teaching for Mission

Educational Theory and Practice: Anthropological Considerations for Mission Education among different Ethnics in Myanmar

COPE SUAN PAU

DOI: 10.7252/Paper.000032

About the Author

Cope Suan Pau is Research Professor of Christian Mission Studies at All Nations Theological Seminary in Yangon, Myanmar. He also serves as Director of the Myanmar Missions Mobilization and the All Racial Mission Studies organization in Myanmar.

Abstract

To a significant extent, Christianity is expressed as a tribal religion among different ethnic groups in Myanmar today. Anthropological study of tribal peoples in Myanmar is critical for mission studies and the continued development of the Christian faith in Myanmar. Each ethnic group has its own distinct culture with varying degrees of similarity with neighboring groups. However, today most tribal peoples have no clear conceptualization of their group's anthropogenesis or their ancestral progenitor. The Union of Myanmar has eight major tribes. Among these, more than one hundred sub-ethnic groups still speak their own languages in their communities though Burmese is the official language in the country. These linguistic and cultural differences among groups further accentuate the differences which exist in Chin Christianity, Kachin Christianity, and so on. Therefore, doing mission studies with anthropological attentiveness toward different ethnic groups is needed and will help improve future Christian mission education. To promote these goals, the "All Racial Mission Studies," a study group for Myanmar Christian mission, has now been initiated for the anthropological study of tribal expressions of Christianity. It is hoped that our study will contribute to the health of the Christian church, to mission studies, and to secular research efforts as well.

Introduction

Protestant mission commemorated its bicentenary anniversary recently in Myanmar. Catholic mission will also soon commemorate its 500th anniversary. Christianity is no longer alien in the Union of Myanmar today. Western-led Christianity had to cease in 1967 when Gen. Ne Win took power and expelled all foreigners – including missionaries – out of the country. Since then, self-governing local churches have been growing among different ethnic peoples of the Union of Myanmar. Christianity continues to spread among the different tribal peoples and thus it has become, to a significant extent, a tribal religion. The expression of Christianity differs significantly from one tribe to another because of linguistic and cultural differences, which anthropological studies have identified for decades. Even among one major tribe, many sub-ethnic groups may have significant linguistic and cultural differences among themselves. Today, Myanmar Christianity as a whole may equally be thought of as differentiated ethnic Christianity. This paper argues that more attention to anthropological concerns in mission education and Christian Studies in Myanmar is needed in both religious and secular circles. This study probes some of the anthropological distinctiveness of various groups of ethnic peoples in order to begin to trace back their anthropogenesis. It examines the colonial era missionary translation efforts and the conversion of the indigenous peoples out of their primal religions so that one can easily see the differences of Christianity among the ethnic tribes of Myanmar.

I. Burman Intellectual Response to Christian Mission

Before discussing the anthropological distinctiveness of various ethnic peoples, it is important to review the Burman intellectual perspective on Christianity in the Union of Myanmar. When Adoniram Judson, the first overseas missionary from America, started his missionary efforts among the dominant tribe of Myanmar, he first encountered the dominant Burman Buddhist intellectuals. Judson categorized the Burmans into two distinct groups, "the orthodox Buddhists and the skeptical 'semi-atheists.'" By "semi-atheists," Judson meant those who no longer practice the Buddhist rituals but had a more vague notion of "Wisdom," (Maung Shwe Wa 1963: 40) Note that the Theravadins do not believe the Buddha as "a person who exists permanently," (Phra Sriyansophon 2001: 29). Impermanence (*anicca*) is a critical teaching within Theravada Buddhism.

Postcolonial perspectives of Buddhist Burman intellectuals on the work of Judson and the Protestant missionaries are important to consider here. Dr. Htin Aung, formerly Vice-Chancellor of the University of Rangoon, in his Foreword to Helen G. Trager's book, *Burma through Alien Eyes: Missionary Views of the Burmese in the Nineteenth Century*, (Trager 1966:xi) writes:

> Dr. Judson and his missionaries also felt frustrated because they found among the Burmese no religious vacuum which their religion could fill. Since the beginning of their history, the Burmese had professed Buddhism, one of the noblest faiths mankind has ever known; and the Burmese way of life itself had always been under the all-pervading influence of Buddhism.

From the perspective of an indigenous Buddhist intellectual, Judson and his colleagues, the pioneering Protestant missionaries, were frustrated in their missional failure. Dr. Htin Aung asserts, "As years passed and their endeavors among the Burmese continued to meet with failure, the missionaries were forced to seek converts in the remoter areas where Buddhism had not penetrated and where the pre-Buddhist religion of animism still prevailed (Traeger 1966: xi)."[1]

Buddhist Burman intellectuals' critique of Christian mission efforts may be summarized like this: "Your religion is good for you, ours for us. You will be rewarded for your good deeds in your way—we in our way," (1966: 75). They point out that missionaries' approach to "heathens" (due to the latter's atheistic Theravada ideology) was ineffective as a means of translating the Christian faith. Political scientists in the postcolonial era in Myanmar further stress how Westerners and/or Western Powers entered into their colonial territories via three Ms –Merchandise, Missionaries, and Militaries. It is somewhat simplistically argued that Western colonial power made its approach firstly via merchandise; then it sent its Christian missionaries; finally, its military advances caused colonialization. After that, Western powers Christianized the colonized. This has so far been the anticolonial view of Christianity in Myanmar.

The present study seeks to highlight tribal groups' agency by making a more complex argument whereby ethnic peoples through their concepts of primal religious systems assimilated the Christian faith. That has been the main reason why the hill tribe peoples of Myanmar continue to profess Christianity today.

II. Hill Peoples' Christianity: the Case of the Northern Chin Hills

I will investigate the primal beliefs of animistic religious system of the northern Chin people, and thereby provide the context in which missionaries engaged in the vernacular translation of the Christian faith. This analysis will enable scholars to have a more in-depth and nuanced interpretation of how and why people converted to Christianity. Andrew Walls asserts (Walls 2004: 71):

> In primal societies in quite diverse parts of the world, the Christian preachers found God already there, known by a vernacular name. Often associated with the sky, creator of earth and moral governor of humanity, having no altars or priesthood, and perhaps no regular worship, some named Being could be identified behind the whole constitution of the phenomenal and transcendental worlds.

When the American Protestant missionaries first reached the British Chin Hills by the end of the nineteenth century, there had already been *Pathian*, the Supreme Being in the indigenous Chin vernacular.[2] By "translating the message" of the gospel of Jesus Christ, the Chin people came to know the Christian God in the name of *Pathian*, their native animistic Supreme Being. Why did the American Protestant missionaries employ *Pathian*, the theistic name of spiritism to be identified with the Christian God in the British Chin Hills? What does *Pathian* mean in the primal belief system of the Chin/Zo people? What is *Pathian's* role and significance? Who was *Pathian* to the Chins or Zo-mi? Who are the Zo-mi? Where did they come from? What are the origins of this name for the deity? It appears that no one fully understands the meaning of *Pathian* in the Chin primal religion. No one is able to say with certainty today the origin and the genesis of *Pathian*. The northern Chin peoples who are Christian worship *Pathian*, but the origin of the term remains obscure.

Since we have little knowledge of animistic beliefs concerning *Pathian* in the Chin/Zo people today, researchers must rely on archival research and oral tradition to articulate the Zo worship and thereby to interpret their conversion to Christianity.[3] We shall trace back the origin of the Chin/Zo people and their cultural background so that we shall be able to interpret their conversion to Christianity out of their animistic religion. What was the nature of their belief in animism? How was the Gospel made intelligible to the primal religious understanding of the Chin/Zo people?

Western Christian missionaries' point of view on the conversions of the people is revealing as much as it also poses new questions. Over a hundred years ago, Anglican Bishop Arthur M. Knight noted that the hill tribes of Myanmar are easier to convert. In the preface of the book *Christian Misisons in Burma,* he asserted, "The Animist tribes are always ready to accept higher religious teachings, Buddhists, Mohammedan, or Christian. The question is, which will reach them first?" (Purser 1911: x). Does he mean that the ethnic, animistic tribes of Myanmar are keen to adopt world religions including Christianity? He quotes the Deputy Commissioner of the British colonial rule with regard to the Chin people: "You are too late to catch the Chins who are now by thousands living in the plains among the Burman." The Commissioner's suggestion to the missionaries was, "[Y]ou must go to those who remain in the hills away from the Buddhists." "He was right," the Anglican bishop agreed with the British colonial official (1911: x).

But what does the Anglican bishop mean by "He was right?" Does he mean that he "must go to those who remain in the hills away from the Buddhists" so that he might Christianize the colonized hill tribes? How did he regard the conversion of hill people at the time in colonial Burma? How shall we describe and understand the conversion of the Chins and the other hill tribes to Christianity in the British colonial era? Was it Christianization into a form of Westernized Christianity? Alternatively, was it happening in the process of religious assimilation? Lewis Rambo (Rambo 1993: 5) asserts, "Such a problem is a classic issue in missions.

Western missionaries seek to find the 'pure' convert, while the converts themselves assimilate the faith in the categories relevant to them." Could one say then that the conversions of the hill tribes in colonial Burma was a "pure" conversion, which the Western missionaries sought? Or shall we say it was the converts themselves who assimilated the faith in ways the missionaries neither anticipated nor fully understood?

In order to understand the conversion of the hill tribes of Myanmar, one must study "the four components: cultural, social, personal, and religious systems" of the hill peoples as Lewis Rambo (1993: 7) believes "to be the most crucial to an understanding of conversion." I will provide a necessarily brief exploration of these various dimensions with regard to the Chin people. The origins and the nature of their primal religious beliefs and practices must be explored in order to comprehend their forms of religious cognition and their meaning and modes of religious change from animism to Christianity.

We must begin with history. Who are the Chins? The Chins are Tibeto-Bumese speaking people who originated from the Tibetan plateau. They are believed to have migrated into the plain region of the Irrawaddy River in Myanmar before the Burman dominant tribe migrated. Generally speaking, the Chins in the Chin Hills of Myanmar are classified politically into three groups: the northern, the central, and the southern people. The Chin tribal sub ethnic peoples are called, Zo-mi, Lai-mi, and Khu-mi respectively, meaning Zo people, Lai people, and Khu people. Mizo (aka Lushai) in the Mizoram State of India, is the same tribe of Zo people who share the Ciim Nuai chronicles and genealogy.[4] Besides the hill-dwellers, there have also been other tribal Chins in the plains, namely Asho, and Yaw, meaning the Sho people and the Yaw people respectively. Vum Ko Hau, (Vum Ko Hau 1963) a native scholar, believes that all the tribes and sub-ethnic clans of the Chins are descendants of one progenitor—Zo; since the various tribal names sound closely similar in the monotone of one syllable "Zo, Yo, Yaw, Cho, Sho, etc."[5] He anthropologically sees all the sub-ethnic tribes of the Chins as "one and the same Zo (Yaw, Jo) race" under the umbrella of Zo (Hau 1963:297-312). He confidently asserts, "From time immemorial we call ourselves Zo (Jo, Yaw). This fact had been admirably recorded by Father V. Sangermano since the year 1783 when he made his headquarters at Ava A few early writers also recorded the fact that we Zo (Jo, Yaw) people inhabited areas between Assam and the Irrawaddy River," (Hau 1963b:238).

Therefore, Zo-mi or Zo people simply mean the descendants of Zo the progenitor. Thus, in any case, generally speaking, a Zo person or a Zo-mi implies any person who belongs to any sub-clan of the Zo people such as Zo, Yo, Yaw, Cho, Sho, etc. The 'northerners' genealogically believe that they are offspring of a progenitor, namely Zo who was the founder of the Zo people. Even though Zo people have many different dialects and clans, in Christianity they hold in common their name for the Supreme Being, namely *Pathian*. Who then was *Pathian*? What is the meaning of the word *Pathian*? Before Christianity came into the territories, the Zo/Chin people worshiped independently following their own form of tribal religious belief. In their animistic belief *Pathian* was the kind and gracious Supreme Being. Did they then worship *Pathian*? What was the relationship between the Zo people and *Pathian*? Vumson asserts, "Zo believe in a supreme God or *Pathian*. God [*Pathian*] is good. He gives health, richness, children and other human wishes. God [*Pathian*] is never cruel and never hurts people. Therefore Zo people never sacrifice or offer anything to appease God [*Pathian*]," (VumSon 1986: 16). However, in practice the Zo worshiped *Zinmang / Zinleng* or *Khuazing* as the supreme one in their social and religious systems. They never had any sacrificial worship ceremonies to *Pathian* in their social and religious life. For the Chins/Zo people[6] *Pathian* was not a regional supreme one, but rather a universal being in their cosmology. While they believed in *Pathian* on the one hand, they also trusted in traditional priests or shamans to worship or appease the local spirits in order that *dawi*, the evil spirits, might not be harmful to them. It will be more correct to say that Chins made bargains with the regional *dawi* to gain advantage. Vum Son rightly interprets, "Zo people fear spirits or devils who are under the rule of the king of spirits. The spirits (*dawi, huai, khuazing*) brings sickness and misery [*sic*] unless treated with due respect. Rituals have to be performed and sacrifices made so as to appease the spirits" (VumSon 1986: 16).

Given this complex picture, can one say that the animistic Chins were monotheist? How did they understand and deal with their deities? In fact, the compound word *Pathian* – the name of the Chin deity – seems to have been derived from the Chinese 天 T'ien [*Thian*] which implies heaven or heavenly deity. Chin language and the Chinese language here are pronounced the same: θ *i-an*. Etymologically speaking, the 天 T'ien [*Thian*], meaning heavenly, with the prefix *Pa* simply means father and/or masculine, the compound term *Pathian* thus implies heavenly father which has made it an apt use as the term for the Christian God.

Sing Khaw Khai suggests (Sing Khaw Khai 1995: 112, 117) that the term *Pathian* "seems to have had originated with the concept to Heaven" since the word *Pathian* originally represents "an object sacrifice" to Heaven, and *Pathian* "was never viewed as bearing demonic characteristic features although the deity was not clearly conceptualized" (Sing Khaw Khai 1995: 112, 117).

Does this mean that the Chins had adopted their traditional deities from the ancient Chinese? Alternatively, are the Chins themselves the lineage of the Chinese or the Jewish Chinese? Interestingly, the beliefs of the hill tribes of Myanmar contain biblical legends in their theistic religions of animism. When the missionaries reduced the vernacular language systems into Roman script, to their surprise they discovered that some biblical legends existed among these hill tribes of Myanmar. Some missionaries wondered if these groups were descendants of the lost tribes of the Jews. The hill tribes were still preliterate as the missionaries first reached them in the nineteenth century and early twentieth century colonial era. Since they had no written records of their history, only oral traditions have been available to be documented in recent decades.

Many animistic beliefs and practices among the hill tribes are held in common though particularities differ in many areas. Regarding the commonality of the hill tribes, Purser rightly asserts his missiological perspective in his book *Christian Missions in Burma*: "The habits, the language, and the physical appearance of these various tribes are widely dissimilar. But while they differ in almost every other particular, they are united by their religion: they are all possessed with a common reverence and fear of the spirits; they are all Animists (1911: 22)." It may be that their animistic beliefs, "with a common reverence and fear of the spirits" in their social and religious life, did in fact make the hill tribes easier to convert to Christianity in colonial Burma. The present study argues that the primal beliefs and animistic religious cognitions of the hills tribes in the spirits had been one of the most helpful basic conditions for the missionary translation of the Christian faith in colonial Burma in the early twentieth century.

III. In Search of the "Strange Names of God": Other Ethnic and Sub-ethnic Peoples

When the Protestant missionaries first arrived at the hill villages of the Chin Hills during the last year of the nineteenth century, they had three options to transliterate the divine name of the Christian God for the people of the Chins: *Pathian*, *Zinmang* and *Khuazing*. The missionaries chose *Pathian* (the Universal Supreme Being) as the most proper word for the Christian God, and their choice has turned out to be an appropriate one for the political "northerners." In other words, the Protestant missionaries "Pathianized" all the deities of the different sub-ethnic Chin peoples into one divine name of God—*Pathian*. Pathianization of Chin Christianity, however, is problematic among the other sub-ethnic groups of the Chin/Zo peoples. It seems that *Pathian* is intelligible only among the "northerners" Zo-mi and the so-called 'southerners' Lai-mi. The real southerners such as the Matu, Dai, Khumi, Asho, and so on have no indigenous connection to *Pathian*; they have their own deities with different names in their primal religious system.

I argue that the "missionary translation" of the name of the Supreme Being for these ethnic groups should be indigenized. The Christian God should correspond with the term for Supreme Being held by these regional groups so that the people might worship the Christian God in their own vernacular understanding. This is unfortunately not the case today. "Southerners" have to worship God in the name of *Pathian*, the Supreme Being of the "northerners." For example, Matu people have their own Supreme Being in the name of *Khoo* who created the universe and rules over it. The Matu Christians should worship God in the name of *Khoo* in their vernacular. However, they worship God today in the name of *Pathian* instead of *Khoo*. By employing *Khoo* as the Christian God among the Matu people, Christianity and Christian mission education might have a transformational effect for Matu theologizing – in theory as well as in practice. In fact, *Pathian* seems to be meaningless or unintelligible today among the southern Chin sub-ethnic groups. For each sub-ethnic group of the southern Chin tribes the names of their primal deities ought to be employed and semantically reconfigured as to convey that of the Christian God today so that they might worship God in a way more fully indigenized in their culture and tradition.

There are similar examples to the problem experienced by the Matu in other groups as well. The Asho, another sub-ethnic tribe of Chin people, has a belief in the existence of a Supreme Being, namely *Hli* in their primal religious system. According to Taw Sein Ko (Taw Sein Ko 1913: 8), a Burman scholar in the early colonial era, *Hli* is a goddess. Today, however, the Asho people worship God in Christianity in the name of formulated *A Pa Hli Bway*, simply meaning "Father God."[7]

In the case of the Kachin people, just like their cousins the Tibeto-Burman-speaking Chin/Zo people, the American Protestant missionaries Christianized them in the name of *Karai-Kasang* the Jingphaw vernacular Supreme Being.[8] Thus, all Kachin sub-ethnic peoples today worship *Karai-Kasang* in Christianity. Kachin peoples today profess Christianity and worship God in the common name of *Karai-Kasang*. In fact, all the sub-ethnic groups of the Kachin peoples surely would have had a belief in the existence of a Supreme Being whom they would rather pronounce in the almost common *Hpan Ningsang - Chye Ningchyang*. *Hpan Ningsang* means "the Almighty One who creates" and *Chye Ningchyang* means "the Almighty One who knows." A Kachin would pray uttering "*Hpan Ningsang – Chye Ningchyang*" especially when he encounters danger and difficulty.

Just as their cousins the Chins did not worship *Pathian* in their primal religious system, the Kachins did not worship *Karai-Kasang*. Rather, they would appease the other evil spirits simply because of fear. Gilhodes (1995: 94-95) advocates for *Karai-Kasang* regarding him as "a good being" in the primal religious system of the Kachins. Eventually, the Kachins worship *Karai-Kasang* in Christianity. Today, a Christian Kachin, in whatever sub-ethnic group, will surely say in his prayer, "*Wa Karai-Kasang e!*" saying, "Oh, Father God!" Alternatively, one may also utter, "*Phan Wa Ningsang e!*" Or, "*Chye Wa Ningchyang!*" Here *Wa* means father: the missionaries seemed to introduce the Christian God as the heavenly father *Wa* to the Kachin peoples. Note that, like the Chins, almost a hundred percent of the Kachins today profess Christianity in the name of *Karai-Kasang* the primal deity. Here we would argue that the Protestant missionaries' transliteration of the name of God among the hill tribes is appropriate. One obviously sees that Christianity has been expanding in the different vernacular names of God.[9]

With regard to the study of religious conversion and in search of the Supreme Being among the Karens, Rev. Harry Ignatiuis Marshall's book *The Karen People of Burma: A Study in Anthropology and Ethnology* (Marshall 1922: 211), is the best. When the American Protestant missionaries reached the Karen jungle dwellers, they found three distinct spiritual concepts of religion, namely, 1) *Pgho* referred to magical power or force; 2) *Hpi Bi Yaw* referred to an animistic goddess; 3) *Y'wa* referred to the Creator. Marshall explained, "Among the Karen we find traces of three distinct religious conceptions, which have left their impress upon the people," (211). Accordingly, Marshall explains the Karen believe that the deities have *pgho* the power or force to perform wonderful things. A person who performs a magical works is called "*pgha a pgho*" meaning a man of power—*pgho*. In their primal animistic beliefs of their religious system, the Karens had numerable spirits with various powers including the goddess *Hpi Bi Yaw*. The Karens, like the Chins and Kachins, would appease the spirits "by continual offerings, sacrifices, and tabus" as Marshall says. With regard to the animistic religious thought of the Karens, Marshall asserts, "To keep on good terms with these numerable spirits consumes a large part of the time and thought of the Karen" (1922: 211). The third and most vital conception of the Karen primal religious system is the belief of the existence of a Supreme Being, namely, *Y'wa* in the Karen vernacular. Today, a Christian Karen would pray to God saying, "Maw Y'wa" meaning "Father God" in its English translation.

Conclusion

Today one sees that Christianity has become a tribal religion in the Union of Myanmar. It is critical to recognize the different expressions of the Christian faith in the many different ethnic groups in Myanmar: Chin Christianity, Kachin Christianity, Karen Christianity, etc. This paper has illustrated that even among these ethnicities, there are sub-ethnics and sub-clans which differ from one another linguistically and culturally and that these differences must be well-understood in order for Christian mission and the Gospel to be more faithfully appropriated by various groups. For example, Chin Christianity should be differentiated as Zo-mi Christianity, Lai-mi Christianity, Cho Christianity, etc.

This paper claims that greater attention to anthropological research in Christian mission studies will make mission education and Christian Studies more vital both in terms of religious practice and in the secular understanding of people in Myanmar. By doing so, Christianity and/or Christian mission studies will surely grow as an exciting subject in Myanmar and Southeast Asia. Deeper anthropological insight will also further strengthen future Christian mission in theory and in practice.

Notes

1.   Dr. Htin Aung was formerly Vice-Chancellor of the University of Yangon, and Chairman of Burma Historical Commission. He had been to Columbia University in New York in 1964.

2.   The Chin Hills became well known in 1896 when the British decreed the "Chin Hills Regulations". For details of the regulations, see Khup Za Go, *Zo Chronicle: A Documentary Study of History and Culture of the Kuki-Chin-Lushei Tribe* (New Delhi: Mittal Publications, First Published 2008: 61-71). Zo people, who call themselves Zo-mi, *mi* meaning man or people, have been known as Chin people. The present study shall use the term Zo people, Zo-mi, and Chin /Chin people interchangeably. For a more detailed study of the Chin people, see Vum Ko Hau, "History of the Zo Mi (Chin) Race" in *Profile of a Burma Frontier Man* (Bandung, Indonesia: Self-published 1963: 297-312); and Vum Son, *Zo History: With an Introduction to Zo Culture, Economy, Religion and Their Status as an Ethnic Minority in India, Burma, and Bangladesh* (Aizawl, Mizoram: Self-published, 1986).

3.   We are especially thankful and indebted to Robert G. Johnson who distinctively accomplished a complete Christian mission history of the Zo people; and to Chester U. Strait whose research has been in both Master of Theology and Doctor of Theology studies of the Chin animistic religion. We also would like to thank and credit some Zo-mi native scholars particularly to Vum Son, Vum Ko Hau and Sing Khaw Khai, whose scholarly contributions provide us with valuable studies concerning the origin and culture of the Zo people.

4.   *Ciim Nuai* is reported as the first migration location for the Zo-mi the "northerners" from the Kale-Kabaw valley. The time line is estimated about C.E. 1500 that the Zo people moved away from the Kale-Kabaw valley to the hilly regions of the Chin Hills. A group of them who call themselves Zo-mi first settled at the valley named "*Ciim Nuai*," meaning "underneath the *Ciim* plants," in the northern region of the present Chin State in Myanmar.

5.   Vum Ko Hau is a scholar of the Chin/Zo people: he received his PhD in Anthropology from Charles University, Prague whilst he served as the Ambassador of the Union of Myanmar to Hungary, Czechoslovakia, and Austria. He was well-known as a frontier leader in unifying the union together with Aung San.

6.   The present study employs the term "Chin" and "Zo people" interchangeably.

7.   Via correspondence with Salai Htun Hlaing, an Asho elder, ex. Head of State and Division level Education Department, he asserts that there had been the belief in the existence of a Supreme Being in Asho primal religion. According to him, the deity name "*Hli*" is used as the Christian God, and thus "*A Pa Hli Bway*" meaning Father God, is applied today not only in the Holy Bible, but also is everyday use in the Asho dialect as well.

8.   Kachin peoples are also called Jingphaw in the tribal name of the majority. There are at least six more sub-ethnic groups among the Kachins, namely, Jingphaw, Maru (Lawngvaw), Atzi, Lashi (La chid), Hkahku, and Rawang.

9.   There also are other minority ethnic groups among the hill tribes of Myanmar who profess Christianity: for instance, the Lisu, Lahu, Akha, Pa-O, Wa, etc., who have their own vernacular names of God. The present study has been challenged to investigate also the other tribal peoples' anthropogenesis and their religious conversions to the Christian faith.

Works Cited:

Gilhodes, C.
    1995   *The Kachins: Religion and Customs*. New Delhi: Mittal
            Publication.

Khup, Za Go.
    2008   *Zo Chronicle: A Documentary Study of History and Culture
            of the Kuki-Chin-Lushei Tribe*. New Delhi: Mittal
            Publications.

Marshall, Harry Ignatius
    1922   *The Karen People of Burma: A Study in Anthropology and
            Ethnology*. Columbus, OH: Ohio State University Press.

Maung Shwe Wa
    1963   *Burma Baptist Chronicle*. Rangoon: Burma Baptist
            Convention, Board of Publication.

Phra Sriyansophon, Bhikkhu Sugandha, and Paul Dennison ed.
    2001   *Phra Buddha Dhammacakra*. Bangkok: Phra Buddha
            Dhammacakra Creation Committee.

Purser, W. C. B.
    1911   *Christian Missions in Burma*. 2nd ed. Westminster: Society
            for the Propagation of the Gospel in Foreign Parts.

Rambo, Lewis R.
    1993   *Understanding Religious Conversion*. New Haven: Yale
            University Press.

Sing Khaw Khai
    1995   *Zo People and Their Culture, A Historical, Cultural Study and
            Critical Analysis of Zo and Its Ethnic Tribes*. New Lamka,
            Manipur: Khampu Hatzaw.

Taw Sein Ko
    1913   *Burmese Sketches*. Rangoon: British Burma Press.

Trager, Helen G.

  1966   *Burma through Alien Eyes: Missionary Views of the Burmese in the Nineteenth Century.* Bombay: Asia Publishing House.

Vum Ko Hau

  1963   "History of the Zo Mi (Chin) Race" in *Profile of A Burma Frontier Man.* Bandung, Indonesia: Self-published.

  1963b "The First Printed Burmese Book," in *Profile of A Burma Frontier Man.* Bandung, Indonesia: Self-published.

VumSon

  1986   *Zo History: With an Introduction to Zo Culture, Economy, Religion and Their Status as an Ethnic Minority in India, Burma, and Bangladesh.* Aizawl, Mizoram: Self-published.

Walls, Andrew F.

  2004   *The Missionary Movement In Christian History: Studies in the Transmission of Faith.* Maryknoll, New York: Orbis Books.

Preparing Melanesians for Missions

DOUG HANSON

DOI: 10.7252/Paper.000029

About the Author

Doug Hanson is a missionary to Papua New Guinea, teaching missions, Bible and theology at the Christian Leaders' Training College. He earned a DMiss from Western Seminary in Oregon.

Introduction

Melanesia is the area of the South Pacific that is northeast of Australia and includes the countries of Papua New Guinea, Solomon Islands, New Caledonia, Vanuatu, and Fiji.[1] Christianity came to Melanesia recently in world history, arriving on the shores in the nineteenth century and penetrating into the interiors in the twentieth century. Christianity has grown tremendously since its introduction in Melanesia, to the point that countries in Melanesia are referred to as "Christian nations." There are few Western missionaries still working in Melanesia, most having left to concentrate their efforts in "non-Christian nations." The churches in Melanesia are now starting to send out their own missionaries to play their part in global missions. That brings us to the focus of this paper, preparing Melanesians for missions. There are two goals for this paper. The first goal is to evaluate the strengths and weaknesses of Melanesians as missionaries in light of their cultural background. Based on that evaluation, the second goal is to determine how best to prepare Melanesians for missions based on these – admittedly generalized – strengths and weaknesses.

Before we begin, a bit of background information is needed. I am an American missionary serving with the mission agency Pioneers and teaching in Papua New Guinea at a Bible college called the Christian Leaders' Training College. I have been at the Bible college for thirteen years (discounting study leaves), and I teach a variety of Bible, theology, and missions courses. The college is an accredited educational institution which offers undergraduate and graduate degrees. We are seeking to increase our missions training to help churches in Melanesia fulfill the Great Commission, which makes the opportunity to write and present this paper both timely and relevant to the work of my college.

Melanesia is a kinship culture where tribal allegiance is paramount. Despite the prevalence of Christianity in Melanesia, there is still an undercurrent of animism. From an economic standpoint, many Melanesians live in villages and rely on subsistence farming.[2] Within this cultural context of tribalism, animism, and subsistence agriculture, the Christian Leaders' Training College seeks to provide education pertinent to the background and needs of the students.

Before we continue, a caveat is in order. In this paper I use the singular phrase "Melanesian culture" for the sake of simplicity. This is not to deny that cultural variations exist within Melanesia. This is perhaps most strongly exhibited in cultural distinctions between people from the coast and those from the highlands of Papua New Guinea. Despite these variations, there are many cultural commonalities across Melanesia which permit me to speak of the culture as somewhat of a whole. Still, generalizations which I make in this paper may surely be contested by some readers, and I welcome further dialogue in this regard.

Melanesians as Missionaries

A few graduates of the Christian Leaders' Training College serve with the mission organization SIM Australia. As part of my research for this paper, I asked David Hammer, Pacific Region Ministry Director for SIM Australia, three questions: What are Melanesians' strengths for mission work? What are Melanesians' weaknesses for mission work? What definitely should be included in training Melanesians for missions? He queried his co-workers at SIM Australia and then formed a response based on SIM's collective experience in sending out Melanesians as missionaries.[3]

Strengths to Applaud

Melanesians bring a number of strengths to the mission field. They value prayer and spend a great deal of time communicating with God. Rather than being individualistic and standoffish, they are more collectivistic and relationally-oriented than persons in the west. Melanesians are also conscious of the spirit world, realizing its potential significance. Melanesians are also generally adaptable, tough, and easy-going, able to live frugally and exhibit patience in adverse circumstances. Finally, they have a deep concern for the lost; they want to reach the unreached for Christ.

Challenges to Overcome

The challenges facing Melanesians on the mission field in addition to the strengths just named – which could surely be elaborated upon – should be the key drivers for designing a missionary training program.

Communication. Melanesians prefer personal verbal communication to non-personal written communication. They also prefer to communicate indirectly and frequently talk around an issue while at the same time talking about the issue. Since English is a second or third language for most Melanesians, they can struggle with English, especially in writing and reading.

Technology. The modern missionary movement is highly technical and missionaries are required to have skills in this area. However, most Melanesians lack sufficient word processing, spreadsheet, and internet skills that are necessary for missions today. Compounding this fact is the challenge they face in communicating with their supporters in Melanesia. Supporters who live in rural environments normally do not have access to technology. Technology also plays a role today in the transference of money. A lack of on-line banking expertise affects both missionaries and their supporters.

Allegiance. Melanesians come from a tribal background where tribal loyalty is paramount. This emphasis can carry over to devotion to their denominations and can become a new sort of tribalism which limits collaborative mission efforts across denominations. This emphasis on allegiance can also influence relationships among Melanesian missionaries – especially those relationships comprised of people from different tribes and geographical locations, most notably between those from the coastal areas and those from the highlands in Papua New Guinea.

Cultural Personality. Melanesians are not as concerned about clock time as Westerners. This can result in such things as neglected e-mails or text messages. Moreover, if Melanesians feel offended by the communication, they will not answer e-mails. Melanesians focus on events rather than the clock, which influences the process of giving financial support in Melanesia. The concept of regular support is not practiced, with churches preferring to give one big offering in lieu of regular monthly giving. Church financial support often is inadequate. Additionally, Melanesians tend to be compliant and reactive in hierarchical structures, rather than proactive.

Exposure. Most Melanesians have not traveled outside of their own countries, which limits their exposure to other religions, worldviews, and cultures. People who live in towns and cities may have access to television, which would be their primary "window" to the world. Some of the population also has access to daily newspapers which offers further exposure. Related to exposure, in a sense, is education. Primary and secondary formal education standards may not be on par with educational systems of the West. Melanesians, therefore, may not be as formally prepared educationally for missions as needed. One way this is particularly evident is in the lack of qualifications for entry into some countries; frequently persons have few verifiable professional skills to gain an entry visa.

Requirements. With this in mind, SIM Australia is working towards a standard of requirements for those coming from Melanesia as missionaries. Future requirements will include the following:

1. Proven English proficiency – verbal and written;
2. Good communication skills;
3. Minimum Information Technology skills – email, Word, Excel;
4. Proven cross-cultural adjustments;
5. Ability to fight spiritual warfare, but avoid over-emphasizing or under-emphasizing this reality;
6. Healthy – psychologically and medically (need culturally appropriate psychological assessment and medical, dental and optical assessments);
7. Interdenominational in doctrine and practice.

For the time being, SIM Australia has arranged with a Bible college in Australia for candidates to attend a TESOL course and to do their practical work there. The Bible college will also make sure that their English skills are good and that their computer skills are further developed. This would prove unnecessary if Melanesians with more exposure to formal education applied for service.

Preparing Melanesians for Missions

We can learn several things about Melanesian culture – and preparing Melanesians for missions – from the above discussion. Framing our discussion within cultural-descriptive terms such as high vs. low context, polychronic vs. monochromic, collectivism vs. individualism, and high vs. low power distance will shed light on the challenges Melanesians face as missionaries.

Recently, I heard of specific challenges that Melanesian missionaries face when serving on multi-cultural teams on the mission field. The following discussion often relates to preparing Melanesians to operate effectively within a multi-cultural team environment, a field practice increasingly followed by mission organizations today.

High-Context Culture

In SIM discussions of challenges to overcome, we saw that Melanesians favour personal, verbal, and indirect communication. This places them firmly within the high-context communication category.[4] According to Edward T. Hall, "A high-context (HC) communication or message is one in which most of the information is either in the physical context or internalized in the person, while very little is in the coded, explicit, transmitted part of the message" (1989: 91). Knowing this is significant in several ways.

High-Context Based Training. Effective training for missions for Melanesians would be one that uses high-context communication. This suggests verbal- and activity-based training utilizing case studies that involve role-playing. Kenneth Cushner mentions a distinction that some scholars make between "field-independent" and "field-dependent" learners, with the former characterized by "parts-specific," linear, factual learning and the latter by "big picture," relational, personally-relevant learning (1994:121). I would classify Melanesians as field-dependent learners, reinforcing the need for high-context based training.

Furthermore, Jon Paschke emphasizes the importance of training Melanesians in small groups. He refers to seminal research by Earle and Dorothy Bowen on learning style preferences among African students. "The Bowens have noted that East and West African students typically demonstrate 'field-sensitive' characteristics, remarkably similar to observations of students from other non-western countries in Asia, Africa, Latin America, and Oceania" (2004: 60). Paschke notes nine such "field characteristics," including the realities that Melanesians relate well interpersonally, enjoy being with people, and value social acceptance over autonomy (2004: 61).

Communication / English Training. Prospective Melanesian missionaries need training in communicating with low-context co-workers and within low-context organizations. In mission agencies that are multi-culturally team-oriented, Melanesian missionaries may often team with missionaries from low-context cultures on the mission field. This suggests specific training on communication principles, but training that builds upon the high vs. low context communication model.[5]

It is also necessary for Melanesians to acquire solid English skills in order to operate within the global environment that exists today. Whether it is travelling internationally, or communicating within a multi-cultural mission organization, English is often the language of choice.[6] On a related note, one of the challenges facing Melanesian missionaries is the lack of skills needed to obtain visas in many countries. This is due in part to limited access to professional training in the countries of Melanesia. One common solution for obtaining visas is entering a country as an English teacher. The Christian Leaders' Training College could offer TESOL training towards an internationally recognized certificate. Securing qualified TESOL teachers to provide the training remains the biggest obstacle.

Technology Training. Most mission organizations are driven by technology for communication and are consequently low-context operations. Technology training is therefore imperative since Melanesian missionaries must operate competently within mission agencies in today's technology-driven environment. They need to understand the nuances of doing low-context communication despite coming from a high-context culture. Necessary technology training includes word processing, spreadsheet, e-mail, and internet. One should not overlook specific training on e-mail and social networking etiquette either.

Polychronic Culture

SIM also noted that Melanesians are relational and event oriented rather than activity and clock-oriented.[7] This falls squarely within Hall's definition of polychronic: "High-context people also tend to be polychronic; that is, they are apt to be involved in a lot of different activities with several different people at any given time" (1989: 150). "Furthermore," Hall states, "polychronic cultures often place completion of the job in a special category much below the importance of being nice, courteous, considerate, kind, and sociable to other human beings" (1989: 150). There are several implications of this for training Melanesians for missions.

Cultural Training. When serving cross-culturally it is imperative that missionaries understand the cultural blinders they wear. This is no less true for Melanesians serving in cultures which differ from their own. "Without culture-sensitive *knowledge,*" according to Stella Ting-Toomey and John G. Oetzel, "disputants cannot learn to uncover the implicit ethnocentric lenses they use to evaluate behaviors in an intercultural conflict situation" (2001: 174, italics in the original). There are at least two coordinate ways to provide culture training. Providing formal cultural anthropology training exposes students to characteristics of differing cultures. The second option is to expose students to cross-cultural internships during their training. In our own efforts in this regard we are considering having students do their cross-cultural internship in eastern Indonesia, primarily for economic reasons. Such an internship would give them the opportunity to learn more about Islam and, at the same time, expose them to an Asian culture other than their own.

Interpersonal Relationship Training. It is important for prospective missionaries to understand themselves. This is often accomplished through psychological testing, which, unfortunately, is often designed by and geared for populations in the West. In spite of the cultural bias in many of these tools, learning to decipher and relate to others based on their psychological and cultural make-up is imperative to the successful operation of a multi-cultural team.[8] Training that increases Melanesians' self-awareness and awareness of others "plants seeds" which will hopefully bear fruit through more healthy relationships throughout the missionaries' ministries.[9]

Leadership Training. It is important for Melanesias to better understand various leadership models as they relate to persons from diverse cultures. A polychronic leader views success as maintaining human relationships. A monochronic leader, by contrast, views success as the accomplishment of tasks. This can create team tension on the mission field if leadership goals are misunderstood. The concept of "power distance" has been a useful interpretive framework in this regard. James E. Plueddemann explains:

> Some cultures assume a large status gap between those who have power and those who don't. In these cultures, both leaders and followers assume that the power gap is natural and good. These societies are called *high-power-distance* cultures. Other cultures value lesser power distance and seek to minimize status symbols and inequalities between people. These are called *low-power-distance* cultures. All cultures fit along a power-distance continuum (2009:93).

The Melanesian culture falls in the middle spectrum of the power distance continuum, a mid-power distance culture (Kavanamur and Esonu 2011:115). The two Melanesian leadership practices of big-men and chiefs favour a high-power distance classification, while the collective Melanesian culture (as discussed below) favours a low-power distance culture.

Remember also that one of the challenges to overcome was the Melanesian tendency to be compliant and reactive in hierarchical structures. Such a challenge can be mitigated by understanding leadership structures and their relationship to culture. In many ways then, training in leadership – from both time and power perspectives – would minimize potential problems on the mission field.

Collectivist Culture

Melanesians are quite community and relationally oriented rather than being individualistic and standoffish. This characteristic lends itself to relational evangelism, especially when combined with Melanesians' deep concern for the lost. Negatively, the high value Melanesians place on allegiance can be detrimental when working on teams. Therefore, Melanesians' relational focus is both a benefit and a challenge, which should not surprise us if we understand the comparison of individualist vs. collectivist cultures. David A. Livermore describes a collectivist culture, which typifies Melanesian culture,

> In these places, people view themselves less autonomously and more as members of groups. They're concerned about the effects of actions upon the group as a whole, and decisions are made by consensus rather than individualistically. This isn't to say people living in collectivist cultures are purely unselfish. Rather they're programmed to think about the goals and needs of the groups of which they're a part rather than to consider their own individual needs first (2006:122).

One of the challenges noted earlier was that if Melanesians feel offended by an e-mail communication, they would not answer e-mails. Because Melanesian culture is a collectivist culture, this should not surprise us. Collectivist cultures are built around human relations; therefore, when relationships are broken people are "much more vulnerable to anger" (Hall, 1989:150). This example and others presented earlier, show that the ramifications of training for missions within a collectivist culture are significant. For example, Neal R. Goodman notes "societies that are strong on Collectivism," prefer group work when given assignments (1994:138).

Teamwork Training. Understanding group dynamics is foundational to teamwork (Ting-Toomey and Oetzal 2001:132-135). Appreciating individual personalities, cultural backgrounds, the purpose of the team, and individual roles in the team are all vital to making a team successful (Hooker 2008:4-6). The training should include formal study of group dynamics, combined with mimicking real life cross-cultural situations through case studies and role-playing. Intercultural conflict often begins with different cultural expectations (Ting-Toomey and Oetzal 2001:1). The case studies should include high context and low context, polychronic and monochronic, and collectivist and individualist players. In addition, training in truths such the unity of the body of Christ, including reconciliation among members, is vital (Lundy 1999:152).

Spiritual Warfare Training. In addition to things that are visible in this world, an important part of the collectivist culture in Melanesia includes things that cannot be seen. Relating appropriately to both visible and non-visible entities is significant in Melanesian traditional beliefs. A Melanesian Christian needs to be prepared to deal with the spirit world, both from a theological and practical perspective. Comprehensive training in world religions must include both formal doctrine of the world religions and associated folk religion practices, since folk religions often emphasize the spirit world.

Conclusion

The training recommendations above grew directly out of the challenges that Melanesians face on the mission field. In addition to the areas discussed in this paper one ought not overlook other standard training relevant to missions such as theology of mission, history of mission, and other areas. However, the purpose of this paper was to highlight the training needs that are specific to Melanesians, training that should not be overlooked before Melanesians go to the field. We classified Melanesian culture as high-context, polychronic, mid-power distance, and collectivist, finding that Melanesians have cultural strengths to applaud and cultural challenges to overcome on the mission field.

One of the emphases in this paper was training Melanesians to work in multi-cultural teams on the mission field. With that emphasis in mind, it should not surprise us that much of the proposed training involved practical life-skills, including communication, English, interpersonal relationships, teamwork, and leadership. The remaining proposed training – cultural, TESOL, and spiritual warfare – are less surprising since we might find them in missions training programs in the West. Most surprising to me, though, was the importance of technology training. As a missionary from the West who has been the recipient of formal educational systems that prize such training, it is second nature to use technology. Training Melanesians, however, requires attention to such topics which may not be as necessary in the West.

Historically, the mission education we have offered to our students at the Christian Leaders' Training College has focused on the importance of "going" to the mission field. We have sought to convince students and churches in Melanesia that they needed to play an increasingly prominent role in worldwide missions. However, based on the above feedback from SIM Australia, we now need to focus on the "doing" of the mission field. Our training needs to include practical skills necessary for working on multi-cultural teams which operate within the influences of globalization. In conclusion, let each of us be wise in our mission education efforts, no matter what culture we come from, or in what culture we teach!

Notes

1.   Irian Jaya, although part of the nation of Indonesia, is also considered part of Melanesia. Irian Jaya occupies the western half of the island of New Guinea, while the nation of Papua New Guinea occupies the eastern half.

2.   One estimate is that 87% of the population of Papua New Guinea lives in rural areas. See David Kavanamur and Bernard Esonu (2011), "Culture and Strategic Alliance Management in Papua New Guinea," *International Public Management Review*, 12(2): 116. <www.ipmr.net>.

3.   In addition to the insightful information provided by David Hammer of SIM Australia, I also appreciated comments on drafts of this paper by Tema Manko, Director of PNG World Mission (an indigenous missions agency), George Mombi of the Christian Leaders' Training College, and Patrick Hall, also of the Christian Leaders' Training College.

4.   Low-context communication, generally speaking, occurs in nations that have European roots, including Australia, Canada, New Zealand, the United States, and much of Europe. High-context communication is often prevalent in the rest of the world. See John N. Hooker (2008), "Cultural Differences in Business Communication," Carnegie Mellon University, Tepper School of Business, Paper 152:2. <http://repository/cmu.edu/tepper/152>.

5.   The operative phrase "global fluency" captures the importance of being able to communicate across contexts. See "Selected Cross-Cultural Factors in Human Resource Management," *The Society for Human Resource Management Quarterly Journal* (Third Quarter, 2008): 3.

6.   Lundy, however, challenges mission agencies to progress in their internationalization by "compensating for English having to be the lingua franca of the mission." J. David Lundy, "Moving Beyond Internationalizing the Mission Force," *International Journal of Frontier Missions* 16:3 (Fall 1999): 148.

7.   Sarah H. Lanier uses the more popular terms "hot" and "cold" climate cultures to represent relationship-based and task-oriented cultures respectively. See (2012) *Foreign to Familiar* Rev. ed., Hagerstown, Maryland: McDougal Publishing, pg. 15-16.

8.   Lundy observes, "Studies in cross-cultural psychology supports the thesis that there are fewer universal commonalities in human thought processes than most people think." J. David Lundy, "Moving Beyond Internationalizing the Mission Force," *International Journal of Frontier Missions* 16:3 (Fall 1999): 150.

9.   Stella Ting-Toomey and John G. Oetzel offer seven intercultural conflict assumptions, which lay a ground work for deciphering and addressing conflicts in cross-cultural situations. They rightly stress that intercultural conflict is situation-dependent and responding appropriately requires "system thinking," which includes considering "perceptions, thinking patterns, emotions, behaviors, meanings, and embedded contexts." See (2001) *Managing Intercultural Conflict Effectively.* (London: Sage Publications, pg. 23-24.

Works Cited

Bertuzzi, Federico A.
    2005   "Internationalization or 'Anglonization' of Missions." *International Journal of Frontier Missions,* 22:1 (Spring): 13-16.

Brislin, Richard W.
    1994   "Individualism and Collectivism as the Source of Many Specific Cultural Differences." *Improving Intercultural Interactions,* edited by Richard W. Brislin and Tomoko Yoshida. London: Sage Publications. pp. 71-88.

Cushner, Kenneth
    1994   "Preparing Teachers for an Intercultural Context." *Improving Intercultural Interactions.* edited by Richard W. Brislin and Tomoko Yoshida. London: Sage Publications. pp. 109-128.

Goodman, Neal R.
    1994   "Intercultural Education at the University Level: Teacher-Student Interaction." *Improving Intercultural Interactions,* edited by Richard W. Brislin and Tomoko Yoshida. London: Sage Publications. pp. 1994, 129-147.

Hall, Edward T.
    1989   *Beyond Culture.* New York: Anchor Books.

Hooker, John N.
    2008   "Cultural Differences in Business Communication." Carnegie Mellon University, Tepper School of Business, Paper 152. http://repository.cmu.edu/tepper/152/. Accessed on 18 September 2014.

Kavanamur, David and Bernard Esonu
  2011   "Culture and Strategic Alliance Management in Papua New Guinea," *International Public Management Review*, 12(2). http://www1.imp.unisg.ch/org/idt/ ipmr.nsf/ac4c1079924cf935c1256c76004ba1a6/ 5436c88f62e78afec125794f00363591/$FILE/ Kavanamur%20&%20Esonu_IPMR_Volume%2012 _Issue%202.pdf. Accessed on 18 September 2014.

Lanier, Sarah A.
  2010   *Foreign to Familiar*. Revised Edition. Hagerstown, Maryland: McDougal Publishing.

Livermore, David A.
  2006   *Serving with Eyes Wide Open: Doing Short-term Missions with Cultural Intelligence*. Grand Rapids: Baker Books.

Lundy, J. David
  1999   "Moving Beyond Internationalizing the Mission Force." *International Journal of Frontier Missions*, 16 (3) (Fall): 147-155.

Paschke, Jon
  2004   "The Small Group as a Learning Environment for Teaching Melanesian Christians: Issues for the Cross-Cultural Facilitator." *Melanesian Journal of Theology*, 20 (2): 54-78.

Plueddemann, James E.
  2009   *Leading Across Cultures: Effective Ministry and Mission in the Global Church*. Downers Grove: InterVarsity Press.

  2008   "Selected Cross-Cultural Factors in Human Resource Management." 2008 *The Society for Human Resource Management Quarterly Journal*, (Third Quarter): 1-9.

Singelis, Ted
  1994   "Nonverbal Communication in Intercultural Interactions." *Improving Intercultural Interactions*. Ed. Richard W. Brislin and Tomoko Yoshida. London: Sage Publications. pp. 268-294.

Ting-Toomey, Stella and John G. Oetzal
    2001   *Managing Intercultural Conflict Effectively*. London: Sage Publications.

APM

Mission Education Outside the Classroom

Nurturing Missionary Learning Communities

RICHARD AND EVELYN HIBBERT

DOI: 10.7252/Paper.000028

About the Authors

Richard and Evelyn served as missionaries for 20 years among Turkish-speaking people in Bulgaria and West Asia, and later as international trainers and strategy advisors. Richard is currently the Director of the School of Cross-Cultural Mission at Sydney Missionary and Bible College, and Evelyn is a Senior Lecturer in Education at the University of Western Sydney. They are both involved in ministry in Western Sydney.

Introduction: The Need for On-the-Job Missionary Training

Many missionaries struggle as they transition from their initial years of language learning and cultural acquisition to engaging in ministry. There is often no clear road map for how to go about their ministry in a new cultural context, especially when they are working among unreached peoples in the pioneering tasks of evangelism, discipling, and planting churches. Along with many of our co-workers in the Middle East, we found that the primary task of learning the local language and culture during the first two years on the field was clearly mapped out for us, but that once we launched into our work of cross-cultural church planting, we had very little idea how to proceed. We wrestled with questions such as "How do we form a church planting team?" "How should we present the Gospel?" "How widely should we share the gospel?" "How should we respond to local cultural practices?" "How should we disciple those who come to faith in Christ?" "How and when should gatherings start?" It was rare to find a team member who had been introduced to these questions in Bible college or seminary classes, and when we began to wrestle with these issues on a day-to-day basis, we had very little input from experts to guide us or to help us reflect on our practice.

This kind of struggle is not limited to us or to the Middle East. For the past 12 years we have been visiting and interacting with missionaries from several mission agencies, listening to the issues they face and giving some training input to them. We have discovered that most of these missionaries have had very little current missiological input to help them develop their ministry or reflect on their task. Those that have received some missiological training before coming to the field have thought through some basic issues of communicating across cultures, learning a new language, and surviving in a new culture which has prepared them relatively well for the first two to three years on the field, but it has not usually equipped them for the work of cross-cultural evangelism, discipling, church planting, or training local leaders.

A survey of active missionaries from WEC International working among unreached people groups in Africa, Asia, Latin America, and Europe (Hibbert and Hibbert 2002) asked them to indicate, from a list of ten possibilities, the three that they believed were the greatest hindrances to their reaching the unreached with the gospel in their area. After "resistance of the people group," (included by 68% of the 63 respondents among their top three hindrances), "lack of experience or training" was the most frequently noted hindrance (indicated by 59% of respondents). Respondents who were members of church planting teams (56 of the 63) reported that "lack of training in evangelism and church planting" was the second most significant hindrance to their work.

Although larger mission agencies usually offer some on-the-job training to their missionaries, this training tends to focus on helping team leaders and field leaders with their leadership task. Occasional workshops on church planting or specific approaches such as Bible storytelling are becoming more widespread, but many missionaries still receive little intentional on-the-job training input from their organizations. As a result, too few field workers are being helped to make sense of what they are doing with the help of missiological tools. A few missionaries engage in further formal missiological study through universities, but many of these move on from active missionary service soon after finishing this formal study.

The work of missionaries could be further enhanced by appropriate on-the-job learning and training. Pre-field training is at best preparatory; much more must be learnt by missionaries after they have left home and started on their cross-cultural ministry in order for them to become effective workers. "In our missionary communities and agencies we urgently need to create a climate of humble, committed, life-long learning, and the willingness to grapple long and hard with deep issues in cross-cultural settings" (Dowsett 2005:41). The thesis of this paper is that collaborative learning communities that connect experienced and novice missionaries and help them connect practice with theory are a particularly adaptable way of meeting this learning need.

Missiological and Educational Assumptions

This paper assumes that the primary purpose of missiology is to improve the practice of mission and that the primary purpose of teaching mission is therefore to enhance the ministry of missionaries. Dwight Baker eloquently expressed this ultimately practical purpose of missiology:

> Missiology does more than simply record missionary practice; it seeks, as stated, to reform or reshape missionary practice, missionary theory, even missionary strategy, and to refine missionary self-understanding in ways that will enhance missionary effectiveness (Baker 2014:17).

Secondly, this paper assumes that good education helps learners make strong and multiple connections between theory and practice which help them enhance their life and work. This connection-making process occurs when learners reflect on their practice in the light of theory and apply the insights they gain from this reflection. Ted Ward and Samuel Rowen conceptualised this process using a split-rail fence in which the top rail represents theory and cognive input, the bottom rail represents ongoing practice or field experience, and the vertical fence posts represent the making of solid connections between cognitive input and field experience through dynamic reflection (Ward and Rowen 1972:24-27). Many other educational theorists confirm that connecting theory with practice is fundamental to learning (e.g., Kolb 1984; Schon 1983). This understanding of learning is depicted in figure 1.

Figure 1. Learning as connection-making between theory and practice (based on Ward and Rowen 1972: 24-27, and Plueddemann 1972:89-90).

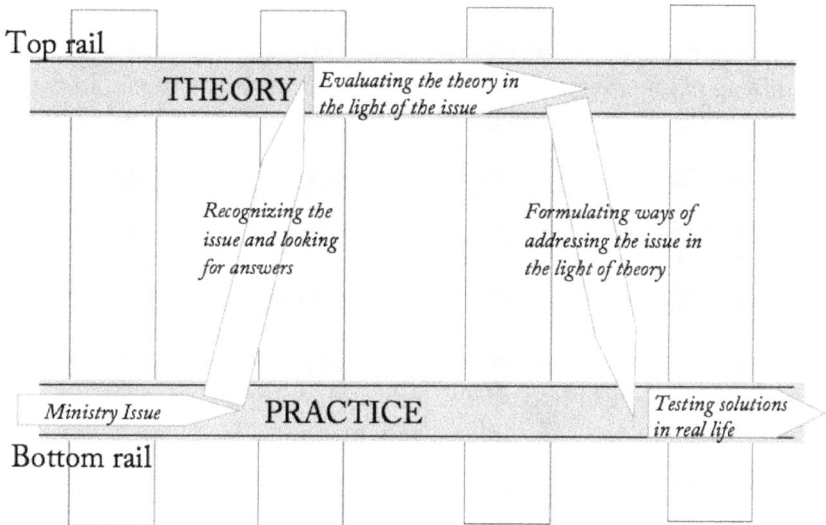

A third assumption of this paper is that good education is holistic and integrated. Learning should include not only dynamic reflection that connects theory and practice, but must also involve the development of essential character qualities and attitudes. Good education is holistic, then, in the sense that it integrates knowing, being, and doing (Brynjolfson 2006:27-36).

The Purpose of On-the-Job Training: Nurturing Reflective Practitioners

The most helpful kinds of training help learners to keep on learning. On-the-job training for missionaries should therefore ideally inculcate in trainees the ability to connect missiological theory with their own field experience. Such training nurtures reflective mission practitioners. Reflective practitioner missionaries reflect on their ministry experience, experiment with new ways of doing things as a result of that reflection, and in the process acquire a special kind of practical understanding that Donald

Schön calls "knowing-in-action" (Schön 1983). This practical knowledge enables reflective practitioner missionaries to navigate their way through ambiguous and complex ministry situations.

Reflecting on action, adjusting ministry approaches in the light of this, and evaluating those adjustments is an iterative process. Reflective practitioner missionaries are therefore lifelong learners. They are constantly open to knowledge that may help them to see their work in new ways and eventually help them become more effective. They look for help from many sources: they read the Bible to find insight about their ministry, they immerse themselves in the local culture to gain insights about it, and they listen carefully to local Christians and to fellow missionaries to understand their perspectives and practices. This kind of openness to new knowledge is a *habitus*, a habitual attitidunal posture. It is more than just wanting to study courses or read books; it is a disposition of continual openness to new experiences, ways of thinking, and intentional learning.

The ability to think and act missiologically is best developed by a combination of engaging in missions practice and reflecting on that practice in the light of missiological theory (Ward and Rowen 1972; Schon 1983; Kolb 1984). Both good theory and ongoing practice are essential to good missiology. Theory helps improve practice. "There is nothing more practical than a good theory," argued Kurt Lewin (Lewin, 1951:169). Missiologists, as developers and teachers of mission theory, should therefore provide ways of understanding problematic missions situations that will help practitioners solve those problems (cf. Vansteenkiste and Sheldon 2006: 63). But missiological theory does not stand alone; ongoing mission practice is also essential to the process of effective learning both for the field missionary and the missiologist. Ongoing practice forces missiologists to remain earthed by making them engage with the complex dilemmas that characterise missionary work and resist simplistic solutions.

The Role of Communities of Practice in Nurturing Reflective Practitioners

Some missionaries are able to engage in on-the-job learning without much support from a group. They reflect on their experience largely on their own in the light of reading and non-formal or formal seminars. For the majority of missionaries, however, solitary reflection does not come naturally. Social interaction is a key stimulus to their learning, and they learn most through being part of a learning community of fellow missionaries who are reflecting on their missionary practice. Ward and Rowen (1972: 275) put it like this: "If a student is to make a solid connection between cognitive input and his field experiences, he needs someone to talk to—preferably someone who is learning along with him."

The concept of learning communities has been gaining traction in many areas, particularly in the fields of business and education, as learning is increasingly being understood as a social process (Streumer and Kho 2006:23-24). College faculty, school principals, and business managers, for example, are encouraging the formation of learning communities to enhance the pre-service and in-service training of teachers and corporate employees (e.g., Whitford and Wood 2010; Yendol-Hoppey and Dana 2008).

Etienne Wenger and Jean Lave coined the term "communities of practice" to describe these learning communities in order to emphasize their ongoing commitment to and engagement with a particular practice that the members of the community are engaged in. Communities of practice are "groups of people who share a concern or a passion for something they do and learn how to do it better as they interact regularly" (Wenger 2014). They have three key dimensions: (1) a joint enterprise—in this case their missionary work; (2) mutual engagement, meaning that the members keep interacting with each other about the work they are engaged in; and (3) a shared repertoire of values, stories, concepts and ways of talking about and doing things that the group develops over time (Wenger 1998: 72-85).

Advocates of communities of practice suggest they are particularly powerful vehicles for helping their members connect theory with practice (Islam 2008:279-280). Their argument is based on a social theory of learning that sees learning as primarily a social process that occurs through the communicative practices of people who share similar goals and interests. This is in contrast to the classical paradigm of learning, in which individual learners internalise a largely cerebral and decontextualized body of knowledge from a teacher or expert usually in a classroom (Lave and Wenger 1991: 15, 47-49). Lave and Wenger found through their ethnographic study of apprentices in several countries that learning was happening not mainly by formal instruction but by participating in the community of fellow apprentices engaged together in their particular trade. The combination of active social participation and mutual engagement in a work practice was the primary vehicle of learning. In addition to small amounts of teaching by the master trainer, apprentices were continuously engaged in learning as they tried out aspects of the new practice and were caught up in the circulation of knowledge among their peer group of apprentices (Lave and Wenger 1991: 61-87; 92-93).

The members of a community of practice are not primarily theorists but practitioners of shared practice. Members of a missionary community of practice are therefore engaged in mission work themselves. The ultimate purpose of a missionary community of practice is to learn how to better engage in mission. This kind of learning is not defined as knowing about something but as competence—the ability to do the task well. "What they learn is not a static subject matter but the very process of being engaged in, and participating in developing, an ongoing practice" (Wenger 1998: 95).

In order to learn—to become more competent at their task—members of a missiological community of practice meet together to talk about the enterprise (missions) they are concerned about and engaged in. They help each other solve problems that arise as they go about engaging in missions, and they share information, insights, and advice. They think together about common issues and explore ideas and new ways of doing things. They hone their understanding of their task by generating multiple perspectives on their task and work to reconcile conflicting perspectives. Over time they develop a shared perspective on their specific missions context and a body of shared stories, knowledge, approaches, and practices.

Advantages of Learning in Communities of Practice

The kind of learning that occurs in communities of practice has several advantages over the traditional model of in-service professional development. First, because it is focussed practice, putting improved practice at the centre of its concern, it honours the contributions of each of the practitioners who comprise its membership (cf. Palmer 1998:115-138). Subject matter experts such as missiologists from the academy may contribute to the learning from their reading and research, but their contribution is of equal value to the practitioner who has not formally studied missiology but is *doing* the subject.

A second advantage of this kind of communal learning is that it is holistic. "As an aspect of social practice, learning involves the whole person; it implies not only a relation to specific activities, but also a relation to social communities" (Lave and Wenger 1991: 53). The process of engaging in learning as a group helps to overcome a tendency to perceive learning as primarily intellectual because not only cognitive abilities but character qualities and social skills are needed for this kind of learning. *How* members learn together in these communities is as important as *what* they learn. Attitudes of openness, acceptance, and respect, and skills of listening and negotiating in participants that are necessary for and enhance all aspects of missionary life and work are developed (Elmer 2002: 87-97). Through the process of discussion, listening to the perspectives of other group members and of the missiological literature, and negotiating an integration of these perspectives, members grow in their capacity to carefully listen to others, value their perspectives, agree or disagree respectfully, and negotiate a common outcome (cf. Lave and Wenger 1991: 15-16).

A third benefit of learning in communities of practice is that it encourages experimentation. Learning in these communities is framed in terms of developing, testing out, and evaluating the implementation of new ideas and approaches. Openness to experimentation and taking risks is engendered through this approach. The learning community not only allows members to try out innovative solutions to problems but also provides a supportive community which can allay the stress and anxiety of trying new things. If innovations fail, the community can share responsibility for the experiment and frame it in terms of ongoing learning rather than failure.

Fourthly, in contrast to traditional models of on-the-job or in-service training that are focussed primarily on the individual's acquisition of knowledge, learning in communities of practice is a social process that benefits not just the individual but a whole group of people (Yildirim 2008: 234). What any one member learns belongs to the group and therefore is shared with them. Being part of a community of practice therefore provides to its members personal experience of a collective learning approach that will enhance their ministry to people from collectivistic societies and help them relate better to team members from collectivistic cultures.

A fifth advantage of this kind of learning is that it is contextualised. It is situated in a specific context that includes both the learner's community of co-learners and teachers and the practice in which they are all engaged. This is in contrast to the traditional model of on-the-job training which usually involves in-service workshops and seminars in which the content is often decontextualized, disconnected from daily practice, and focussed on correcting deficiencies as perceived by governing bodies away from the front line of practice (Yildirim 2008:234). In response to objections that their theory seems to make knowledge and learning too parochial and limited to a given time and task, Lave and Wenger argue that every kind of learning must eventually be contextualised to be useful: "Abstract representations are meaningless unless they can be made specific to the situation at hand" (1991:33-34). Learning is an "indigenous enterprise" in that the group that is learning together responds to local conditions that are not determined by outside authorities (Wenger 1998:79).

Sixth, this kind of learning is highly accessible to missionaries. Learning communities can gather wherever learners are, at times that suit the participants. These communities are not dependent on large facilities and can regroup wherever participants find themselves. Also, as learning communities focus on learning *together* they are more amenable to incorporating learners from all stages of practice, in distinct contrast to the competitive, hierarchical and often exclusive structures traditionally associated with institutionalised learning.

A seventh advantage of communities of practice is they foster a habit of lifelong learning. Stimulated by regular discussion and interaction in the group, members develop the habit of missiological reflection. When a learning community is working well, positive feelings of belonging and being encouraged in their ministry increase members' motivation to learn and keep on learning. This positive experience of learning has the potential to encourage participants to replicate that experience in new situations they move into.

This kind of learning is also consistent with prevailing theories of adult learning developed in the West that propose that adults learn best through an active process driven by the adult learner who brings to it the problems they face in the course of living and working (Knowles 2011:67). Every member of the learning community is an active participant who brings the dilemmas they are facing in their work to the thinking and learning process, in contrast with the traditional model of on-the-job training in which seminar attendees can easily become passive recipients of knowledge (Yildirim 2008:234). Communities of practice allow learners to be self-directed (Knowles 2011:65), but to do this in community with a group of other self-directed learners. They organize themselves, take the initiative to diagnose their learning needs, shape their learning goals, discover and employ strategies for learning, and evaluate their learning (Hansman 2008:301).

The learning that occurs in a community of practice also accords with recent thinking about missions education. David Fenrick (2013), for example, convincingly argues that current missiological teaching needs to shift from focussing on cognitive development to a missional pedagogy that develops "missional activists," whose attitudes have been shaped and whose skills developed for effective missional action. The essential ingredients of such a pedagogy, according to Fenrick, include many of the elements that characterize communities of a practice: integrated learning, problem-posing content, reflection and critical analysis of experience, and cooperative learning in community.

Examples of Communities of Practice

Examples of communities of practice can be found in many contexts. They are being started and fostered at various levels—by mission agencies, by individual field and team leaders, and by mission agency executives in sending countries. One interdenominational agency working in community development and church planting in Central Asia, for example, has developed a strong culture of on-the-job training. Each of this agency's eight teams in one country I visited meet once a week as a learning community to discuss an issue they are facing in ministry. Facilitation of these learning sessions is led either by a team member who has been reading about a particular issue such as what the Qur'an says about Jesus or a visitor to the team who has expertise in some area such as teaching cross-culturally. Another example comes from a small group of cross-cultural workers in South Asia who meet once a month at a coffee shop to present and discuss the ideas for ministry that they are working on and approaches they are trying out.

The Church Missionary Society (CMS) in the UK is an example of a mission agency that is nurturing communities of practice. The purpose of these communities is to enable missionaries to learn from one another through discussion of issues, problems and their solutions, ideas, lessons learned, and research findings. Members of these learning communities are expected to share what they learn with others, and it is anticipated that this will "generate innovation and creativity in the practice of mission" (Goh et al. 2003:2).

Seminaries can also foster communities of practice. Andrew Wingate, who served as a theological educator missionary in India in the 1970s, described his seminary as "a laboratory of the gospel" that employed an action-reflection approach to learning. Faculty members and students were "deeply engaged with the world outside, as a learning and acting community" (Wingate 2010:223). Teachers were expected to be involved in practical ministry outside the college. Wingate, for example, was assigned together with a group of students to prison ministry where he recalls experiencing the power of the gospel to change lives and faced the complexity of sharing the gospel with Hindus and discipling life prisoners. Engagement with the practice of ministry outside the classroom enlarged his and his students' appreciation of the gospel and the complexity of human problems, and their ability to minister to people from vastly different religious, cultural, and socio-economic backgrounds than their own. Although Wingate suggests that the whole seminary was a community of practice, he does not give details of how this worked. It seems likely that faculty members formed one learning community as they discussed the issues they faced in their out-of-classroom ministries, and groups of students together with individual faculty members formed another kind of learning community as they engaged in and reflected on ministry they did together, such as the prison ministry.

Nurturing Missions Learning Communities: The Role of Missiologists

Communities of reflective missions practitioners transcend the dichotomy between practical and theoretical knowledge as they intentionally and systematically integrate their mission field experience with missiological theory together with other missionaries. They critically research their context and the practical knowledge generated in it, evaluate insights from theory, and integrate these in a dynamic way. In the process, they become practical missiologists, doing in-context missiological theologising and theorising in a way that shapes their practice and their understanding of the missionary task.

Seminary-based missiologists could have a significant role in nurturing missionary learning communities and thus developing future missiologists as well as a wide-based foundation of missiological expertise across the mission fields of the world. Four steps that missiologists could take towards fostering these communities are: (1) recognizing the need for more integrated missiological education; (2) planting the seeds of learning communities through the way they teach their seminary classes; (3) becoming a resource for field-based missionary learning communities; and (4) establishing local missions practitioner learning communities.

1. Recognize the need for more integrated missiological education

Many Bible college and seminary programs perpetuate a separation between theory and practice. The International Council for Evangelical Theological Education's (ICETE 2013) Manifesto on the Renewal of Theological Education acknowledges this weakness: "We are at fault that we so often focus educational requirements narrowly on cognitive attainments, while we hope for student growth in other dimensions but leave it largely to chance." The need for greater integration between theory and practice has been confirmed by a recent survey that asked more than 1500 theological educators and church leaders from all major Christian traditions in every part of the world, "What are the most important elements in the program of preparation and/or formation for Christian ministry?" Their responses stressed the need for experiential learning in the location of ministry to be integrated with spiritual formation and academic programs (Global Digital Library on Theology and Ecumenism 2013:5).

Despite this widely felt need, some Bible colleges and seminaries continue to resist the kind of rethinking that is needed to integrate theory and practice (Taylor 2006:x). For missiologists to embrace and support missionary learning communities, they need firstly to recognise the need to improve current training models. They need to resist Western education's captivity to ancient Greek educational traditions, in which practical experience is treated as a poor cousin to intellectual learning (Ward 1996:43-44; cf. Elmer 1984: 230-231).

Missiological education and mission professors are not immune to this weakness. The majority of missions classes in both Bible colleges and seminaries focus on cognitive outcomes. Practical engagement with people from other cultures is generally limited to an occasional field trip or short-term trip overseas. While these are steps in the right direction, holistic, integrated development of the whole person's attitudes and abilities in cross-cultural engagement requires further shifts in our approach to teaching and learning.

2. Model reflective practice in classes

Seminary-based missiologists could plant the seed of missionary learning communities through the way they conduct their classes. One way to do this is to model in their classes how to learn together in groups and how to make connections between theory and practice by discussing and critiquing theory together based on students' life and ministry experiences.

Another way of modelling reflective practice and sowing the seeds of missionary learning communities is to make seminary-sponsored seminars, such as doctoral seminars, more accessible for practitioners. Through collaborating with mission agencies, seminars that cover topics that are particularly relevant to practitioners could be opened up to more missionaries for audit, but conducted in a way that models and develops learning community approaches which could then be reproduced and possibly supported on the field. Although seminary courses are not necessarily practical in their focus, by increasing practitioner participation and by missiologists being ready to adjust their teaching according to their students' questions, there is more likelihood that relevant practical issues can be explored and debated together.

3. Become a resource person for field-based learning communities

Communities of Practice require intentional nurturing to help them reach their full potential (Wenger *et al.* 2002:13). One way that missiologists could contribute to their nurture is by offering their expertise to mission agencies to provide input to their field-based learning communities. They could be in direct contact with missionaries about current issues being faced in their ministry and provide relevant resources and teaching. They could also work on joint research projects that seek to address questions that are of current concern to missionaries.

Another way that missions educators could nurture learning communities on mission fields is to act as mentors or guides for the missionaries who facilitate those communities. Facilitators of learning communities fine-tune and nudge discussion and the group's learning in helpful directions (cf. Yildirim 2008:239). They could benefit greatly from the missiological theory and information about recent missiological developments that the missiologist could provide.

4. Start a missions learning community

A final way that seminary-based missiologists could contribute to missions learning communities is to start or become involved in one close to where they are based. Many seminaries and Bible colleges are close to culturally diverse communities which either have or need Christian ministry among them. As a practitioner, the missiologist would engage in sharing the gospel, discipling, planting churches, or training leaders. This group of learner-practitioners could include local Christians wanting to learn how to minister to people from other cultures as well as some of the missiologist's students. As they engage in local ministry, members would also experience a learning community, and some could take this model of learning with them when they move on to cross-cultural ministry elsewhere.

This kind of local learning community would go some way towards addressing the need for greater integration between theory and practice in pre-field training. Most proposals to address this need urge faculty to be holistic examples who are involved in ministry alongside students as mentors and models, sharing not only knowledge but their lives (e.g., Frame 1984:379-380; Jeyeraj 2002:249,264-266; Banks 1999:171-175; cf. 1 Thess. 1:5-6). Professors in such learning communities would spend significant time with students in the community over meals, in their homes, and doing ministry together.

Missions has always been an on-the-edge endevour. Missionaries step into places that the rest of the church does not go and take risks for the sake of the gospel that are unthinkable for many. Perhaps it is time for missiologists to lead in a new paradigm of theological training which integrates the Bible, theology and missiological theory with the kind of missionary attitudes and practices needed for authentic cross-cultural ministry. This requires a paradigm shift towards lifelong learning in which missiologists provide practical, prophetic, and reflective input into real life situations.

Works Cited

Baker, Dwight
    2013   "Missiology as an Interested Discipline--and Where Is It Happening?" *Missiology: An International Review,* 38(1):17-20.

Banks, Robert
    1999   *Reenvisioning Theological Education: Exploring a Missional Alternative to Current Models.* Grand Rapids, MI: Eerdmans.

Brynjolfson, Robert
    2006   "Understanding Integral Ministry Training." In *Integral Ministry Training : Design and Evaluation.* Robert Brynjolfson and Jonathan Lewis, eds. Pp. 27-36. Pasadena, CA: William Carey Library.

Dowsett, Rose
    2005   "Growing in Grace Means Life-Long Learning," *Connections: The Journal of the WEA Mission Commission,* 4(2):41.

Elmer, Duane
    1984   "Education and Service; A Model for Praxis Education." In *Missions and Theological Education in World Perspective.* Harvie Conn and Samuel Rowen, eds. Pp. 226-248. Farmington, MI: Associates of Urbana.

    2002   *Cross-Cultural Connections: Stepping out and Fitting in around the World.* Downers Grove, IL: IVP.

Fenrick, David
    2013   "Missional Education for Social Action." In *Social Engagement: The Challenge of the Social in Missiological Education: The 2013 Proceedings of the Association of Professors for Mission.* Pp. 5-55. Wilmore, KY: First Fruits Press. http://place.asburyseminary.edu/academicbooks/3/

Frame, John
 1984 "Proposals for a New North American Model." In *Missions and Theological Education in World Perspective*. Harvie Conn and Samuel Rowen, eds. Pp. 369-380. Farmington, MI: Associates of Urbana.

Global Digital Library on Theology and Ecumenism
 2012 "Global Survey on Theological Education." http://www.globethics.net/web/gtl/research/global-survey; accessed 9 October, 2013.

Goh, Patrick, Paul Thaxter, and Phil Simpson
 2003 "Building Communities of Mission Practice." http://webarchive.cms-uk.org/_pdf/Building_Communities.pdf.

Hansman, Catherine
 2008 "Adult Learning in Communities of Practice: Situating Theory in Practice." In *Communities of Practice : Creating Learning Environments for Educators*, Vol 1. Chris Kimble, Paul Hildreth, and Isabelle Bourdon, eds. Pp 293-309. Charlotte, NC: Information Age Publishing.

Hibbert, Richard, and Evelyn Hibbert
 2002 "Report on Hindrances to and Needs in Reaching the Unreached and Church Planting in WEC Fields," Unpublished research paper, presented at WEC Intercon, May 2002, Rehe, Germany.

ICETE (International Council for Evangelical Theological Education)
 2013 "ICETE Manifesto on the Renewal of Evangelical Theological Education," http://www.icete-edu.org/manifesto/index.htm; accessed 3 October, 2013.

Islam, Gazi
 2008 "Bridging Two Worlds: Identity Transition in a University-Consulting Community of Practice." In *Communities of Practice : Creating Learning Environments for Educators* , Vol 1. Chris Kimble, Paul Hildreth, and Isabelle Bourdon, eds. Pp. 279-292. Charlotte, NC: Information Age Publishing.

Kolb, David
    1984   *Experiential Learning: Experience as the Source of Learning and Development.* Englewood Cliffs, NJ: Prentice-Hall.

Knowles, Malcolm
    2011   *The Adult Learner: The Definitive Classic in Adult Education and Human Resource Development.* Burlington, MA: Taylor and Francis.

Jeyaraj, Jesudason
    2002   *Christian Ministry: Models of Ministry and Training.* Bangalore: Theological Book Trust.

Lave, Jean, and Etienne Wenger
    1991   *Situated Learning : Legitimate Peripheral Participation.* Cambridge [England]; New York: Cambridge University Press.

Lewin, Kurt
    1951   *Field Theory in Social Science : Selected Theoretical Papers*, Dorwin Cartwright, ed. London: Harper.

Palmer, Parker
    1998   *The Courage to Teach : Exploring the Inner Landscape of a Teacher's Life.* San Francisco, CA: Jossey-Bass.

Plueddemann, James
    1972   "The Real Disease of Sunday School." *Evangelical Missions Quarterly*, 9(2):88-92.

Schön, Donald
    1983   *The Reflective Practitioner : How Professionals Think in Action.* New York: Basic Books.

Streumer, Jan, and and Martin Kho
    2006   "The World of Work-Related Learning." In *Work-Related Learning.* Jan Streumer, ed. Pp. 3-50. Dordretcht: The Netherlands.

Taylor, William
    2006   "Foreword." In *Integral Ministry Training : Design and Evaluation.* Robert Brynjolfson and Jonathan Lewis, eds. Pp. vii-xiv. Pasadena, CA: William Carey Library.

Vansteenkiste, Maarten and Kennon M Sheldon
    2006   "There's Nothing More Practical than a Good Theory: Integrating Motivational Interviewing and Self-Determination Theory." *Br J Clin Psychol,* 45 (1): 63-82.

Ward, Ted
    1996   "Evaluating Metaphors for Education." In *With An Eye on the Future : Development and Mission in the 21st Century: Essays in Honor of Ted W. Ward.* Duane Elmer and Lois McKinney, eds. Pp. 43-52. Monrovia, CA: MARC.

Ward, Ted, and Samuel Rowen
    1972   "The Significance of the Extension Seminary," *Evangelical Missions Quarterly,* 9(4):17-27.

Wenger, Etienne
    1998   *Communities of Practice : Learning, Meaning, and Identity.* Cambridge, UK: Cambridge University Press.

Wenger, Etienne
    2014   "Communities of Practice: A Brief Introduction." http://wenger-trayner.com/theory/; accessed 6 February, 2014.

Wenger, Etienne, Richard McDermott and William Snyder
    2002   *Cultivating Communities of Practice : a Guide to Managing Knowledge.* Boston, MA: Harvard Business School Press.

Wingate, Andrew
    2010   "Training for Ministry in a Multifaith Context: A Case study from Britain." In *Handbook of Theological Education in World Christianity : Theological Perspectives, Regional Surveys, Ecumenical Trends.* Dietrich Werner, ed. Pp. 223-229. Eugene, OR: Wipf & Stock.

Whitford, Betty Lou, and Diane Wood
    2010   *Teachers Learning in Community: Realities and Possibilities.* Albany, NY: State University of New York Press.

Yendol-Hoppey, Diane, and Nancy Fichtman
2008 *The Reflective Educator's Guide to Professional Development: Coaching Inquiry-Oriented Learning Communities.* Thousand Oaks, CA: Corwin Press.

Yildirim, Rana
2008 "Adopting Communities of Practice as a Framework for Teacher Development." In *Communities of Practice : Creating Learning Environments for Educators,* Vol 1. Chris Kimble, Paul Hildreth, and Isabelle Bourdon, eds. Pp. 233-253. Charlotte, NC: Information Age Publishing.

APM

Other Plenary Addresses

Connecting Cultures for Christ

GRACE CAJIUAT

DOI: 10.7252/Paper. 000040

About the Author

Grace Cajiuat is an ordained elder in the Wisconsin Conference of the United Methodist Church and, until recently, served with the General Commission on Religion and Race of the United Methodist Church in Washington D.C. As Training and Development Specialist, Grace works with clergy of color and their congregations in building bridges between cultures in order to move towards an effective ministry. Her intercultural work is informed by her continuing training in intercultural communication and lived experiences as an international conductor/ musician, her first career. Grace is a native of the Philippines. She received her Master of Divinity and Master of Sacred Theology from Boston University. She also has MA degrees in music and earned a Doctor of Musical Arts in conducting from the University of South Carolina.

This is a rough outline by APM President Benjamin L. Hartley of Dr. Grace Cajiuat's presentation based on the handout and powerpoint slides she provided to APM participants.

I.   Introductory Remarks about her experience as a Filipina woman in a wide variety of educational settings. Brief discussion of her work in promoting intercultural awareness in United Methodist churches and Annual Conferences (regional ministry areas).

II. The four layers of diversity

   a.   At the level of one's personality the Myers-Briggs Personal Type Indicator offers a helpful way of thinking about diversity in terms of how one functions according to four scales of behavior (introvert/extravert, intuitive/sensory, feeling/thinking, and perceiving/judging).

   b.   The next layer is the internal dimensions over which one has no control. These include such things as country of origin, gender, race, ethnicity, etc.

   c.   The third layer is the external dimensions where you have made choices—geographic location, income, political affiliation, recreational habits, faith tradition(s), educational background, work experience, appearance, parental status, marital status.

   d.   The outer layer is the organization dimensions which includes the different levels and places of responsibility within that organization that impact your life.

A graphic was utilized depicting these four layers from Lee Gardenswart and Anita Rowe, Diverse Teams at Work, Irwin Professional Publishing, 1994. The image utilized is available at http://www.umassmed.edu/dio/strategy/ layers/

III. Growing in self-knowledge of how one operates: We discussed in small groups in the plenary session how we operated according to various spectrums of individualism – collectivism; low context – high context; egalitarian – hierarchical; task orientation – relationship orientation; directness – indirectness.

IV. Kolb's Learning Style Model

A graphic was utilized here depicting Kolb's Learning Style Model which is available online at http://www.businessballs.com/kolblearningstyles.htm

V. Breaking the Anger Cycle: We discussed in small groups habits of students we experience as teachers which we find most aggravating. A graphic of "the Anger Cycle" by John E. Jones was shared in a handout.

Adult Learning in a World Leaning Into God's Mission

MARY HESS

DOI: 10.7252/Paper. 000041

About the Author

Mary Hess is Associate Professor of Educational Leadership at Luther Seminary in St. Paul, MN, where she has taught since 2000. Mary has a PhD in Religion and Education from Boston College, an MTS from Harvard Divinity School, and a BA from Yale University. Her research focuses on the intersection of media, religion and education, and she is particularly interested in digital storytelling's implications for faith formation. Her most recent books include *Teaching Reflectively in Theological Contexts,* and *Engaging Technology in Theological Education,* and she has developed the website Storyingfaith.org.

This is an outline by APM President Benjamin L. Hartley of Dr. Mary Hess's presentation based on the powerpoint slides she provided to APM participants.

In keeping with our theme of "Transforming Teaching for Mission," Dr. Hess chose to present her topic through the use of images and short video clips which cannot be reproduced in a book. Internet URL's, however, are provided in this outline for the reader who wishes to re-construct at least some of what Dr. Hess presented to the APM at our annual meeting.

I.   Introductory Remarks

    a.   Identifying the "social location" of the presenter as a Roman Catholic laywoman teaching at an Evangelical Lutheran Church in America seminary in Minnesota.

    b.   Goals of presentation:

        i.   To catalyze good questions and to ignite the imagination.

        ii. To have an evening of adult learning rather than "information transfer."

II. What does adult learning look like when we speak of faith?

III. Three shifts which have taken place to which we need to pay attention.

    a.   Widespread epistemological challenges:

        i.   How do we understand authority?

        ii. What is meant by authenticity?

        iii. Who has agency?

    b.   Specific issues in transformative learning

        i.   Learning proceeds through an ongoing spiral of "confirmation," "contradiction," and "continuity."

        ii. "Spreadable media" is implicated in all three of these dynamics.

iii. If we don't understand this cycle, we find ourselves stuck in places where fundamentalism or relativism are evoked, rather than deep adult learning.

Two youtube videos were displayed offering two different views of ecclesiology which may be utilized to promote "transformative learning":

- "Why I hate religion, but love Jesus" - http://youtu.be/1IAhDGYlpqY

- "Why I love religion, and love Jesus" - http://youtu.be/Ru_tC4fv6FEc.

c. The rise of "maker" culture. What is this?

    i. The participatory, active forms of culture-creation.

    ii. Easily shared – "spreadable." Spreadable media are resonant, address meaningful issues, evoke relationship, are easily shared. Theologically we may understand this as "create, share, believe."

    iii. "Value and meaning get created as grassroots communities tap into creative products as resources for their own conversations and spread them to others who share their interests." -- Henry Jenkins, Spreadable Media, (2013).

Youtube videos to illustrate "spreadable media," "disruptive innovation," and "maker culture" were shared:

- "The Innovators' Bible": https://vimeo.com/77818196

- "Woman at the Well": http://youtu.be/Q49BbfgJbto

- "Finding Hope in the Holy": http://youtu.be/WQ4nF07IC7U

Following Dr. Mary Hess's presentation APM member Dr. Stanley Skreslet responded to her lecture. One of the items he offered by way of critique was to briefly discuss a recent article in the *New Yorker* by Jill Lapore on the problem of "disruptive innovation." The link to that article, "The Disruption Machine," is here: http://www.newyorker.com/magazine/2014/06/23/the-disruption-machine.

APM

Conference Proceedings

Conference Program

Thursday, June 19

2:00pm Meeting of APM Advisory Board and Executive Committee, Blue Room Nazareth Hall

4:00-6:00 Registration, Robertson Student Center

6:00 Dinner, Dining Hall of Billy Graham Commons

7:00 Welcome and Introduction to the 2014 Conference, Blue Room, Nazareth Hall
Benjamin L. Hartley, Palmer Theological Seminary, the Seminary of Eastern University

7:15 Worship, Blue Room, Nazareth Hall
Grace Cajiuat, Wisconsin Annual Conference of the United Methodist Church; Robin Harris, Accompanist, Graduate Institute of Applied Linguistics; Ernest Chung, Preacher, Overseas Ministries Study Center

| 7:45 | Plenary Address, Blue Room, Nazareth Hall
"Leaning in with God's Mission: Thinking Afresh about Adult Learning."
Mary Hess, Luther Theological Seminary, St. Paul, MN |

| 8:30 | APM respondent to address / Plenary discussion
Stanley H. Skreslet, Union Presbyterian Seminary |

| 8:45 | Announcements / APM Reception with Light Refreshments
Weather permitting, refreshments will be served on the veranda outside of Nazareth Hall |

Friday, June 20

| 7:00am | Breakfast, Dining Hall, Billy Graham Commons
Optional: "Conversations about Teaching with Senior Mission Educators": A few tables in the dining hall will be designated as places of informal conversation about teaching mission facilitated by senior mission scholar/teachers. Participants who are new(er) to teaching mission may find these conversations particularly fruitful. |

| 8:15 | Worship, Blue Room, Nazareth Hall
Grace Cajiuat and Robin Harris, Worship leaders |

| 8:30 | Plenary Address, Blue Room, Nazareth Hall
"Great Books and Missionary Fictions."
Daniel Born, Northwestern University |

| 9:15 | APM Respondent to address / Plenary discussion.
Paul Kollman, University of Notre Dame |

9:30   Break

9:45   Paper Sessions, Billy Graham Commons rooms 115, 140, 205, 210, 227
(See parallel bellow)

11:15   Conversations about Teaching, Blue Room, Nazareth Hall
Lisa Beth White, Boston University School of Theology
Participants will be invited to discuss with one another their teaching practices and philosophy as these pertain to courses in mission studies. Tables will be designated to focus discussion on four different course types: Introduction to mission, mission theology, anthropology and mission, and world Christianity. Participants are encouraged to bring syllabi to the conference or otherwise access them online while there.

12:00pm   Lunch, Dining Hall, Billy Graham Commons
"Orientation Lunch" for first-time attendees will be held at designated tables in the Billy Graham Commons Dining Hall.

1:00   Plenary Address, Blue Room, Nazareth Hall
"Connecting Cultures for Christ." Grace Cajiuat, Ordained Elder, Wisconsin Conference, UMC

1:45   APM respondent / Plenary Discussion
Elizabeth "Betsy" Glanville, Fuller Theological Seminary

2:00   Break

2:20   Business Meeting and Conclusion

Parallel Paper Sessions

Track 1: Classroom Case Studies and Strategies for Mission Education
Billy Graham: 227

9:45-10:10   *Transformative Learning versus Informative Learning in Facilitating Mission Studies*
Glory Dharmaraj, Interfaith Mission Institute of the Asian American Federation

10:15-10:40   *The Pedagogy of Hip Hop in Teaching Missiology: Exploring a Project Based Learning Environment using Elements of Hip Hop Culture as the Curriculum*
Daniel White Hodge, North Park University

10:45-11:10   *Jesus and the Gospels: A Compelling Oral Training*
Kevin Olson, Bethel Theological Seminary

Track 2: Theological Considerations for Mission Education
Billy Graham: 115

9:45-10:10   *A Wesleyan Theology of Cultural Competency*
                  Esther D. Jadhav, Asbury Theological Seminary

10:15-10:40   *Engaging in Pneumatic Mission Theology*
                  Robert Gallagher, Wheaton College

10:45-11:10   *A Heuristic Model for Conceptualizing Evangelism*
                  Mark Teasdale, Garrett-Evangelical Theological
                  Seminary

Track 3: Rethinking the Mission Curriculum
Billy Graham: 140

9:45-10:10   *Redesigning Missiological Education for the
                  Twenty-first Century: International Joint Degrees in
                  International Development and Missiology*
                  Kevin Book-Satterlee, William Carey
                  International University

10:15-10:40   *The Integration of Spirituality with the Study
                  of Missiology: A Case Study of Practices for the
                  Cohort-Based DMiss Program at Fuller School of
                  Intercultural Studies*
                  Elizabeth "Betsy" Glanville, Fuller Theological
                  Seminary

10:45-11:10   *Cultural Bias in Missionary Education: The
                  Unintentional Dynamic of Trained Incapacity*
                  Birgit Herppich

Track 4: Anthropolgical/Sociological Considerations in Mission Education
Billy Graham: 205

9:45-10:10
Anthropological Considerations for Mission Education among different Ethnics in Myanmar
Cope Suan Pau, All Nations Theological Seminary, Yangon, Myanmar

10:15-10:40
Preparing Melanesians for Missions
Doug Hanson, Christian Leaders' Training College, Papua New Guinea

10:45-11:10
Teaching a Two Course Sequence in Quantitative Research Methods that Includes Real, Missiologically-Relevant Research
David Dunaetz, Azusa Pacific University

Track 5: Mission Education Outside the Classroom
Billy Graham: 210

9:45-10:10
Sharing Best Practices in Travel Courses
Paul H. de Neui, North Park University

10:15-10:40
Nurturing Missiological Practitioner Learning Communities
Richard Hibbert, Sydney (Australia) Missionary and Bible College

10:45-11:10
Equipping Ordinary Practitioners for Entry Level Missiological Field Research
Stan Nussbaum, Global Mapping International

Business Meeting Agenda

Association of Professors of Mission
2014 Annual Business Meeting
June 19-20 – University of Northwestern, St. Paul, MN

1. Call to Order – Ben Hartley, APM President

2. Secretary/Treasurer's Report – David Fenrick

3. Venue and date for 2015 Annual Meeting (with ASM)

   a. Wheaton College, Wheaton, IL; June 18-21, 2015

4. Executive Committee's Report – Ben Hartley

5. Advisory Board Structure for the APM

   a. It was agreed in 2012 to implement this new structure for three years and then to revisit the matter at the 2015 Business Meeting.

6. New Business and Announcements – Ben Hartley, Robert Danielson (APM Advisory Board member)

7. Election of Officers for Advisory Board and Exec Committee – Ben Hartley

8. Recognition of 2014-2015 APM President Nelson Jennings

9.   Adjournment – Nelson Jennings

Secretary-Treasurer's Report

	Credit	Debit	Balance
Opening Balance: June 19, 2013			5,687.46
Receipts			
Membership Dues Received			
125.00			
Transfer from ASM			
(Less Conference Expenses)	2,325.00		
Grant for APM Executive Meeting			
Expenses			
APM 2013 Meeting Honorarium & Expenses		1,442.00	
Mission Studies Renewal		304.00	
Total			6,391.46

Balance at Wells Fargo Bank,
Minneapolis, MN, as of June 19, 2014: $6,391.46

Respectfully Submitted,
David E. Fenrick
Secretary-Treasurer

Executive Committee Report

The Executive Committee met on three occasions in 2013-2014 (June 2013 at Wheaton College; January 2014 at Perkins Theological Seminary, Southern Methodist University; June 2014 at the University of Northwestern) in order to engage in a common research effort, plan for the 2014 APM Conference, and to discuss and implement recommendations from the 2013 Annual Meeting at Wheaton College.

January Meeting of Executive Committee and Advisory Board members

For the second year in a row the APM Executive Committee and a few Advisory Board members met in January in Dallas, Texas at Perkins School of Theology. Persons present were Robert Hunt, Kevin Lines, David Fenrick, Stephen Bevans, Nelson Jennings, Lisa Beth White, and Ben Hartley.

Director of Global Theological Education Robert Hunt of Perkins School of Theology (and APM member) has received a grant to collaborate with APM leadership in designing a resource(s) for short-term mission education. The first day of our meeting was spent with area United Methodist church leaders at Perkins School of Theology. With them we discussed ideas to strengthen short-term mission education/ preparation/debrief so as to make such experiences as transformative for the sake of God's mission as possible. The following early morning was spent visiting an intentional Christian community (comprised of Perkins seminary students) in a poor neighborhood of Dallas over which Professor Elaine Heath of Perkins School of Theology has oversight.

The late morning was spent discussing the upcoming APM conference in June 19-20 in St. Paul, MN. The following new ideas to implement at the 2014 APM Conference were discussed:

1. We discussed inviting a resident from the Overseas Ministries Study Center in New Haven, CT to serve as our preacher at the APM. We raised the possibility of making this a regular component of the APM June meetings each year.

2. We discussed how we might do plenary presentations somewhat differently in 2014 through the use of long-standing APM members as respondents to addresses.

3. We discussed implementing as part of the June Conference program a "Conversations about Teaching" segment to focus more intentionally on pedagogy in specific types of courses. At the very first program year for the APM in 1954 a time for "syllabus sharing" was the focus of the meeting. 2014 will be the 60th anniversary of that first programming year of the APM.

Advisory Committee

The new leadership structure instituted in 2012 now includes both an Advisory Board – comprised of seven persons serving three-year terms – and an Executive Committee (President, 1st Vice President, 2nd Vice President, and Secretary/Treasurer). The Advisory Board currently includes the following persons: Robbie Danielson; Paul Kollman, Steven Bevans, Paul Hertig, Lisa Beth White, Sarita Gallagher, and Kevin Lines. Lisa Beth White's and Steven Bevans' terms of service end in June 2014.

The new Advisory Board structure appears to be working well as it allows for more continuity and greater breadth and depth of experience about the work of the APM which was lacking in the previous Executive

Committee-only structure. As decided at the 2012 Business meeting, in 2015 the APM will need to vote on whether to continue the Advisory Board structure, modify it, or eliminate it.

Administrative Organization

In October 2014 Sr. Madge Karecki, SSJ-TOSF, D.Th., announced her departure from the Chicago Archdiocese to serve as president of St. Augustine's College in South Africa. The Executive Committee of the APM wished Sr. Madge well in this new mission "into the deep" (as she put it in her departure letter), but it left the Executive Committee with three persons instead of four.

As a result of the smaller Executive Committee, two major tasks I (Ben Hartley) had hoped to focus on in the 2013-2014 academic year as first Vice President were left undone because of the more immediate need to organize the 2014 conference. These tasks included 1) the development of a database of APM members to make the nominations process a bit easier and 2) investigation into how the APM might better be in service to mission professors outside of North America. Both of these items were discussed at the 2013 planning meeting in Dallas, TX. I do believe that the persons who have been nominated (and will likely be elected) to serve as new members of the Executive Committee and Advisory Board will strengthen the APM's ability to further these goals.

The continued growth of the ASM, the APM's and ASM's introduction of parallel paper sessions, and our change of conference venue after our decades-long residence at the Society of Divine Word Techny Towers Retreat and Conference Center have resulted in an increase in the organizing work needing to be performed by the President of the APM and the Executive Committee / Advisory Board. This is, on the whole, a very good thing! However, it will require continued dialogue among APM and ASM leadership to ensure the continued smooth operation of APM Conference planning. If the ASM growth pattern continues, it will be important to re-examine the way the APM relates to the ASM to minimize conference organizing redundancies and to ensure that this relationship continues to be mutually beneficial.

"First Fruits" Open-Access Press

In 2013 the APM instituted the practice of publishing the papers presented at the APM conference – both plenary and parallel sessions. The online publication of conference proceedings will occur in 2014 as well. The number of free downloads of individual papers and the full book of the 2013 conference proceedings from Asbury Theological Seminary's First Fruits website has far exceeded expectations; over three thousand downloads have occurred. The details of this will be discussed in a report given by Dr. Robert Danielson of Asbury Theological Seminary during the APM Business Meeting.

Conclusion

There remains a great deal of work to do to make the Association of Professors of Mission even better than it is. The 2013 Executive Committee Report noted the importance of exploring how the APM may grow in its encouragement of excellence in the teaching of mission in North America and elsewhere. The research project on short-term mission education currently underway in collaboration with APM member Robert Hunt is just one example of the resources the APM could develop in the future. Other resources include open-access courses, bibliographies, digitization of mission-related documents, online video resources for teaching and any number of other online resources.

If the APM chooses to continue to expand beyond a North American constituency we will need to proceed in such a way as to best encourage – and not overwhelm – the networks of professors of mission which already exist in many parts of the world. The structural problems in mission studies Professor Andrew Walls wrote about decades ago remain an item of concern with which this professional society ought to work to address for the sake of God's mission in the world today.

Respectfully submitted,
The Executive Committee of the APM

Benjamin L. Hartley, President
Nelson Jennings, First Vice President
David Fenrick, Secretary/Treasurer

Report on Electronic Version of APM Papers

ROBERT DANIELSON

During the 2013 APM Conference in Wheaton, we experimented with making papers electronically available before, during, and for a short time, after, the conference. Initial papers were posted as they were received by the presenters (one month to two weeks before the conference), and following the conference, the presenters could have their papers removed at their request (if they wanted to publish them elsewhere), or they could send in corrections based on feedback from the conference to update their work, which remained on First Fruits as individual papers. The papers were then compiled with additional reports from the conference into the Proceedings, entitled *Social Engagement: The Challenge of the Social in Missiological Education*, which is available through First Fruits Press for free download or for purchase as a print book for the cost of the on demand printer (http://place.asburyseminary.edu/academicbooks/3/).

First Fruits pulled the statistics from the conference about one or two weeks after the conference. The following is a brief overview of the numbers.

1. There were 239 downloads of individual articles, with the highest being 85 downloads and the lowest being 9 downloads for any one article.

2.	There were 258 downloads of the entire collection of articles. This includes 10 in the ePub format, 44 in the Mobi format (Kindle), and 204 in PDF.

3.	We had an all time high number of people registered for the conference in 2013 with 116 people in attendance.

Even at our most conservative guess, if everyone attending the conference downloaded the papers as a complete set to their computer or digital device just once, this would only account for 116 of the 258 downloads. We do not really rely on the 239 downloads of individual papers, since people might have downloaded them multiple times or during the course of a presentation. However, if someone downloaded the complete collection, it is less likely that they would have downloaded it multiple times. We also know that not everyone attending probably downloaded the material. By providing electronic versions of the papers, APM was able to reach a broader audience than just the 116 who physically attended the conference. It is possible we reached at least the same amount of people or more than those who physically attended through electronic access.

Just by physical observation during the conference, I noticed a number of people following along with presenters on mobile devices or looking over papers when we were in our general meeting space. I also had several members of the ASM inquiring about what we were doing and expressing an interest in the project. General feedback I heard was entirely positive.

First Fruits pulled the same statistics in early June 2014 to look at usage from the entire year before the 2014 APM Conference. The following is a brief overview of the numbers.

1.	There were a total of 738 downloads of individual articles, with 132 being the highest number of individual downloads and 29 being the lowest.

2.	The entire collection of articles was replaced by the book, *Social Engagement: The Challenge of the Social in Missiological Education* in October of 2013. In addition to the downloads mentioned above immediately after the conference, there were 3,587 downloads of the finished book. This includes 32 in the ePub format, 67 in the Mobi format (Kindle), and 302 in PDF. In addition, 32 physical copies of the book have been sold.

The success of this project goes beyond my own expectations. APM has provided a valuable resource for global use. In a report of statistics done back in March, we were able to see that 82.22% of the downloads of the papers came from the Americas, 8.45% from Africa, 5.10% from Europe, 3.06% from Asia, and 1.17% from Australia. Due to a change in the analytical tools we are able to use, I am not able to update these statistics, however these initial findings seem to clearly indicate that APM papers are being accessed outside of North America.

We look forward to continuing this project with APM for 2014.

Robert Danielson
Advisory Committee Member

2014 Business Meeting Minutes

DAVID E. FENRICK

1. The APM meeting was held at the University of Northwestern, St. Paul, MN. The meeting was called to order and opened with prayer on Friday, June 20, 2014, 2:25 p.m. by Ben Hartley, President.

2. The minutes for the 2013 meeting were submitted by David Fenrick, Secretary-Treasurer, and approved.

3. The Secretary-Treasurer's financial report was submitted and approved.

4. Ben Hartley announced the 2015 APM Annual Meeting location – Wheaton College, Wheaton, IL, June 18-21, 2015. Wheaton College was set as the location for the 2015 annual meeting due to scheduling conflicts. Ben Hartley also reviewed the process and decision regarding the future venue for annual APM (with ASM and AETE) meetings. The ASM Board of Directors, with APM representation, will decide on the permanent venue for our annual meetings at their Board of Directors meeting in October 2014. Members will participate in the final selection by providing feedback on each site.

5. Ben Hartley presented the Executive Committee's Report. (See 2014 Executive Committee Report)

a.   It was noted that Madge Karecki resigned as APM President due to her appointment as the President of St. Augustine College, South Africa. Consequently, Ben Hartley became APM President. This left the Executive Committee with extra work in preparation for the annual meeting, thus not all of the projects set for the past year were completed.

b.   The relationship between APM and international associations of professors of mission continues to be discussed and explored.

c.   Discussion regarding member services beyond the annual meeting continues to be discussed, such as, online publishing.

d.   A motion was made and approved to accept the Executive Committee's report.

6.   Ben Hartley reviewed the Advisory Board structure, reflecting the mandate given by the APM membership at the 2012 Annual Meeting.

a.   The Executive and Advisory Committees held three meetings this past year. Of particular importance was the strategic vision and planning meeting at the Perkins School of Theology in Dallas, TX, January 29-30, 2014. Through Robert Hunt at the Perkins School of Theology, the Grimes Foundation has continued to extend its grant to facilitate meetings. This allows the APM Executive and Advisory Committees to meet, provide education for pastors and lay-leaders, as well as APM and Perkins School of Theology to collaborate in the development of educational resources for short-term missions.

7.   New Business and Announcements:

a.   Robert Danielson reviewed a proposal for member services and gave a report of the present partnership with First Fruits Press at Asbury Theological Seminary. This includes online services and paper publication of the proceedings and papers presented at APM annual meetings, as well as an APM handbook which will include guidance on developing curricula and course syllabi. The 2014 APM Annual Meeting reports and paper presentations are available from First Fruits. In regards to the 2013 online publication, there were 215 downloads of papers prior to the 2013 annual meeting. There have been 3,587downloads following the 2013 annual meeting, in addition to numerous purchases of printed copies (book) of the papers and proceedings in their entirety. A significant number of those downloads have come from countries outside the U.S.

b. APM noted the retirement of the following colleagues this past year, and their unique and enduring contributions to the field of missiology and the proclamation of the Gospel:

   i. Craig Van Gelder, Luther Seminary.

   ii. Daniel Shaw, Fuller Theological Seminary.

8. The report of the Nominating Committee regarding the election of officers was submitted by Ben Hartley and J. Nelson Jennings, First Vice President.

   a. David Fenrick, University of Northwestern, St. Paul, MN, was reelected Secretary-Treasurer.

   b. J. Nelson Jennings, Overseas Ministry Study Center, New Haven, CT, was elected President.

   c. Angel D. Santiago-Vendrell, Asbury Theological Seminary, was elected First-Vice President.

   d. Larry Caldwell, Sioux Falls Seminary, was elected Second Vice-President.

   e. The new members of the APM Advisory Board were introduced and approved:

      i. Elizabeth Glanville, Fuller Theological Seminary

      ii.   Haemin Lee, Presbyterian Church USA - World Mission

9.   Ben Hartley thanked the Executive and Advisory Committees for their hard work on the Executive Report and contribution to the Annual Meeting. He also introduced the new APM President, J. Nelson Jennings.

10.   J. Nelson Jennings thanked outgoing President, Ben Hartley, and the Executive Committee for their outstanding work in organizing an excellent and memorable conference. He also presented the theme of the 2015 Annual Meeting – "What's in a Name? Assessing Mission Educational and Program Titles."

11.   J. Nelson Jennings closed with prayer at 3:00 pm.

Respectfully Submitted,
David E. Fenrick
Secretary-Treasurer

2014-2015 Leadership Roster

Executive Committee Officers

President:

Nelson Jennings (Independent Protestant)

jennings@omsc.org *Overseas Ministries Study Center*

First Vice President:

Angel Satiago-Vendrell (Conciliar Protestant)

angel.santiago-vendrell@asburyseminary.edu
Asbury Theological Seminary

Second Vice President:

Larry Caldwell (Independent Protestant)

lwcald@yahoo.com *Sioux Falls Seminary*

Secretary-Treasurer:

David Fenrick (Independent Protestant)

defenrick@unwsp.edu *University of Northwestern*

Advisory Committee

Robert Danielson
> robert.danielson@asburyseminary.edu
> *Asbury Theological Seminary*

Paul Kollman
> pkollman@nd.edu *Notre Dame*

Paul Hertig
> phertig@apu.edu *Azusa Pacific University*

Sarita Gallagher
> sgallagher@georgefox.edu *George Fox University*

Kevin Lines
> kplines@hiu.edu *Hope International University*

Betsy Glanville
> eglanville@fuller.edu *Fuller Theological Seminary*

Haemin Lee
> haeminster@gmail.com

www.ingramcontent.com/pod-product-compliance
Lightning Source LLC
La Vergne TN
LVHW051621080426
835511LV00016B/2108